Chicago Jazz: the Second Line

The authors with John Steiner, Chicago jazz historian (centre).

***

"Elementary"

"On one of the occasions that the authors met the renowned Max Jones, the *Melody Maker* journalist, he greeted us with, 'Ah, the Holmes and Watson of discography!' He never did say who was who, but as Bert was a little taller and I was the one usually holding a notebook, I guess that Bert qualified as the master detective."

Chicago Jazz: the Second Line

A compilation by
Derek Coller and Bert Whyatt

Hardinge Simpole

Published by:

Hardinge Simpole
An imprint of Zeticula Ltd
Unit 13
196 Rose Street
Edinburgh
EH2 4AT
Scotland
http://www.hardingesimpole.co.uk

First published in 2018

ISBN 978-1-84382-226-4 hardback
ISBN 978-1-84382-227-1 paperback

In Memory of

Bert Whyatt

a dedicated jazz collector and researcher,

the best of companions and a true gentleman

A gathering of jazzmen at the Club Silhouette, Chicago, 1949.
Left to right: Brad Gowans, at the piano; (standing) Brownie McGhee, Danny Alvin, Miff Mole, Doc Cenardo, Jimmy Jones, Bill Pfeiffer, Bill Tinkler, Herb Ward, Mama Yancey, Bud Jacobson, Art Hodes, Jimmy Yancey; (kneeling) John Schenck, Doc Evans, Tony Parenti, Wild Bill Davison, Chet Roble, Johnny Lane, Lee Collins, and Freddy Flynn.

Contents

New Orleans Rhythm Kings, 1922.
Left to right: George Brunies, Paul Mares, Ben Pollack, Leon Roppolo,
Mel Stitzel, Volly De Faut, Lou Black, Steve Brown.

New Orleans Rhythm Kings (Friars Society Orchestra), 1922.
Left to right: George Brunies, Frank Snyder, Paul Mares, Arnold
Loyacano, Elmer Schoebel, Jack Pettis, Leon Roppolo.

Illustrations

Introduction

The purpose of this compilation is to pay tribute to Bert Whyatt (1920-2013), author, biographer, discographer, researcher, for his important contribution to our knowledge of the history of early and middle-period jazz.

A secondary purpose was to gather together those of our articles which could be grouped together under a common heading. That heading proved to be Chicago. All the musicians chronicled here had strong connections with the Windy City. Most of them are lesser-known but nevertheless had fascinating lives within the world of jazz. Another sub-title for this collection could have been "The Unsung White Jazzmen of Chicago".

So it was that Bert Whyatt and I, though fully appreciative of the wonderful music of the black musicians from New Orleans, gravitated in our research activities towards the white players from the Crescent City and from Chicago, and to those who rallied around the figurehead of Eddie Condon.

Two trips to the U.S.A. led to meetings and/or correspondence with some of the men in this compilation, as well as memories of many others. Our interest in Chicago jazz can be seen by the subjects of the first books we had published. Bert's was a bio-discography of *Muggsy Spanier: Lonesome Road* (Jazzology Press, 1995); mine was of *Jess Stacy: The Quiet Man of Jazz* (Jazzology Press, 1997). Much more about Bert's jazz activities can be found in his autobiography, *Jazz: So Much In My Life* (The Grimsay Press, 2014).

The possibility of such a book as this was discussed over a period of about four years, prior to Bert's death. During that time some ambitious ideas were considered, even though it may have needed three or four books to encompass them all. Perhaps it is well for our readers that they are faced by just this one volume.

Of the articles herewith, some appeared under a dual by-line, others as by either Whyatt or Coller, but in all instances there was consultation and discussion prior to publication.

Some of these stories are about pioneers. Elmer Schoebel, Jack Pettis and Frank Snyder, for example, were in the New Orleans

Rhythm Kings in 1923. Another member of that band was trombonist George Brunis, also chronicled here, though his long career has been more widely documented. There are connections between most of these articles, an over-lapping of jobs, leaders and clubs. Brunis, for example, also played with Muggsy Spanier, as did Rod Cless and George Zack, in the Spanier Ragtime Band of "Great Sixteen" fame. Floyd Bean and Tut Soper were also Spanier alumni.

The musicians whose biographies are documented here are a small percentage of those who played jazz in Chicago, but they are representative of a long and proud tradition.

Derek Coller
November 2017

Acknowledgements

First, our most important thanks are to the many musicians featured here who have given us, and so many more, listening pleasure over the years.

Grateful thanks go to *Jazz Journal* (editor, Mark Gilbert at jazzjournal.co.uk) and to the *I.A.J.R.C. Journal* (editor, Ian Tiele) for the use of material originally published in their magazines. Sadly, *The Mississippi Rag* and *Storyville* ceased publication many years ago, though both remain essential reference sources.

Thanks also go to the following for the reprinting of the Muggsy Spanier essays: American Music AMCD1-109, Lars Edegran of Jazzology Records: Retrieval FJ-108, Chris Ellis; and Avid AMSC 695, reproduced courtesy of AVID Ltd – www.avidgroup.co.uk.

The acknowledgements accompanying individual articles are gathered here.

Frank Snyder: Rhythm King Drummer

We am deeply grateful to Mrs. Peggie Snyder for the time and thought which she gave in answering numerous questions. Without her friendly response our knowledge of another of our music's pioneers would be limited to a name in a discography.

The following contributed valuable facts and guidance: John Chilton, Charlie Crump, Jim Gordon, Art Hodes, Catherine Jacobson, Wayne Jones, Warren Plath, William Russell, Hal Smith, Tut Soper, Jess Stacy and Bert Whyatt.

Other references used for this article were:

Squirrel Ashcraft – unpublished notes on an interview with Jack Pettis, 1936, courtesy of William Russell. [see also Jack Pettis chapter.]

John Steiner – chapter in *Jazz*, edited by Nat Hentoff and Albert J. McCarthy.

Richard Sudhalter and Phillip Evans – *Bix: Man and Legend*.

Eddie Condon, with Thomas Sugrue – *We Called It Music*.

Richard Hadlock – *Jazz Masters of The Twenties*.

C.E. Smith – chapter in *Jazzmen*, edited by Frederick Ramsey, Jr. and Charles Edward Smith.

George Brunies – transcript of interview with William Russell.

George Beall – chapter in *Frontiers of Jazz*, edited by Ralph de Toledano.

Whitney Balliett – chapter on Lou Black in *Such Sweet Thunder*.

Brian Rust – *Jazz Records 1897-1942*.

John Hammond (with Irving Townsend) – *John Hammond on Record*.

John Chilton – *Who's Who of Jazz*.

Bob Thiele – article in *American Jazz Quarterly, No. 1*.

Elmer Schoebel: Pianist, Composer, Pioneer Arranger

Buhmann, Tom: *The New Orleans Rhythm Kings, Storyville* 2000-1.

Chilton, John: *Who's Who Of Jazz*.

Dapogny, James: *notes to* A Tribute to Elmer Schoebel, Stomp Off CD 1407.

Janis, Conrad: e-mails, January 2006.

Kenney, William Howland: *Chicago Jazz*

Maher, James T. and Sultanof, Jeffery: *The Oxford Companion To Jazz*

Meyer, Ed: *Giant Strides*

Morgenstern, Dan: for copies of the Leonard Feather questionnaire and ASCAP entry.

Peerless, Brian: *Observations on a Life in Jazz* (Kenny Davern), *Jazz Journal,* March 2007.

Schoebel, Elmer: questionnaire for Leonard Feather (c. 1955).

Schoebel, Elmer and Openneer, Jr, Herman: *Doctor Jazz*. Nr. 32, October 1968.

Sharpsteen, Tom: e-mails, March 2006.

Sudhalter, Richard M: *Lost Chords*.

Vaché, Warren, Sr: *The Unsung Songwriters*

van Delden, Ate: notes for *Early Chicago Jazz,* Timeless CBC1-071.

ASCAP Biographical Directory, *1980*.

Down Beat: various issues, 1951-1953, and April 15, 1971 (obituary).

Library of Congress website (Performing Arts Reading Room).

George Snurpus: Elusive Jazzman

Our thanks to George Snurpus for his patience in answering questions during a series of letters in 1993 and 1994.

Maurie Bercov: Following Tesch

Bercov's nickname has been spelt variously as Maurie, Morrey and Morrie: Tut Soper – letter to Bert Whyatt, dated August 18, 1986, Frank Powers - notes to IAJRC CD 1007, Marty Grosz - notes to Time-Life Giants of Jazz series - Frank Teschemacher LP set.

Richard M. Sudhalter - *Lost Chords: White Musicians and Their Contribution to Jazz, 1915-1945,* (Oxford University Press, 1999).

AFM Handbook Local 47: Morris L Bercov.

Special thanks to Peter Hanley for providing the Bercov family details, using the 1910 and 1920 U.S. Census, Illinois, Cook County, Chicago 2nd Ward; and the California Death Index 1940-1997.

Brian Ross Bercov - letters to Bert Whyatt dated May 25, 1985 and September 1, 1992. Unfortunately offers by Brian Bercov to provide further information and photographs failed to materialise.

Floyd O'Brien: He Played Jazz Chicago Style

Thanks go to the following for their generous help: Florence O'Brien, so patient in both letters and interview, and Jim Gordon, the Chicago jazz collector supreme. Other material in this article has been quoted from correspondence with:

Jim Beebe, Ron Clough, John Dengler, Marty Grosz, Wayne Jones, Bob Koester, Chuck Sweningsen, John Stock, Bill Tinkler, Iris Town, Jack Tracy, C.K. Bozy White.

And special thanks to trombonists Jim Beebe, Geoff Cole and Campbell Burnap for giving their perspective on Floyd O'Brien's recordings.

Numerous issues of *Down Beat* were consulted, including O'Brien's obituary, which appeared in the January 9, 1969, issue. Particularly helpful were *The Mississippi Rag* for August 1987 and March 1992 (Tut Soper articles by Bert Whyatt), *Record Research* for August *1960, Jazz* for December 1943 (Tut Soper article by Catherine Jacobson), *Cadence* for October 1980 (Marty Grosz interview), *The Jazz Record* for June 1945 (Earl Wiley story) and *Jazz Report* for August 1962. Art Hodes' column for *Jazz Report* (Volume 8, Number 6, 1975) was devoted to Floyd O'Brien. George Avakian's article, "Why Bury O'Brien?", appeared in *Jazz*

Information ii/2, 1940. W.H. Miller's tribute to O'Brien was self-published in Australia in the booklet "Three Brass,"August 1945.

The following books provided quotations and useful background information: Eddie Condon: *We Called It Music.* Phil Evans and Dick Sudhalter: *Bix: Man and Legend.* Bud Freeman: *Crazeology.* Mike Hazeldine and Barry Martyn: *Bunk Johnson: Song of the Wanderer.* Art Hodes: *Hot Man.* Max Jones: *Talking Jazz* (Jimmy McPartland interview}. Laurie Wright, ed.: *Storyville 1998-89* (Harold S. Kaye article on Dave Tough). Max Kaminsky: *My Life in Jazz.* Mezz Mezzrow: *Really the Blues.* Hugues Panassie: *Dictionary of Jazz.* Hugues Panassie: *The Real Jazz.* Artie Shaw: *The Trouble with Cinderella.* Laurie Wright: *'Fats' in Fact.*

Johnny Lane: "Played With Gusto"

Grateful thanks are expressed to all those musicians and collectors named in the text, and to the following: American Federation of Musicians (Local 407), Nick and Jean Carter, Dick Cary, Gilbert M. Erskine, Marty Grosz, Pete Goulding, Merrill M. Hammond, Wayne Jones, Bob Koester, Gene Kramer, Floyd Levin, Paige van Vorst.

References:

The Chicago Reader, January 23, 1981: "Leona and Johnny Were Sweethearts" (Chuck Sweningsen).

Autonetics Skywriter, 1960s: "John Italiane of Purchasing Known as 'Banker' with a Beat' (anonymous).

The Second line, Sep/Oct 1963: "The Saga of Johnny Lane's Clarinet: as told by Johnny himself".

Chicago Sun-Times, October 4, 1977: "Clarinetist Lane Returns For A Set" (Jerry De Muth.)

The Mississippi Rag, February 1990: "Floyd Town: His Story" (Derek Coller).

The Mississippi Rag, May 1992: "Reminders of a Forgotten Era" (Warren Vache, Snr).

The Mississippi Rag, August 1992: "Coming of Age in the 1950s: Chicago Traditional Jazz Clubs" (Thomas B. Gilmore).

Johnny Lane (excerpt from interview) with unidentified interviewer, Downey, CA, early 1960s.

Buzz Knudsen interview with Jim Gordon.

Down Beat numerous issues.

Jack Gardner: "A Truly Lusty Pianist"

Thanks to correspondence and or interviews with Jim Gordon, George Hulme, Merrill Hammond, Bob Koester (Delmark Records), Tor Magnusson, John Miner, Bill Reinhardt, Chuck Sweningsen, John Steiner, Les Strand.

To various issues of *Down Beat*, including the writings of George Hoefer, John Lucas and Sharon Pease.

To Ian Crosbie, Jim Gordon, George Hulme and, particularly, Charlie Crump for help with the recordings and supplying the label images for this article.

Chet Roble: A Chicago Pianist

To the following sources, and with special thanks to the correspondents mentioned: Various issues of *Down Beat*, including 6 April 1951 and 6 December 1962. Obituary written by Will Leonard for *The Chicago Tribune*, 1 November 1962. Sleeve note written by Don Gold for Argo LP-616 (provided by John Dever). 'Chicago Jazz' chapter by John Steiner, in *Jazz*, edited by Nat Hentoff & Albert McCarthy. Ed Ward, Chicago Federation of Musicians.

Also Sammy Aron, Nick and Jean Carter, John Cowley, Charles Cruttenden, Marty Grosz, Merrill Hammond, Ross Kailey, Bob Koester, John Miner, Howard Rye, Tut Soper, John Steiner, Bill Tinkler, Jack Tracy, Bob Weir, and Bozy White.

Floyd Bean: The Forgotten Ones

Floyd Bean. *Jazz Record*, July 1945 and correspondence 1970; *Cedar Rapids Gazette* 1963: Jim Beebe.

Dan Lipscomb: Talk About Two-Handed Piano

This article was greatly assisted by Howard Rye. Thanks also to Rob Ford for contributions to the Lipscomb family tree.

Frank Chace: Chicago Clarinet

Without input from Wayne Jones, Hal Smith and, in particular Michael Steinman, this article would not have happened. Wayne often worked with Chace and he and Michael knew him well. The latter taped several telephone conversations with him in 1998/9 and we have drawn on Michael's transcriptions of these.

Certainly without Martin Richards's interview with Marty Grosz, published in *Jazz Journal International*, October 1992, it would have been thinner. Correspondence with Marty included great help in clarifying the background to the Gaslight period. Also helping is the co-operation of Terry Martin, of the University of Chicago, as are the quotes from John Dengler, Butch Thompson and from letters from Frank Chace to Derek Coller.

A shorter version of this biography of appeared in the *IAJRC Journal* for June 2009, titled *Frank Chace: Clarinet Ace*. This was published with a discography by Bert Whyatt.

Jimmy Ille: Cornet Player From Biwabik
Thanks to John Miner for supplying a number of personnels for the Chicago bands, and to Ken Whitten for the "Circus, Circus" information.

Paul Jordan: Another Unsung Jazzman
For help with cassettes and CD-Rs, my thanks to George Hulme and Charlie Crump.

Acknowledgements to the usual reference works, including Rust, Delaunay, Jepsen and Lord.

Substantial Additions received from Chris Kaufmann and Robert L. Campbell.

Chicago Style Jazz

Chicago Jazz style was the music created by the young white musicians from that city and its environs as they listened to and learned from the pioneer black stylists, many of them the greatest jazz players to emigrate from New Orleans - King Oliver, Louis Armstrong, Johnny and Baby Dodds and Jimmy Noone among them. There are numerous stories of novice players such as Muggsy Spanier, cornet, Frank Teschemacher, clarinet, Jess Stacy, piano, Gene Krupa, drums, and Dave Tough, drums, listening to the King Oliver Creole Jazz Band at the Lincoln Gardens dance hall in 1923. Even, on occasion, sitting-in, to give their idols a short break.

A shorthand name for the musicians playing Chicago jazz was the Austin High Gang, as several of them were pupils at Austin High School, including Bud Freeman, Frank Teschemacher, Jimmy and Dick McPartland and bassist, or pianist as he was then, Jim Lanigan.

The Friars Society Orchestra, which became the New Orleans Rhythm Kings, was a band of young white musicians playing in Chicago and which became a strong influence on their contemporaries. The front-line came from the Crescent City, Paul Mares on cornet, George Brunies on trombone and Leon Roppolo on clarinet. A few years later, in December 1927, what we now call Chicago style was caught on record, when McKenzie and Condon's Chicagoans recorded China Boy, Sugar, Nobody's Sweetheart and Liza. On these sides was heard the flare-ups, the shuffle rhythm, the breaks, the explosions which typified the style. The personnel were Jimmy McPartland, cornet, Frank Teschemacher, clarinet, Bud Freeman, tenor, Joe Sullivan, piano; Eddie Condon, banjo, Jim Lanigan, bass, Gene Krupa, drums, Red McKenzie, vocal, all key members at this time, with Teschemacher and Condon the most influential.

George Avakian's notes for the album issue of these titles state: "The unusual characteristics in these performances not only set them apart stylistically, but also serve as checkpoints for the 'Chicago' elements ...." He continues by talking of the 'Chicago shuffle', the two-bar flares, the varying dynamics and "... the solos are almost agonised. Phrases are short, jagged, almost spit out. There is a Chicago tone, too – tart, slightly off-pitch, with a buzzy rough edge."

A note from Pete Goulding suggests that

> Perhaps Chicago Jazz could be described as less flowing, rhythmically, than the best New Orleans variety. It is also tough, jagged, more shrill, more sour ....

> Mezz Mezzrow in *Really The Blues* goes into the use of the saxophone more and the trombone less, which I believe was associated with a shortage of trombone players amongst the youthful protagonists. Centred on the Austin High School Gang and Condon, also on Muggsy, Tesch was probably the most important and distinctive member. The style had a very short shelf-life, since the originators started to drift to New York in 1928 and merge with other styles, while those that stayed behind in Chicago came under commercial pressures. Also, Tesch died in 1932.

Cornetist Bix Beiderbecke died in 1931. Though a contemporary, he had a strong influence on these young musicians out of all proportion to the time he spent in Chicago.

Of the clarinettists, Maurie Bercov was a Teschemacher follower for only a short period, while Rod Cless and Frank Chace retained his influence all their lives. Pee Wee Russell was not from Chicago, but never wavered from the "tough, jagged" style. Benny Goodman was influenced by the men he heard in Chicago, both black and white, but later developed the smoother style which made him 'The King of Swing'.

In an essay on Chicago Jazz, tenor player Frank Powers comments:

> When one listens to the Chicagoan's recordings, it isn't a stylistic adaptation that you note; it is an emotional intensity – a driving, hard-boiled quality, with an honest earthiness, that distinguishes their music. Many of them did play in the black style, but they were musical originals. A case in point might be Bud Freeman ...

He suggests that "these were very young people who might be labelled as juvenile delinquents today." Regarding the musical devices mentioned above, he asserts that these had largely been abandoned by 1930, appearing only occasionally on a recording by

Bob Crosby's Bob Cats or Eddie Condon. Also, he draws attention to the fact that though the Chicagoans did play standards like Jazz Me Blues and Sister Kate, more often than not they concentrated on pop tunes.

He concludes:

> Some Chicagoans, like reedman Bud Jacobson, never left town. Others such as Goodman, Stacy, Krupa, Freeman, Tough, Sullivan and Spanier became internationally famous during the Swing Era and remained revered figures in jazz. Later, younger musicians like Frank Chace, Bobby Gordon and Marty Grosz would revive the older Chicago traditions and play in the idiom with surviving veterans like Tut Soper, Art Gronwall and Johnny Mendell. But, for the most part, these veterans are gone and today Chicago Style is seldom played in the form in which it was conceived.

After the early 1930s, certainly, the Chicago jazz style as epitomised by the recordings of McKenzie and Condon's Chicagoans, the Chicago Rhythm Kings, The Jungle Kings and The Cellar Boys had run its course. Thereafter the music was affected by many influences; by what was happening in New York, by new musicians arriving in the city and by the revivalist movement which began with Bunk Johnson and Lu Watters.

One of the new enthusiasts searching for Chicago jazz was guitarist, vocalist and raconteur Marty Grosz, who lived in Chicago for twenty years, having moved there in 1954. He went to the city in search of a dream: "I had this kind of vision in my head. I thought that I could find the ghost of Tesch and the ghost of the Three Deuces. Of course, it was gone, they were all parking lots ..." and "All the time dreaming that somewhere in the distance ... there was a Summa Cum Laude band waiting ... Not realising of course that these things were becoming scarcer and scarcer ... that things in jazz don't last very long. But we were young and full of beans."

The Summa Cum Laude band was Bud Freeman's eight-piece group which included Max Kaminsky, trumpet, Brad Gowans, valve-trombone, Pee Wee Russell, clarinet and Eddie Condon, guitar. It survived just over a year between 1939 and 1940.

Grosz expresses the view that the last gasp of Chicago jazz was "when [George] Avakian went there and recorded Jimmy McPartland and Boyce [Brown] and so forth." That was for Decca

Records in 1939 and may well be a suitable cut-off line for the style known as Chicago, but related jazz continued to be played there for the decades after and into the 21st Century, as proven by Grosz himself and, to name just five others, musicians like trombonist Jim Beebe, reed player John Otto, trumpeter Bob Neighbor, drummer Wayne Jones and cornetist Andy Schumm. Whatever the style, a great deal of quality jazz was played and continues to be played.

George Brunies: The tailgate supremo

February 2002 saw the centenary of the birth of the New Orleans born trombonist who, being of a superstitious nature, changed his name to Georg Brunis when it was pointed out that he'd been saddled with a 13-letter name. The revised surname stayed, as inevitably the revised given didn't because, he said, no one knew how to pronounce 'Georg'.

His parents were musical, as were his sister and five brothers, but he was the only one to move from New Orleans in pursuit of a career in jazz. (Brother Merritt, also a trombonist plus playing cornet, led the band at Chicago's Friars Inn after the New Orleans Rhythm Kings broke-up; this was a comparatively brief spell away from his home town). But earlier George played alto horn in 1910 in the band led by Jack Laine and, later, trombone in the Pantsy Laine (Jack's son) band as well as working with other groups in the area. Around 1920 he was in Chicago, again jobbing, until becoming a member of the Friars Society Orchestra, the house band at the Friars Inn on the North Side of the city. By the summer of 1922 the band included fellow New Orleanians cornetist Paul Mares and clarinettist Leon Roppolo and such was its success that Gennett recorded two batches which sold well enough, though probably principally in the Chicago area. Certainly enough for Gennett to have the band back several times the following year when the records appeared as being by the New Orleans Rhythm Kings.

This is the name by which the band is generally known to record collectors and jazz buffs and must be considered the first by a band playing jazz in the New Orleans style. King Oliver's band with Louis Armstrong and much admired by the NORK men, followed quite soon and this suggests that Gennett was happy with sales of these now primitive-sounding discs. For all that, they repay listening today, 80 years on, for the nicely balanced ensembles and lively rhythm. Brunies played perfect tailgate and simple but effective harmonics and a few solos of which that on Tin Roof Blues became the set version down the years.

The NORK disbanded early in 1924 and by April Brunies was a member of Ted Lewis's touring 'show-biz' band, staying for 10

Left to right: George Brunies, Muggsy Spanier, Darnell Howard, Chicago, 1950.

Muggsy Spanier and George Brunies, Chicago, 1939. (Courtesy of Jim Gordon Collection)

years. Most of the band's records are very commercial with, for us today, too many 'vocals' by the leader. Carefully put together LPs and CDs are worthwhile if only because many tracks include solos, albeit mostly of eight bars, by Brunies who can be heard from time to time pumping little bits of New Orleans trombone into the ensembles.

Generally rather more interesting for us are the Deccas of September 1934 and 8 February 1935 which appeared as being by the NORK. Wingy Manone and Sidney Arodin fitted the billing well enough as did Eddie Miller in the later session. These are likable performances, if perhaps a little too refined, but Brunies does his stuff just like he always did, including on Tin Roof Blues (which he also made with the Lewis band in 1925). And from this period, as part of his regular job with trumpeter Louis Prima, and with Arodin and Miller, were more records which have been much reissued on CD in recent times.

Brunies spent most of the second half of the 1930s in the house band at Nick's in New York's Greenwich Village. In 1938, Bobby Hackett was the leader and Brunies recorded with the band and, with much the same front line under Eddie Condon's name, as he also did in this period with Wingy Manone. But it was the band led by Muggsy Spanier, in Chicago and, later, New York in 1939, that produced the records by which both the leader and Brunies, as well as clarinettist Rod Cless, are particularly remembered. These classic sides have been reissued countless times down the years and need no analysis here. Suffice to say that Brunies fits perfectly, just as he never failed to do, in the ensembles. Spanier and Brunies worked together several times in later years and always happily, though the trombonist, a steady drinker who never got really drunk, was inclined to take over the leadership as he mellowed. Spanier had difficulty controlling him.

The 1940s passed in New York, again at Nick's and other clubs such as the Famous Door and with leaders Art Hodes and Eddie Condon. There were records under his own name as well as Wild Bill Davison's for Commodore in 1943 and again in 1946. Brunies had been taking vocal choruses, famously first in 1939 on Spanier's Sister Kate and Dinah, on gigs and Milt Gabler had him perform his parody of Clarence Williams's 1917 hit, Pretty Doll. The words were Brunies's own - he called it Ugly Child and it sold well. The later dates brought vocals on several others including a 'comic' version of

Shade Of The Old Apple Tree. All these sessions provided typical hard-blowing jazz which became known as 'Nicksieland' with Brunies's trombone exuberant and not yielding an inch to Davison's cornet.

He was a regular on Rudi Blesh's *This Is Jazz* radio half hour in 1947. By the 1950s, Brunies was back in Chicago where he led the band at Club 11-11 on Bryn Mawr Avenue for about eight years. He made the trip to New Orleans in 1955 when he recorded for the Southland label. There were briefer engagements elsewhere but by the 1960s his health was in decline, though he did work from time to time. He died in Chicago on November 19, 1974.

George Brunies was self-taught and never learned to read music. Like others, including Louis Armstrong, he never forgot a tune: once heard, it was in his repertoire. Added to which, he was one of the very few who didn't need to warm up: he put the trombone to his mouth and played hot jazz from cold. He was not a great soloist but impressed with his carefree *joie de vivre* as he swung mightily in the fast pieces and quite tenderly in the slow.

As already remarked, his real forte was his ability in ensemble Dixieland/New Orleans style jazz. He seemed to have that instinctive know-how of where to place a few notes in the right spots so that the performance is propelled. Here it can be said that he played rhythm on his trombone as though part of the rhythm section. In the 1930s, *the* white trombonist was Jack Teagarden, a stunning soloist. His ensemble playing, rarely heard in Dixie/NO, was indifferent. Miff Mole was eclipsed and Brunies soldiered on and then came the Revival and Jim Robinson and, for traditional buffs, the others were nowhere.

Even so, there were those who never lost their admiration for little Brunies. If you haven't listened recently and wish to refresh memory of what real ensemble trombone is all about, get out those Spanier 1939 albums and just listen to George Brunies telling us. He was the master.

Records: New Orleans Rhythm Kings: Classics 1129. Ted Lewis: Living Era CDAJA5273, JSP CD326 and Retrieval RTR79014 are recommended; Muggsy Spanier: Bluebird 07863 66550-2. Bill Davison Commodores: Commodore CMD14052. This is Jazz (Blesh): Jazzology J CD 1025/1026 onwards in 2-CD sets.

Jack Pettis: More on …

"Nobody seems to know about Jack Pettis, but he was the first swinging tenor player I ever heard. Since there was no one before him, playing that style, I have to call him a master."
— *Bud Freeman (Talking Jazz to Max Jones)*

While researching the career of Frank Snyder (*The Mississippi Rag*, April 1983), the original drummer with the New Orleans Rhythm Kings, I wrote to William Russell in order to follow a lead that Snyder's drum set was on display somewhere in New Orleans. Although the lead led nowhere, Bill Russell kindly sent me some NORK material. This was a summary by Squirrel Ashcraft of an interview he had with Jack Pettis on August 14, 1936. Last year I contacted Squirrel Ashcraft's widow, "Patter" Ashcraft, who kindly agreed that the interview notes could be published.

Ashcraft sent this summary to Bill Russell at the time when the book *Jazzmen* was being prepared. The notes, reprinted exactly as written, begin:

Jack Pettis originally came from Danville, Illinois,[1] but came to Chicago and worked on the Board of Trade as an office boy. At the age of about 18, when he was then working for the Hoover Food Administration, on the day of the Armistice, he and a friend of his, in the course of their celebration, both bought saxophones (C Melody) at Lyon and Healy's. He had monkeyed around with a piano to a certain extent before this, but not seriously, and had never played a saxophone or heard one played by anybody. The following morning his friend returned his saxophone but Jack decided to keep the one that he had bought, and he spent every afternoon from two to four, after the Market had closed, in the office vault practicing.

Some time later, when he had learned something about the instrument, Sammy Weinstein asked him if he would play a job with a band that was then playing at the Erie Cafe.

After having tried to handle both jobs at the same time, he finally quit his Board of Trade job since he was making $20 a week there and the band was paying him $45. This band was composed of a

Jack Pettis.

violin, saxophone, clarinet, banjo and piano. The clarinetist was called 'nigger' and came from New Orleans. The pianist was Elmer Schoebel. Some time later some one brought George Brunies arid Paul Mares to them (they were working at another cafe) so that Pettis and Schoebel could hear some "New Orleans music." Every Sunday after that Mares and Brunies jammed with them at one of the band members' house until finally they decided to substitute them for the banjo and violin. They then wired Frank Snyder in Danville to come up, which he did, and added Johnny Provozano on clarinet instead of 'nigger' and Arnold Loycano *(sic)* on bass. They jobbed around Chicago for a while and then got a job on a river boat where they played on the sister ship of a boat that Louis Armstrong was playing on, and frequently jammed with his band whenever they had a chance. Bix used to come down to the boat when they were in Davenport and hear both their band and Louis'. He had just gotten a trumpet and could play Fidgety Feet and only one other tune - (and four pieces on the piano) - so they would let him sit in with their band for those pieces only.

Bee Palmer came up north with an act which included Leon Rappolo. After Pettis' band had gone back to Chicago and the Palmer act had broken up they got Rappolo to come to Chicago and join them. He sent to New Orleans for a friend of his, named (Lou) Black, to play banjo. Later, Steve Brown joined the band on bass when they first got the job at the Friars Inn. They started at $90 a week and were raised to $125 after the first month.

Pettis was the first to leave the band, because he wanted to put some money in the band and go to New York, and the others were unwilling to leave Chicago. His place was taken by Valle Devoe *(sic)* for a short time. Don Murray and Mel Stitzel, who lived in Chicago, were playing in a small band at Round Lake, Wisconsin, in the summer time. (Don's father was a minister and his only previous experience on saxophone had been playing in church). The Friars band played a job near Round Lake, and Don came down to hear them regularly when he came back to town, and ultimately took Devoe's place on tenor.

Later, Stitzel took Schoebel's place on piano and later was succeeded himself by Carl Pierce. Glen Scoville was later added as an additional tenor sax, and Benny Pollack took Snyder's place after all of the Friars records had been made and the first set of New Orleans Rhythm Kings numbers. Stitzel played piano in Tin Roof Blues. Bix and Mesirow used to hang around the band all the time.

Pettis played a tenor by accident; he had never heard any jazz tenor player before. He sent his C Melody to be repaired and, since the job took a week; they sent him a tenor to use during the interval. He liked the tenor better because it was better voicing for their combination. Pettis and the boys in the band had heard very little colored music prior to encountering Louis on the river boat, which was for a relatively short time, though they all had heard, on some occasions, Baby Dodds and Joe Oliver who were then playing in Chicago. At the time the Friars were playing, practically the only other orchestras in Chicago were Isham Jones and the Oriole Terrace.

In Pettis' opinion, the styles of all the members of their orchestra and the orchestra as a whole was determined before they had had any negro influence to amount to anything, and their basic style remained the same even though the band used a number of negro licks and figures after their contact with Louis and the others. He thinks that up until the end they were playing basically white music with the actual figures greatly influenced by the negroes, but that this influence had no very substantial effect on their original idea.

The above summary is also held at Rutgers Institute of Jazz Studies in Newark, and at the William Ransom Hogan Jazz Archive at Tulane University in New Orleans. The Rutgers copy contains the following postscript: "This was dictated just after Jack left the office & there is a lot of extraneous stuff. The spelling of names is doubtful. Sq."

Today we know the correct spellings for Arnold Loyacano, Volly De Faut, Leon Roppolo, Mezz Mezzrow and Johnny Provenzano. And the final paragraph could no doubt be the basis for prolonged discussion.

Conclusion

John Chilton's *Who's Who Of Jazz* supplements the above summary of Pettis and his early career by telling us that he was born in 1902 and that prior to joining the NORK he worked for a spell in Dixon's band on the S.S. Capitol. After the NORK Pettis formed his own band to accompany singer Ann Pennington on vaudeville circuits, and he stayed on in New York after engagements at the Palace theatre. He joined the Ben Bernie orchestra and was principal saxist and arranger for about five years. Worked under

Bernie's auspices as leader aboard the Atlantic liner *S.S. Leviathan*. He led a band accompanying singer Morton Downey, then had long residencies at the Hotel New Yorker and in Hollywood.

It seems likely that Pettis left New York about 1934, possibly after the Hotel New Yorker engagement. An item in the February 1935 issue of *Metronome*, under a Pittsburgh heading, states:

> Jack Pettis, whose music and booking office was the rage of the town for awhile, has departed for an engagement in the midwest.

As Cody Morgan, who found this reference, comments, an item like this raises more questions than it answers. But it does suggest that after leaving New York, Pettis became a booker, rather than continuing as a full-time musician. Reports in *Down Beat* confirm that he was in Chicago during the latter half of 1936, though he is only mentioned in references to jam sessions and concerts. Early in January, 1937, just before a Chicago Rhythm Club concert scheduled for the 24th, the program tells us that Pettis "had to leave for the coast."

Ed Ward, of the Chicago Federation of Musicians, advises that there is no birthdate for Pettis in the union's files, but his membership record shows that he was elected to the Chicago Local on October 21, 1921, and that his membership was erased on January 8, 1938. At the time he was elected, Pettis was living on N. Keating Avenue.

Local 47 of the AFM in Los Angeles has no record of Pettis at all. ("We have no information on a Jack Pettis in our active, inactive, or deceased files.") This probably confirms that Pettis left music towards the end of 1937 but would also suggest that any work in Hollywood was very limited, perhaps even restricted to the four titles made at a recording session for Variety in April of 1937.

What is surprising is that we do not know his precise date of birth. Even the year 1902 is surmised from a note on the Ashcraft summary of 1936 which states: "Pettis is 34 now." Neither has any information been found about the date and place of his death, assuming the likelihood that he is no longer alive.

In *The Mississippi Rag* for December, 1985, Warren Vaché, Sr., posed "The Piquant Puzzle of Jack Pettis," examining the Pettis-related recordings made between December 1926 and March 1930. Readers are referred to this extremely useful survey and discography, which attempts to distinguish between those recordings with Ben Bernie sidemen and those with Ben Pollack's. Names such as Benny Goodman, Tony Parenti, Eddie Lang, Don Murray, and the Dorseys abound. Brian Rust's *Jazz Records 1897-1942* adds to this discography a New Orleans Ramblers session in January 1931 and the Variety date mentioned above. In the Vaché listing there is confusion between the 1929 sessions of February 8 and c. February 14, leading to the omission of Jack Teagarden's name.

Another useful source of information on Pettis recordings was "A Discography of Jack Pettis and his Orchestra" by R.G.V. Venables, published by *The Jazzfinder* in November 1948. This was compiled with the assistance of Al Goering and includes a note that the trumpet obbligato behind the vocal on Baby is by Tommy Dorsey.

The reasons for Pettis' retirement and for his impact on jazz saxophone playing may be inferred from the following quotations by two disparate musicians:

Bud Freeman, in conversation with Max Jones (*Talking Jazz*), said:

> It must be realized that there was a Chicago school of tenor. There were many players who played in that style and didn't become well-known. Pettis was the king of that style. They called the style North-western then. It had the cool sound and a Louis-King Oliver beat. Lester Young, though he may not have known Pettis, was influenced by that particular school of tenor. A lot of saxophone players in the early Twenties were pretty corny, and this swinging was played by very few.

Making similar comments in his autobiography, *Crazeology*, Freeman writes: "I was hardly the only musician to have lived off a rich woman. I could name seven other tenor-saxists who have done it. Jack Pettis... was one. He married an heiress."

And in *Twenty Years On Wheels* Andy Kirk wrote: "There was a tenor man with (Ben) Bernie who was my first big jazz influence. His name was Jack Pettis. I even copied some of his solos."

If hearsay evidence is allowed, Bill Challis told Norman Gentieu that Don Murray thought highly of Jack Pettis's playing.

In his *Rag* article, Warren Vaché, Sr., commented of Pettis,

> He was also a talented composer and is listed, with Elmer Schoebel, as co-composer of the jazz standard Bugle Call Rag. He

went on to turn out a number of jazz-flavored instrumentals with pianist Al Goering.

(Goering was a colleague and collaborator of long standing.) These instrumental included Bag O' Blues, Spanish Dream, Stockholm Stomp, Freshman Hop, and Sweetest Melody, all pleasantly typical of their time. It is interesting to note that two titles (St. Louis Shuffle and Shufflin' Sadie), recorded by Fletcher Henderson, are credited to Pettis and Fats Waller. Intriguing to consider the circumstances which brought about a collaboration between Fats Waller and a member of showman Ben Bernie's orchestra.

Individual Pettis titles have been released on French RCA and other labels, while Neovox in England have put ten of the better known titles onto cassette, coupled with eight by Jack Purvis (Neovox 742). There is also an album on Broadway BR115. Now Retrieval is planning three volumes of Pettis material. Volumes one and two are in abeyance until better copies of some of the original 78s can be found, but volume three (Retrieval FH-129), containing titles from July 1928 to May 1929, was recently issued. The final title on this album is At The Prom by Irving Mills and his Modernists, a Mills-Pettis composition, while the May 9, 1929, session features both Benny Goodman and Tony Parenti as clarinet soloists. FR-129 is a required acquisition for anyone wishing to discover more about this pioneer of jazz saxophone.

One of the difficulties when trying to assess Jack Pettis as a player and as an influence is deciding which instrument he actually plays on his recordings. An *ad hoc* panel of John Chilton, Bert Whyatt, Bob Wilber and this writer listened to 16 titles from the Neovox and Retrieval reissues with only partial agreement. John Chilton commented: "I have noticed before that it is very difficult to distinguish between 'C' melody sax and someone playing in a 'light toned' manner in the upper registers of the tenor sax." Bob Wilber echoed this with: "It's pretty hard to tell what Pettis plays sometimes, (particularly when he doesn't have a solo)..."

There was unanimity on just two titles. On Bugle Call Blues it was agreed that Pettis played tenor, and on the 1929 version of Bag O' Blues he played alto.

Whether playing alto, C-melody or tenor, the solos by Jack Pettis are technical rather than rhythmical. This would confirm that Pettis was not strictly a jazzman, but that his main influence was in his sound and his skill on what was, at that time, an instrument trying to find its place in jazz.

Edwin "Squirrel" Ashcraft (1907-1981) was an attorney whose home near Chicago became famous for its weekly "Sessions at Squirrel's". He played piano accordion with the Princeton Triangle Club Jazz Band from 1926 to 1928. Many of the Monday night sessions were recorded by John Steiner and selections were issued in limited edition albums as "More Informal Sessions". Squirrel Ashcraft is heard on piano on some titles.

Postscript:

Since the above was written, Retrieval has released, in LP form, Volume Two (FJ-130) of their Jack Pettis series. There are 17 tracks, recorded between November 1924 and February 1929, featuring sessions by The Ambassadors, Jack Pettis and His Pets, Bert Bernie and his orchestra, The Whoopee Makers and Mills' Musical Clowns.

*

1   Later information shows that Jack Baber Pettis was born, not in Danville, Illinois, but in Ermandale, Vigo County, Indiana on February 10, 1902.
In 1929 he married Catherine Ann Lynch, whose professional name was Taddy Keller, one of the Keller Sisters vocal group. They had a daughter, Barbara (1930-2002), were divorced in 1932, but then moved together to Oklahoma City about 1956. His occupation was shown as "salesman". Taddy died there on July 2, 1962, aged 53, followed by Jack, "somewhat penniless", on August 24, 1963 from cirrhosis of the liver. He was buried in an unmarked grave, but in March 2017, thanks to well-wishers, a proper headstone was laid. These facts may be found on the David Garrick website, www.jazzage1920s.com/jackpettis/jackpettis/php, a comprehensive survey of the Pettis career, with many photographs of the Pettis family, and other memorabilia. The entry acknowledges the Pettis and Lynch families, a second cousin, Jay McKay, and researchers Enrico Borsetti and John Liefert.
A check of sailings by the *S.S. Leviathan*, researched by Howard Rye, confirms that Pettis was employed as a member of the luxury ship's orchestra for the trans-Atlantic crossings between April and October 1930. His final voyage ended on October 13 and he was discharged on the 19th.

Frank Snyder: Rhythm King drummer

In the history of jazz played by white musicians it is accepted that the most influential group in the early 1920s was the New Orleans Rhythm Kings, known originally as the Friars Society Orchestra. King Oliver's Creole Jazz Band's influence upon them, followed by their own impact on younger musicians such as the Austin High Gang and Bix Beiderbecke, were significant events in early jazz history. Of the members of the band who recorded for Gennett in August 1922 most, including Paul Mares, George Brunies and Leon Roppolo, went on to jazz fame, if not fortune. Perhaps because of the outstanding career of his replacement, Ben Pollack, Frank Snyder was the least publicised member, though he worked as a band-leader throughout the 1930s, employing some of the best musicians in Chicago.

Frank Martin Snyder was born May 21, 1899 in Champaign, Illinois. His parents moved to Danville, Illinois, when he was quite young and he always regarded Danville as his home town. His father played clarinet and flute, passing on his love of music to his two daughters and four sons. Both girls played piano. Harry played alto saxophone, Earl, trumpet, Ralph and Frank (the youngest) drums. Frank's original tutoring came from his father, but he received formal training at the University of Illinois. There he played in the marching band, which he loved. All the sons played with Merle Evans in the Ringling Brothers Circus Band.

While Frank Snyder was learning his trade, another Danville youngster named Jack Pettis was at work in Chicago and practicing on the C-melody saxophone. He later obtained work at the Erie Café on Clark Street in a band which included pianist Elmer Schoebel, plus a violinist, clarinetist and banjoist.

> Some time later someone brought George Brunies and Paul Mares to them so that Pettis and Schoebl could hear some 'New Orleans music'. Every Sunday after that Mares and Brunies jammed with them at one of the band members' house until they finally decided to substitute them for the banjo and violin.

Frank Snyder, in his late 20s. (Courtesy of Peggy Snyder).

Paul Mares had arrived in Chicago from New Orleans in 1920, probably during the fall, to join New Orleans drummer Joe "Ragababy" Stevens' small band at the Campbell Gardens on Campbell and Madison. Satisfied with the prospects he sent a telegram to George Brunies, who joined Stevens in the winter of 1920.

Jack Pettis wired his friend Frank Snyder in Danville to come and join the new group. At the same time Arnold Loyacano was added on bass and Johnny Provenzano on clarinet. They jobbed around Chicago for a while then got a job on a riverboat. John Steiner refers to the band working at the Erie Café and jamming at a beer garden, the Blatz Palm Gardens. He continues: "When faced with the usual summer layoff, a group consisting of Jack Pettis, alto, Elmer Schoebel, piano, Lew (sic) Black, banjo, George Brunies, trombone, Paul Mares, trumpet, and --- Ayres, drums, found a Mississippi riverboat job". The summer job was for the Streckfus company and Brunies in an interview suggested it was on the *S.S. J.S. Streckfus.*

Whoever Mr. Ayres may have been it is probably that Frank Snyder replaced him at an early stage. Peggie Snyder, Frank's widow, says that her husband worked on a riverboat with Paul Mares.

In *Bix: Man and Legend*, details of Leon Roppolo's 1921 itinerary include a mention of George Brunies and trumpeter Emmett Hardy leaving Albert 'Doc' Wrixon's band on the *S.S. Capitol* in July, indicating that Mares and Brunies were not inseparable at this time. Before this, it seems that Brunies and Mares had renewed their New Orleans friendship with Roppolo when their boat took them to Davenport, where Roppolo and Lou Black were members of the Carlisle Evans band.

Early in August 1921 Mares, Brunies Roppolo and Black accompanied Bee Palmer at the Friars Inn, a basement cabaret at Wabash and Van Buren (60 East Van Buren) in Chicago. In January that year Roppolo, with Emmett Hardy, had worked with Bee Palmer in Davenport. Steiner said: "When, after several weeks, she and her husband, pianist Al Siegel, departed, Mares rounded out his Friars Society Orchestra with some Chicago musicians and settled in for a long residency at the cabaret."

The Chicago musicians were Frank Snyder, drums, Jack Pettis, C-melody and tenor, Elmer Schoebel, piano, joining Mares, Brunies, Black and Loyacano. Most sources list Leon Roppolo as present from the beginning, but John Steiner names Johnny Provenzano as the clarinettist, soon to be replaced by Roppolo, with Steve Brown coming in as bassist. This became the personnel which sparked the young apprentice musicians of Chicago from about October 1921 through 1922. They recorded the first influential Gennett titles in August 1922. (Schoebel at 26 and Brown at 32 were the veterans in the band; the average age of the other members was 21.)

In his autobiography, Eddie Condon refers to hearing reed player Don Murray in the band with Frank Snyder, but if Condon's recollection is correct it may have been an occasion when Murray was sitting-in. This practice was a common one, with Bix Beiderbecke and composer Julie Stein just two of those involved.

Richard Hadlock reports that the Friars Inn was managed by Mike Fritzel,

> ... who tried to give the place a high-toned atmosphere, hence the 'Society' orchestra. But before long it had become a hangout for big-time, high-spending gangsters, and even Al Capone and Dion O'Bannion started to come in." *Jazzmen* quotes one of the musicians as saying it was for "the big money people; you had to spend money there. Nevertheless, it was a 'cheap' joint."

For her part, Peggie Snyder says that the Friars Inn was not a cheap joint and the gangsters were real gentlemen. George Brunies recalls that the hoods included Terry Drogg, Nails Martin, Vincent "The Schemer" Drucci, and Frank "Legs Diamond" (Maritote). "It was a place where the boys hung out and it was run pretty nice, there was never any trouble. It was owned by Fritzel alone, no syndicate."

Because of this success, the Gennett record company was interested in recording the band. At this point Husk O'Hare appeared on the scene. According to George Beall, O'Hare represented himself as leader of the band to Gennett, while at the same time telling the musicians that he was a stockholder in the Gennett company and could arrange very favourable terms for them. None of these claims was true, but O'Hare got some publicity and, no doubt, a percentage. By the time of their 1923 recording sessions the band knew the truth; they rejected all references to O'Hare, even to the extent of changing the band name to the New Orleans Rhythm Kings. But in August 1922 they recorded as The Friars Society Orchestra.

As with most recordings of the period, it is difficult to comment on the drumming. Woodblocks predominate, competing with the sound of the banjo, but there is some driving drumming in the final ensemble of Bugle Call Blues, a composition by Pettis, Brunies and Snyder. (As Bugle Call Rag it is usually credited to Pettis, Schoebel and Meyers, with the occasional addition of famed composer Irving Mills!) George Beall, writing more than fifty years ago, said, "Black and Pollack are particularly effective on Bugle Call Blues." Unwittingly he had paid a tribute to the work of Frank Snyder.

Towards the end of 1922 there appears to have been some dissension within the ranks of the Rhythm Kings and early in 1923 "the rhythm section moved over to the Midway Gardens, where Schoebel became the house bandleader". Lou Black went as far as to say; "Well, the Rhythm Kings broke up in 1923 – largely for personal reasons – and some of us joined the Memphis Melody Boys. It was a dance band – an eight-forty-five to eleven-forty-five band."

The front line of this band was normally led by cornetist Murphy Steinberg, with reedmen Phil Wing, Art Kassel and Roy Kramer part of the collective personnel. Records made during 1923 used a variety of band names: the Chicago Blues Dance Orchestra (Columbia), Original Memphis Melody Boys (Gennett), Midway Dance Orchestra (Columbia) and Midway Gardens Orchestra (Paramount). Brian Rust lists Snyder as present only for the Chicago Blues Dance Orchestra titles recorded May 30/31, 1923, but reasonably the Fountain reissue album also lists him for the Gennett session of April 1923. Snyder is listed as co-composer with Elmer Schoebel of Wonderful Dream recorded at this date.

Just when Snyder left the Midway is uncertain, but it was before the end of 1923. His wife says he "went to Providence, Rhode Island, with Arnold Johnson and stayed east for some years, I guess."

In *Rust* there is a quotation from *Variety* for November 24, 1926, which lists a personnel for Ralph Williams and his Rainbo Orchestra, including Frank Snyder.No other information is known, though Peggie Snyder remembers that the Rainbo Gardens in Chicago were beautiful. The ballroom was on Clark Street and Lawrence Avenue.

Peggie Snyder continues:

I met Frank in 1930, when he was playing a dance marathon at the Merry Garden (Sheffield at Belmont), the longest marathon in history. The band was led by Shorty Williamson, a piano player from Frank's home town of Danville. Bix played in the band every night. The Merry Garden were owned by Ethel Kendall and Jack Lund, whom Frank knew well.

In 1931 or 1932 Frank played with Dave Rose (piano) in a band at the Victor Vienna Gardens during our World's Fair.

Around the beginning of 1933 Snyder became leader of the band at the Subway Café, 507 N. Wabash Avenue, in Chicago. Johnny Patterson, the owner, started it in two rooms below street level and built it up into one of the best steak house and bars in town. Advertised as "the longest bar in the world," John Hammond refers to it in his autobiography as "famous for having the longest bar in Chicago." It seems that Frank Snyder contracted the two bands which played in the Café, for a total of 14 hours of band music each day. Snyder's Rhythm Kings played the 11 p.m. to 7 a.m. stint. The bands were in addition to the singers and pianists employed.

Catherine Jacobson recalls that the personnel for the band were virtually unchanged from its opening in early 1933 to its closing in 1936. The regulars were Carl Rinker, trumpet, George Lugg, trombone, Bud Jacobson, clarinet, tenor, Frank Snyder, drums. Jess Stacy was the pianist for a time, with Art Hodes subbing for him for a few days. Stacy was replaced by Tut Soper, who also recalls bassist Bill Foley joining for a while. John Chilton lists George Lugg as working intermittently with the group, but Mrs Jacobson, Bud Jacobson's widow, is certain he was a regular. She is also sceptical of the Chilton entries which show Larry Shields and Rod Cless playing at the Subway, as is Tut Soper.

Eventually an attempt was made to share in the success of the Subway. Peggie Snyder remembers that "a political person told Johnny he wanted 60% of the operation and John to pay all expenses out of the 40%. Johnny just closed the doors and left the person out on a limb. He took over a place out of town called Scarlett's." Tut Soper's memory of this is that Federal agents used pick-axes to destroy the place, "all because our boss refused to pay blackmail money to those powers ... when he was running a legitimate bar." This was in early January 1936.

Frank Snyder did not follow Patterson out of town. Instead he accepted a residency at the Winona Gardens at 5120 N. Broadway.

The *1946 Esquire Jazz Book* says: "late that year (suggesting 1935) Snyder moved his Rhythm Kings to the Winona Gardens, using Rod Cless on clarinet, Bud Hunter on tenor, Carl Rinker on trumpet and Art Gronwall on piano." This personnel was still present in January 1937. A concert held there on Sunday, January 24, 1937 was organised by the Chicago Rhythm Club to feature a revived New Orleans Rhythm Kings – Paul Mares, Rod Cless, Bud Hunter, Kyle Pierce (listed as Carl Pierce) on piano, Arnold Loyacano and Frank Snyder. The support band was Frank Snyder's Rhythm Kings.

Of the Snyder band, the program notes state:

Several years ago (he) organized his Rhythm Kings and it is one of the few good bands in the country to continue the old tradition ... They are now engaged permanently at the Winona Gardens. Most of the band arrangements are by Gruenwald and Hunter and various members of the band have composed Monotony, Don't Lose It, Down Beat Swing and Friday the 13th.

The last was named for the Snyder's wedding date, November 13, 1936.

An invitation card for an "informal Annual Dinner Dance" at the Winona Gardens lists Frank Snyder and his Rhythm Kings and announces a "Grand Opening" on Tuesday, May 22 and Wednesday, May 24, 1939". It is likely that this was a re-opening after redecoration, but it is not known if Snyder worked elsewhere during the time the club was closed.

The chronology hereabouts is a shade uncertain, but Peggie Snyder's recollections are that her husband worked at the Winona Gardens from 1936 to 1939/1940, then led at the Club Silhouette. John Chilton lists Mel Henke [piano] playing with Frank Snyder in the late 1930s and Catherine Jacobson says that her husband was in the band at the Winona Gardens for a while.

Peggie Snyder recalls the Club Silhouette engagement lasting until 1943 or thereabouts, followed by two years at the 5100 Club (5100N. Broadway) where Danny Thomas was the headliner. He and Frank were great golf partners until Thomas left for California.

For the next two years or so Frank did club and show dates until, in 1947, he left full-time music. (Though Catherine Jacobson recalls her husband playing with him in Frank Marshall's band on the "City of Grand Rapids" lake excursion boat between Chicago and Grand

Rapids, Michigan, in the summers of 1946 and 1947.) To quote Peggie Snyder again: "Music took a nosedive and Frank became associated with the radio and TV department in the Fair Store on State Street in Chicago and used music as a secondary. This required another band and for seventeen years he just played shows and country club weekends, and did very well, too." Regular members of this band included Lyle Siske, trumpet, Marshall Maybie, sax, Ange Costalanno, piano, Art Groah, bass, Frank Snyder, drums, with trombonist Charlie Barber added from time to time.

Circumstances also meant a change in style. Frank Snyder's notepaper was now headed: "Chicagoland's Most Danceable Band" and "Music For All Occasions".

For a short spell, after leaving the Fair Store, he worked in the TV department at the Lyon and Healy store on Wabash and Jackson, then, said Peggy Snyder: "Frank retired in 1964 and we moved to Tucson, Arizona, for a warmer climate where we could play golf, hunt and fish."

Frank Snyder died in Tucson, June 17, 1976, and was buried in Danville, Illinois.

In *Jelly Roll, Bix and Hoagy: Gennett Studios and the Birth of Record Jazz* by Rick Kennedy mention is made of an interview with Frank Snyder which appeared in an issue of the *Richmond Palladium-Item* in 1963. Mr. Kennedy did not have a copy of the interview and one has not been traced.

The fifth edition of *Jazz Records 1897-1942* omits the *Variety* quote. Frank Snyder is shown with Ralph Williams and his Orchestra when it recorded three titles for Victor in St. Louis on December 16, 1925.

"Jack Teagarden's Music" by Howard Waters stated that Jack and Charlie Teagarden played in the Eddie Sheasby band at the Vienna Gardens in 1933, with Frank Snyder on the drums.

Down Beat for June 1937 reported that Snyder had left the Club Silhouette to spend the summer season in Charlevioux, Michigan. Reedman Joe Rushton was in the band.

In a letter to Bert Whyatt, dated May 18, 1982, Tut Soper talked about Snyder:

His energies went into outdoor sports – golf, fishing, hunting and the pleasant habit of tilting glass after glass ... He just didn't seem to want to drive the band – too much effort. He could play however, if he wanted to. When you're the leader and you don't seem to want to, especially on drums, you have a non-swinging band and ... we didn't swing 'cause the drummer didn't feel like inspiring the beat. I don't mean to be uncritical and unkind but this is the way it was and he had no fears, as the bosses and owners loved him and truthfully, so did we. I especially loved his human qualities and his compassion and understanding. Very frustrating musically but very secure and safe socially.

N⁰ 25 $2.00 Per Plate
informal
ANNUAL DINNER DANCE
GRAND OPENING
15 Big   Heinie
Vaudeville   beautiful   Cramer
Acts   New Outdoor & Indoor   Master of
                                          Ceremonies
Winona Gardens 5120 Broadway
TUESDAY, MAY 23 & WEDNESDAY, MAY 24, 1989
FRANK SNYDER AND HIS RHYTHM KINGS
DINNER 6 to 12 P. M.

Records

The New Orleans Rhythm Kings (double album, Milestone M-47020)
The Midway Special (double album, Fountain DFJ-115)

Notes

In outlining the events leading to the formation of the New Orleans Rhythm Kings I have been guided by the Jack Pettis interview.
Arnold Johnson is a bandleader of whom little is known. In *Hear Me Talkin' To Ya* Ralph Berton is quoted as asking: "Do you know the name of Arnold Johnson, an excellent pianist of that time?" Danny Polo [clarinet] had his first professional job with the Midway Gardens Orchestra about 1923 and not long after played with Johnson's large band in Florida. Benny Goodman was with Johnson from late 1923 into 1924. Johnson later became well-known in New York with a society-type orchestra.

The photograph of the Frank Snyder Rhythm Kings (with Tut Soper) on page 78 of *Black Beauty, White Heat* by Frank Driggs and Harris Lewine is accompanied by a note that the band was at Harry's New York Bar. Frank Snyder did not lead at this bar. The photograph was taken at The Subway.

Art Gruenwald, the pianist, changed his name to Art Gronwall.

Bob Thiele, in an article about Rod Cless, reported him at the Club Silhouette in late 1937 with Carl Rinker, Bud Hunter and Frank Snyder. "Later in the year the band was augmented by the presence of such notables as Paul Jordan, Bill Dohler, Don Carter and Floyd Town (piano, alto, drums, tenor, respectively). This location lasted about a year and a half when he went back to the Winona Gardens." Thiele fails to mention that Frank Snyder was the leader at both locations. It may be that Cless returned to the Winona Gardens as leader or sideman with another group. Or perhaps the Snyder band played the Silhouette while the Winona was being redecorated? Rod Cless joined the Muggsy Spanier band in April 1939. Bill Dohler told Tut Soper that neither he, Paul Jordan, Don Carter or Floyd Town played the Club Silhouette.

Tut Soper said that Bix Beiderbecke did not play in Shorty Williamson's band.

The Frank Snyder Band at the Subway Cafe, 1934. Left to right: Tut Soper, p; Carl Rinker, tp; Bud Jacobson, ts; Frank Snyder, d; George Lugg, tb. (Courtesy of Peggy Snyder)

Elmer Schoebel: Pianist, composer, pioneer arranger

The purpose of this article is to reconsider the life and music of Elmer Schoebel, looking at his work as pianist, composer and arranger, as well as adding to the details of his later career.

Schoebel was famous in jazz history by reason of his association with the Friars Society Orchestra/New Orleans Rhythm Kings and as a composer for Bugle Call Rag, Farewell Blues, Prince of Wails and Nobody's Sweetheart.

It is surprising that upon his return to playing with jazz groups in New York during the 1950s, when the surge of interest in the music's pioneers was at a peak, no one took advantage of this to interview him in depth. The available information about his career is based upon the questionnaire which he completed (probably in 1955) for Leonard Feather's *The Encyclopedia of Jazz* and, more extensively, upon his exchange of letters with Herman Openneer Jr. This correspondence resulted in "The Elmer Schoebel Story", published in the Dutch magazine, *Doctor Jazz*, in October 1968.

From these sources we know that Alexander Peter Schoebel was born in East St. Louis, Illinois, on September 8, 1896, with no explanation for the "Elmer". He had a high school education, studied the guitar, then switched to the piano. In 1910 he began playing piano and organ in film theatres, and from 1912-1917 he worked in vaudeville. He joined ASCAP in 1927 and an ASCAP entry refers to service in WWI. He moved to Chicago in 1919, with the 20th Century Jazz Band, where he joined (1921-23) the Friars Society Orchestra, later the New Orleans Rhythm Kings. He led the orchestra at the Midway Garden (1923-25), followed by work with Isham Jones (1925 in New York), Louis Panico (1926 at Guyon's Paradise, Chicago), his own orchestra (1927, also at Guyon's) and Art Kassel (1928 at the Morrison Hotel, Chicago). "Later in 1927/28 I had my own radio show called 'Schoebel's Shower Hour' on which I did the announcing but no musicians that you will remember."

In the *Doctor Jazz* article Schoebel tells how, when working as arranger and editor for Walter Melrose, the Louis Armstrong

Midway Dance Orchestra, 1923.

Left to right: Bobby de Lys, Elmer Schoebel, Otto Barberino, Lou Black, Steve Brown, Phil Wing, Mel Stitzel, Art Kassel, Charlie Bezimek, Jesse Barnes, Murphy Steinberg.

cylinders came to be made in 1927. He transcribed the Armstrong improvisations for publication as *50 Hot Choruses For Cornet* ($2.00) and *125 Jazz Breaks For Cornet* ($1.00). Early in 1927 (the contract was signed on February 14) another sheet music album was published by Melrose, entitled *Benny Goodman's 125 Jazz Breaks For The Saxophone and Clarinet*. These too were recorded into a Dictaphone and then transcribed for publication, but Schoebel does not mention them, so perhaps was not involved.

If Schoebel's statement is correct, that the dictaphone was purchased in order to record Louis Armstrong, it means that the Louis recordings were made prior to Goodman's, even earlier in 1927. A project to put the Armstrong variations onto record was conceived by the late Swedish collector Gösta Hägglöf for his Kenneth label and recreated by cornetist Bent Persson. The highly interesting results appeared first on LP, then on three CDs, Kenneth CKS3411, 3412, 3413.

Tom Sharpsteen, who roomed with Schoebel in the 1950s when the Conrad Janis band toured, recalled one story he was told: "Walter Melrose took Schoebel on a trip to an Indian reservation in northern Wisconsin where the chief, for $5 and a cigar, would sing native songs. Elmer recorded this via solfeggio, for use by Melrose for possible songs. None was ever used." Schoebel had always had a keen interest in electrical and mechanical engineering. In 1930 he invented the Tunematic radio, which he manufactured in 1933 in his own factory. Schoebel told Tom Sharpsteen that it was a radio that was programmed to tune itself to various stations, which sounds revolutionary for that time. "He was able to buy a foreclosed factory in Chicago and began production. Sales were sparse due to the continuing depression."

In 1935 he worked for Ina Ray Hutton as an arranger for her all-girls orchestra, before becoming chief arranger for a Warner Brothers publishing company in New York, between 1936 and 1945. It is believed that this was the Music Publishers Holding Company, founded in 1929 by Jack Warner to acquire music copyrights to provide inexpensive music for films.

Chilton lists Schoebel as playing regularly in the late 1940s, as Conrad Janis' reference to the Gay Nineties bar at the Metropole (see below) confirms. He was certainly feeling his way back into the New York jazz scene by the end of 1950 when he played in a Friday jam session at the Stuyvesant Casino on November 17,

Elmer Schoebel

1950, alongside Fletcher Henderson, Bud Freeman, Red Allen, and others.

Between 1951 and 1953 Schoebel was with Conrad Janis and his Tailgate Jazz Band, and the band recorded for Circle on May 8, 1951. To quote Conrad Janis, when asked about his association with the pianist:

> Elmer was a very good friend of mine and we had a long musical relationship. I first saw him play in person at the Metropole Cafe on 49th Street and 7th Ave in NYC. He was then working as a pianist for a Gay Nineties Revue which is what the Metropole was featuring at the time (before they got into Jazz and then, years later, Strippers). I used to pass the place and watch Elmer pounding the ivories.
>
> Anyway, my California group (The Tailgate Jazz Band) had entered, and much to our surprise, won the Record Changer Magazine International Jazz Band Contest and now I was back in New York acting on the Broadway stage and in Television and was looking to bring back the rest of the front line from California (R.C.H. Smith on trumpet and Tom Sharpsteen on clarinet) and then use a veteran New Orleans rhythm section. I had Danny Barker on banjo and Freddy Moore on drums and I asked Elmer to join us on piano. He jumped at the chance to play jazz again and we began a very successful 12 week run at Jimmy Ryan's on 52nd Street in New York. After that we went on the road, The Savoy in Boston, the Senator Hotel in Philadelphia and so on.

The Jimmy Ryan's booking, for 12 weeks, began in March 1951, with the band probably leaving towards the end of May to go on the road. The engagement at Lee Guber's Swing Rendezvous, within the Hotel Senator, Philadelphia, was during late July or early August.

Upon his return to New York Janis was unhappy about the manner in which Wilbur De Paris copied the Tailgate Band's style and supplanted them at Ryan's, but he continues:

> Our band went on to play 8 jobs a week for the next several years, Mon and Tue nights at the Metropole (now playing Jazz), Wed in Brooklyn, Thurs in New Jersey, Fri and Sat at the famed Central Plaza (for Jack Crystal, Billy's father and the subject of Billy's one man Broadway hit "700 Sundays"). Jack was the band booker at the Central Plaza for some 15 years. And Sundays in Brooklyn

again but twice, one afternoon gig and one nighttime gig. Elmer was with us all through this and finally we settled into a long running gig (some 14 months) in 1954 at Child's Paramount, a restaurant under the Paramount Theater on 44th Street and Broadway. Elmer was with us through half the Childs gig and then left the band. His replacement was Dick Wellstood who was with us for the next eight years.

Schoebel had a particular style that fit well into a Chicago ensemble. He was adept at arranging and could sound out interesting harmony parts for the front line instruments and bass, when we could afford one. He was not a jazz pianist in the way that Wellstood was, but then almost nobody was a jazz pianist in the way that Wellstood was.

Reviewing the band at the Central Plaza for *Down Beat*, George Hoefer mentioned Schoebel and commented, "This group made up in spirit what they lacked in experience". About January of 1952 the band played an engagement in Boston and *Down Beat* for February 22, 1952 contained a very critical review by Nat Hentoff. Two issues later the Janis band was defended by Rudi Blesh and others. The band was back in New York by February 10th as Schoebel participated that evening in the Sunday jam session at Central Plaza, which included a Dr. Jazz broadcast.

Down Beat does not list other engagements during 1952 and the first mention in 1953 is not until July, when it reports: "Actor-trombonist Conrad Janis doubling between a part in Time Out For Ginger and tail-gating with a combo at Child's Paramount." The six nights a week engagement at Child's probably began in February or March 1953, with Dick Wellstood replacing Schoebel in September of that year.

Schoebel's dismissal from the band came as a surprise to everyone, including the leader:

> Elmer, who had not manifested any proclivity for drink, went off on a two week bender and I, perhaps precipitously, fired him on the spot. It really hurt Elmer, who couldn't believe I would fire him for his two week absence. I was quite upset about it and stood firm. I still feel badly about it and recounting it does not make me feel any better.

In late November or early December 1953 Schoebel played a brief engagement with the Steve Lacey band, Lacey on soprano.

Dick Schwartz, trumpet, Kenny Davern, baritone, Bill Goodall, bass, and Eddie Phyfe, drums. Through Joe Glaser's office they got a booking at the Savoy in Boston, but were cancelled after a week because the owner hated saxophones!

In Leonard Feather's questionnaire Schoebel said that he was accompanist to singer Tommy Lyman at the 5th Avenue Hotel in NYC, 1954-1955.

Schoebel moved to Florida in 1955, presumably straight to St. Petersburg where, he says, "I made good time jazz weekends at the Crystal Bar." In 1958 he played briefly with Blue Steele and his Rhythm Rebels, a group which included cornetist (and cartoonist) Arnold (Arnie) Mossier. He seems to have been a regular partner with Mossier thereafter. There is even a press release from Child's Restaurant in New York for October 1954 which shows he and Mossier in the Riverboat Jazz Six, playing opposite Turk Murphy and his band. (This Child's date confuses the chronology hereabouts.[1]) In his 1968 article Schoebel says that he "played also with the Arnie Mossier band" (the Suncoast Dixielanders), while John Chilton reports him playing with Mossler's Suncoaters (sic) two days before his death.

By the end of the twenties Schoebel's time as a pioneer leader and arranger, and even as a composer, had come to a conclusion. For the next two decades he was away from the jazz scene. When he did return it was in a secondary role to younger musicians recreating the music of his youth.

Elmer Schoebel died in St. Petersburg, Florida, on December 14, 1970.

Pianist

If Schoebel's claim to fame rested upon his ability as a jazz pianist, then he would have no claim at all. The entry in *The New Grove Dictionary of Jazz*, that he was "Scarcely audible as a pianist on most of his recordings" is only too accurate. The titles by The New Orleans Rhythm Kings, The Midway Garden Orchestra, The Original Memphis Melody Boys and the Chicago Blues Dance Orchestra all confirm this. Even the two titles under Schoebel's own name, best remembered for the presence of Frank Teschemacher on clarinet, Prince of Wails and Copenhagen, contain just one short and rather dull solo. The 14 titles which Conrad Janis and his Tailgate Jazz Band taped on May 8, 1951, were probably recorded in Rudi

Blesh's New York apartment, and are available on GHB BCD-71 and BCD-81. Despite his pioneer status Schoebel is hardly featured, the one exception being a short version of Alabama Bound, a piano solo with banjo and drums. This ragtime novelty piece confirms Schoebel's lack of credibility as a jazz pianist, as do his other solos, on the band numbers Snag It and Creole Belles.

Janis himself said,

Elmer was a wonderful pianist, as we all know, and we would feature Nobody's Sweetheart and Farewell Blues and Elmer wrote and arranged new numbers for the band.

He was a gentleman, courtly and well-dressed. with a wonderful and silly sense of humor which I really enjoyed. I had great affection for him." Tom Sharpsteen, clarinetist in the Janis band, was also complimentary, saying: "I remember his playing as a bit more jazz than ragtime. Perhaps through the years his style developed into more of a 'swing' mode. He was wonderful to work with and I think he really liked working with us amateurs.

Less impressed by Schoebel's playing, after making due allowance for the poor piano at the Central Plaza, was Rutger's archivist Dan Morgenstern, who saw the Janis band there on a number of occasions.

Arranger

In the chapter on pre-swing arranging, written for *The Oxford Companion To Jazz*, James T. Maher and Jeffrey Sultanof state that "other active arrangers [of stocks] at that time were Bob Haring, Jack Mason, Elmer Schoebel, Mel Stitzel and Walter Paul." (Schoebel and Stitzel, together with Marty Bloom, all worked for Melrose during the 1920s.)

Dick Sudhalter, in *Lost Chords*, says that "the work of Schoebel, like that of Roy Bargy and Don Bestor, for the 1923 Benson Orchestra of Chicago .... emerges as easily equal to Don Redman's." He also points out that the highlight of Schoebel's 1923 recording of House of David Blues "is a full chorus for clarinet trio, one of the earliest recorded examples of this device in a jazz setting, and clearly predating similar efforts by both Morton and Don Redman."

In *Chicago Jazz* William Kenney writes it was

... Schoebel who, more than any other individual, chartered the major musical course of white jazz in twenties Chicago.... He designed a successful amalgamation of jazz and social dance music at Midway Gardens in 1924-25, creating the hottest white dance band in a major Chicago ballroom, and went on to play and arrange for other top dance bands led by Isham Jones and Louis Panico.

James Dapogny in *The New Grove Dictionary of Jazz* says: "... his work displays a development from his early, rather naive scores to later, more sophisticated ones." In his notes to Stomp Off CD 1407, Dapogny confirms Schoebel's importance during the 1920s, adding:

> Both as an early 20th- century jazz/pop pianist and as an arranger working so much with the music of Jelly Roll Morton and other early jazz composers, Schoebel absorbed the multi-strain format that the music had inherited from ragtime and other sources.

Also, in *Lost Chords*, Dick Sudhalter indicates that Schoebel's time had passed, writing:

> Nostalgia for the early '20s also permeates an October 18 (1929) Brunswick session under Elmer Schoebel's leadership. By then the pianist of the Friars Inn was heavily involved in commercial music; he'd done well as a songwriter and had risen in the Melrose organization as a composer and arranger.
> For his Brunswick date he chose two Melrose catalogue items, Copenhagen and Prince of Wails. In all, the session has a curiously anachronistic feel. Even Schoebel's arrangements seem a bit out of touch; Joe Haymes' scores for the Weems band had more 'modern' voicings, more out-and-out swing, than anything heard here, on what was supposed to be a 'pure' jazz date.

As with the O.D.J.B.'s pianists being the only band members who could read music, so it was with Schoebel and the Friars Society Band. He was the director and arranger, as he was for The Midway Garden Dance Orchestra.

His arrangements would have been used by others, including Isham Jones and Louis Panico, but details are lacking. Among his stock arranging credits we know of two numbers recorded by Fletcher Henderson. One is Dynamite, originally arranged by Harold Arlen. The other is Sugarfoot Stomp (Dippermouth Blues) originally arranged by Don Redman. Schoebel's stock arrangement includes Louis Armstrong's interpretation of the King Oliver solo transcribed note for note.

Arrangements for Walter Melrose

Some information about his more jazz-orientated arranging/ transcribing for the Walter Melrose company is available on the Library of Congress website. Their Music Division states that the first important set of jazz 'stocks' - published sets of parts for jazz orchestra - was the Melrose Syncopation Series. It holds some of these stock arrangements (dated between 1923 and 1937), including the following arranged by Elmer Schoebel and dated between 1924 and 1927. All titles are Jelly Roll Morton compositions, except where otherwise shown.

African Echoes (Luke-Senter)[2]
Black Bottom Stomp
Cafe Capers (Mel Stitzel)[2]
Chicago Breakdown (= Stratford Hunch)
Easy Rider (Thomas A. Dorsey)[2]
Grace and Beauty (James Scott) [2]
Grandpa's Spells
Hyena Stomp
Kansas City Stomp
King Porter Stomp
Maple Leaf Rag (Scott Joplin)[2]
Midnight Mamma
The Pearls
Queen of Spades (= Black Bottom Stomp)
San Sue Strut (Joe "Wingy" Mannone)
Shave 'Em Dry (Sam Wishnuff)
Shreveport Stomp
Slippery Elm (Boyd Senter)
Smoke House Blues (Charlie Luke)
Steady Roll Blues (Geo. Bates and Mel Stitzel)
Steamboat Stomp (Boyd Senter)[3]
Sugar Babe (Walter Melrose and Boyd Senter)
Tom Cat Blues
Weary Blues (Artie Matthews)[2]
29th and Dearborn (Richard M. Jones)

Composer

A provisional listing of Elmer Schoebel's compositions.

Names of co-composers/lyricists are given inside brackets. House of David Blues and Tea Pot Dome Blues were named for famous scandals of the time, while Ten Little Miles From Town was a hit of the day which was not good enough to last.

Ace In The Hole[4] (Louis Panico)
A Minor ThingWith A Major Swing[5]
Blue Grass Blues (Billy Meyers)
Brotherly Love[4] (Billy Meyers)
Bugle Call Rag (Blues) (Jack Pettis, Billy Meyers)
Cotton Pickers' Ball[4] (Billy Meyers)
Discontented Blues[4] (Paul Mares, Leon Roppollo)
Everybody Stomp[4] (?)
Farewell Blues (Paul Mares, Leon Roppollo)
Don't You Shake Me Down (Billy Meyers)
Hot Aire[4] (?)
House Of David Blues (Billy Meyers)
Land O' Lingo Blues[4] (Billy Meyers)
Lots O' Mama (Billy Meyers)
Made A Monkey Out Of Me (Billy Meyers, Lou Black)
Melancholy (Bloom, Melrose)
Nobody's Sweetheart (Now)
          (Billy Meyers-Gus Kahn-Ernie Erdraan)
Oriental[4] (Billy Meyers)
Prince Of Wails[4] (?)
Railroad Man (Billy Meyers, Sid Erdman)
Spanish Shawl[4] (Billy Meyers)
Stomp Off, Let's Go[4] (?)
Suite 16 (Billy Meyers, Art Kassel)
Tampeekoe[4] (Billy Meyers)
Tea Pot Dome Blues[4] (?)
Ten Little Miles From Town[4] (Gus Kahn)
There's Dixieland In Heaven[5]
There's No Gal Like My Gal[4] (Billy Meyers)
T.N.T.[4]
Too Bad[4] (Billy Meyers)
What Can A Poor Fellow Do?[4] (Billy Meyers)
What Shall We Name The Baby?[5]
Wonderful Dream (Snyder, Frank?)

Most of these titles were originally recorded during the 1920s, by the Friars Society Orchestra and The Midway Garden Orchestra, or its various off-shoots. Other bands which recorded Schoebel tunes (number shown in bracket where appropriate) included Abe Lyman, Ben Bernie, Duke Ellington (2), Don Redman, Erskine Tate (Stomp Off, Let's Go, of course), Charlie Elgar, Gene Fosdick, Guy Lombardo, George Olsen, Gene Rodemich, Isham Jones (3), Jack Hylton, Jimmie Joy, King Oliver (Too Bad), Lud Gluskin, Paul Ash, Ray Miller, Richard M. Jones, Sam Lanin, Tennessee Tooters, The Wolverines, Fletcher Henderson (8), New Orleans Owls (3) Original Indiana Five (4), Original Memphis Five (4), and Johnny Dodds (Melancholy). Many of these titles have been recorded also by revivalist bands.

Ten Little Miles From Town was heard in "Our Dancing Daughters", a 1928 Joan Crawford silent film with a synchronized music track, and Spanish Shawl was in the 1929 Marx Brothers' film, "Cocoanuts".

Billy Meyers, who provided the lyrics for the majority of Schoebel's songs, takes a vaudeville style vocal on Made A Monkey Out Of Me by the Original Memphis Melody Boys.

In summary, Elmer Schoebel was only a jazz pianist in the same way that Lil Armstrong, Fletcher Henderson, Arthur Schutt, Frank Signorelli and so many others were jazz players during the 1920s. It was as an arranger and composer that he made his main contributions. Privately tutored, he seems to have had a natural ability for arranging, transcribing and notating, though most of his work is now outmoded. His best compositions remain in the jazz repertoire and his work for Walter Melrose on the Louis Armstrong "Hot Breaks" collection and the stock arrangements of the Jelly Roll Morton numbers undoubtedly helped to disseminate the work of these masters. For these reasons he deserves to be remembered for this strong contribution to the early days of jazz.

The 1933 radio invention may have been called the Tune-O-Matic.

Collector Charlie Crump found a 78 rpm under Elmer Schoebel's name. These details he provided, combined with data from Michel Ruppli's *Savoy* labels discography (Savoy acquired the National label), adds a session to the Elmer Schoebel discography. Ruppli lists it under singer Billy Banks' name, who may also sing on NSC 599 and NSC 602.

(NSC 600) ELMER SCHOEBEL'S DIXIEBAND
(Schoebel, piano, with unidentified trumpet; trombone; clarinet; tenor; guitar; bass; drums).

(NSC 601) BILLY BANKS with E. SCHOEBEL'S DIXIEBAND
(Banks, vocal; with same band)

New York City - c. April 1950

NSC 599	There'll Be Some Changes Made		unissued
NSC 600	Maple Leaf Rag		National 9113
NSC 601	Train's Comin' (Schoebel)	vBB	National 9113
NSC 602	The Joint's A Jinx		unissued

Schoebel is also present on three titles from a broadcast:

HENRY 'RED' ALLEN & CONRAD JANIS
(Allen, trumpet, vocal; Janis, trombone, vocal; Bill Lovett, clarinet; Schoebel, piano; Bill Stafford, drums.)

Central Plaza, New York – April 13, 1952

Clarinet Marmalade	Storyville STCD6049
Sweet Sue	Storyville STCD6049
Eh Las Bas vHRA,CJ & band	Storyville STCD6049

These titles are from a broadcast, originally on WMGM transcriptions.

Notes

1 Did Schoebel move to Florida towards the end of 1954 but return to New York with the Riverboat Jazz Six to appear at Child's? Or was he a sub in the band for this New York appearance, which led to work with Mossier when he did move to St. Petersburg?
2 These titles also listed in a 1926 "Melrose Dixieland Concert Series", arranged by Elmer Schoebel.
3 Usually credited to Jelly Roll Morton.
4 Titles recorded by Les Rois du Fox-Trot and issued on Stomp Off CD 1407
5 Unrecorded titles listed in ASCAP entry. No dates given. See also, on LP, Fountain DFJ-115, "The Midway Special" and "Early Chicago Jazz", Timeless CBC1-071.

Rod Cless: The Forgotten ones

George Roderick Cless appears in the reference books as playing clarinet and saxes and the former is the instrument for which he is known to connoisseurs of jazz of yesteryear. On record, at least, he played alto on a 1928 session while Frank Teschemacher played both clarinet and alto. Later that year Cless played both instruments in a Frankie Quartell session and then, five years later, both again as a member of the reed section in a Jack Teagarden big band. In only the first of those is his alto playing worth more than a passing mention: Teschemacher starts Jazz Me Blues on clarinet, switches to alto and, towards the end, Cless has a half chorus.

As a jobbing musician in the 1920s and 1930s, doubtless he played both and very likely also tenor saxophone. There is some suggestion that Cless may have played in a Ted Lewis Chicago session the day before the Teagarden and further, that the tenor solo in a recently reissued title (Ten Thousand Years Ago) might be by him. There's something of the up-tempo Bud Freeman about the playing but as there is no certain knowledge of anything by Cless on that instrument the chances are we shall never know for sure.

For record collectors there was nothing easily available until the 1939 sessions by the Muggsy Spanier Ragtime band. They were a revelation for many, for there had been little other than the McKenzie-Condon Okeh and the Chicago Rhythm Kings Brunswick sides, of what could be determined as 'Chicago' jazz as opposed to New Orleans influenced 'Dixieland' by such as the Bob Crosby Bob Cats. The Spanier sound was not too far removed from that of such as the Chicago Rhythm Kings, which included Spanier, of little more than a decade earlier. Cless's contributions to the sixteen titles are exemplary examples of the contribution of the clarinet to jazz ensemble playing and his solos attractive variations on themes, especially in Eccentric, almost a showpiece for him. His sound has something of Teschemacher hardness and nothing of Pee Wee Russell's quirkiness. The former probably had some influence on Cless but just compare with Jimmie Noone's and Johnny Dodds's way with the instrument; Cless's clarinet

Rod Cless and George Wettling (and the back of James P. Johnson).

THE METROPOLITAN HOT CLUB
PRESENTS

CHICAGO JAZZMEN

FEATURING

GEORGE BRUNIES -:- ROD CLESS -:- CHELSEA QUALEY

DANNY ALVIN -:- DICK CAREY

AND OTHER FAMOUS MUSICIANS

MALIN STUDIO-THEATRE   SATURDAY 29th
135 WEST 44TH STREET   AUGUST
NEW YORK   AT TWELVE O'CLOCK NOON

flows, seemingly without effort, and in 1939 Spanier would have been hard pressed to find a more suitable sideman.

Rod Cless was born in the tiny town of Lenox in south west Iowa on May 20, 1907. As a boy he learned to play the violin but moved to cornet and then clarinet and saxophone. He played clarinet in his high school band and later in university bands. He did well in his studies but was attracted to jazz so at the age of eighteen he moved to the state capital Des Moines when he learned that the Wolverines were enjoying a long engagement at the Riverview Park Ballroom. By that time, of course, the band did not include Bix Beiderbecke and the personnel is uncertain. However, for that gig at least, the clarinet and alto sax player was Frank Teschemacher and Cless struck up a friendship with him. He doubtless worked as a musician in the area, perhaps supplementing his income with other jobs, before moving to Chicago at the age of twenty. He roomed with Tesch for a spell and worked for much of the next ten years as a jobbing musician, principally as a saxophonist. Employers included Charles Pierce, an amateur musician/bandleader who, on records at least, used Teschemacher, Cless and Spanier, and led dance bands at ballrooms, restaurants and clubs and happily encouraged jazz-minded musicians to enliven brisk numbers with 'hot' solos. Others such were Frank Quartell, a trumpeter whose band, including Cless, played the Little Club on Rampart Street in New Orleans and recorded for Brunswick in December 1928; and Louis Panico, yet another trumpet playing leader.

As the Depression eased, at least some Americans were able to pick up on the nightclub scene and that, coupled with the end of Prohibition, meant more work for bandleaders. One such was Floyd Town whose musicians included Floyd O'Brien, Jess Stacy and George Wettling as well as Cless in 1933. The jobbing continued through the decade with a 1936 spell for drummer Frank Snyder's Rhythm Kings (Snyder had been with the New Orleans Rhythm Kings in 1922). Snyder, along with Paul Mares of that historic band, and various others including Cless, played in the many sessions organised by the Chicago Rhythm Club set up by Squirrel Ashcraft and Helen Oakley. Jimmy McPartland's photograph collection included several at the Three Deuces on Chicago's North State Street in 1937 showing Cless in company with Miff Mole, Joe Rushton and George Wettling.

Cless mixed socially with fellow musicians and their families and had married Bud Freeman's sister. This did not last - he had become an habitual drinker - and they were divorced in 1939 at about the time Muggsy Spanier was looking for the right men for his classic Ragtime Band. Spanier too had had problems relating to his drinking but was (for the time being, at least) in some degree of remission.

Cless remembered he was, 'working in a band at the Silhouette Club on Howard Street and it was pretty commercial. So when Muggsy came along with his proposition for a good small band, I was glad to come along'. Spanier had lined up George Brunies as trombonist and a rhythm team of George Zack, Pat Pattison and Marty Greenberg. A tenor saxist was being sought but, soon after the band opened in the Panther Room of Chicago's Sherman House Hotel Ray McKinstry came in and proved right. The history of the band is recorded elsewhere. There were a few personnel changes but Cless stayed after the move from the Sherman when it carried out several appearances before moving to Nick's in New York City. It closed at Nick's, recorded a couple of days later and then disbanded. As the year ended, Cless was set to lead the club's Tuesday night relief band, including Art Hodes at the piano and Earl Murphy on drums.

The Spaniers sold very well indeed, as they continued to in long-play reissues in later years. Spanier's cornet in ensembles and solos is by no means the sole attraction; every musician's input was important, not least of all Cless's contributions (critic George Avakian, in a *Down Beat* article, was very impressed). They are well documented on the sixteen tracks recorded for the Bluebird label.

Cless, now based in New York, worked intermittently with pianist Art Hodes during 1940-1941. In about May of that first year the pair, with a bassist, recorded for Bob Thiele's Signature label and then, in August, Hodes added trumpeter Marty Marsala and a guitarist, named the little band The Chicago Rhythm Kings and recorded again for Thiele. Thiele was an admirer of Cless's playing, even taking clarinet lessons from him, and suggested the recordings which resulted when Hodes agreed to take part. Perhaps an agent heard the records and thus resulted in Hodes being offered work at Child's Restaurant on the corner of 103rd

Street and Broadway. He played popular music with the rhythm section, including Cless playing bongoes and maracas until ten o'clock. From then until closing time the band - one Duke Du Val on trumpet, George Brunies and Cless - belted out the jazz standards bringing roaring business from students and jazz buffs. After ten weeks, it was fired with two weeks' notice.

The usual routine of sitting in and scuffling for jobs continued with work in bands led by such as Marty Marsala, Art Hodes (including a Decca record deal), Ed Farley, Brunies and, towards the end of 1942, with Bobby Hackett who disbanded when he went to NBC as a contract musician.

1943 brought some work with Wild Bill Davison, Hodes again, and sessions at Jimmy Ryan's, a famous club on 52nd Street. Bob Wilber recalls enthusiastically organising, when still at high school in Scarsdale, a concert for which he invited "New York professionals to play... including Art Hodes, Pops Foster, Danny Alvin, Wilbur De Paris, Sterling Bose, Rod Cless and Mezz Mezzrow". The school band joined in for the grand finale. Record producer Bob Thiele gathered Cless under trumpeter Yank Lawson's leadership in December along with Mole and the great pianist James P Johnson. Over forty years later the results appeared on a long-play compilation with notes by the respected Dan Morgenstern "Rod Cless never got the recognition he deserved. The glimpses you get of him here suffice to identify him as a master of the idiom."

In March 1944, Hodes made the first of his many recording sessions for Blue Note. The band included Cless, Kaminsky and, perhaps strangely, Ray Conniff on trombone. In the event, that last provided no difficulty and, with a fine rhythm section, the two dates produced fine performances in the contemporary 'Chicago' manner using almost all songs not associated with the Condon book. Cless is excellent throughout and outstanding on Yellow Dog Blues.

Hodes was working at La Casita, a nightclub in the Village, where he set up jam sessions to which 'resting' musicians were invited; they usually could be found at Julius's Bar, close by Nick's. Cless was often available though he did at least one gig in Canada before settling in under Kaminsky's leadership at the Pied Piper in the Village. James P Johnson played the intermissions there and was present for a Commodore record date in June under Kaminsky's name with trombonist Frank Orchard and a Condon-driven rhythm section. Without Condon and with Willie The Lion Smith in place of Johnson, the band recorded for Black & White in mid-August; just what caused these records to appear under Smith's name is, at best, uncertain. However, Johnson rejoined Cless for a recording date for the same label in early September when Bose played trumpet. These were Cless's only records where he appeared as leader.

Cless's drinking had continued unabated and Kaminsky was particularly concerned one December night when the clarinettist was very drunk. Cless rejected the offer of help and set off alone to his apartment. It appears that somehow he fell on to some railings and was badly injured. He died in hospital on the eighth of the month [1944].

Other than the Spanier Bluebirds, seemingly always available either officially or otherwise, it is rather sad that Cless's records are rarely available over the counter. One perhaps automatically turns to the French Classics label but there is no sign of anything under Art Hodes's name. Perhaps those early Signature 78s are hard to find? The Blue Notes were in Mosaic's five disc set from 1990. Typing Rod Cless into Google, however, produced a listing of those Signature titles and another of the Blue Notes as being on (presumably) CD albums but both noted at Sony, this product is not available. Apparently the Black & White label is, or was, owned by Capitol but I know of no use of them from that source.

Sometimes we wonder what happens to a musician's instruments when he dies. Jimmy Hamilton, one time clarinet player for Duke Ellington, was a friend of Pee Wee Russell and recalled Mary, Russell's wife, telling him, "When Rod Cless died, Pee Wee was given his clarinet, which he used for a while. But [she] persuaded him to return it to Rod's widow. She felt that the family and not Pee Wee should have the horn." Where is it now?

George Snurpus: Elusive jazzman

Joe "Wingy" Mannone and his Club Royale Orchestra
Wingy Mannone, t/v; Frank Teschemacher, cl; George Snurpus, ts; Art Hodes, p; Ray Biondi, g; Augie Schellange, d.

Chicago 17 December 1928

C-2682-B Trying To Stop my Crying   Vo15797
C-2683   Isn't There A Little Love?   Vo15797

Of the musicians on this Vocalion record, Mannone, Tesch and Hodes became famous in the jazz world, Biondi became well-known, but Schellange and Snurpus remained shadowy figures. Over the years it has even been suggested that George Snurpus was a pseudonym. However, he was and is very much a real person. Surprisingly, he visited Britain several times, during the 1950s and 1960s, as part of his work with travel groups, but even then did not come to the attention of collectors.

The story of the Snurpus family in America actually begins in the early part of the [19th] century. As a fourteen-year-old in East Prussia, Frank Snurpus avoided conscription into the German army by joining the Turnveine, an athletic club. (This was a sensible move; his father and four brothers died fighting the French.) Later, Frank Snurpus was one of several athletes to leave the club to join the Schiller Family Circus, which toured Europe and then the U.S.A. The circus was in Indianapolis when the Civil War began, and many of the troupe, including Frank, joined the Union army. He fought at Shilo, at Winchester, and at the siege of Vicksburg. Shot in the head by a sniper, he survived with a steel plate in his scalp. When he was discharged he settled in Evansville, Indiana, where he married and raised a family.

By the early years of the [20th] century Frank Snurpus had seven grandsons, one of whom was George Marshall Snurpus, born in Evansville on 27 June 1906.

George says that his father, Edward Henry, played fiddle, guitar and harmonica.

He didn't read music but played all the reels. I was 13 or 14 years old when I put on shows with my brother in the stable and charged 2 cents or a sack of rags. One boy didn't have any rags or

George Snurpus (Courtesy of).

2 cents, but was tooting a tin whistle. He gave me that and started me interested in music. I played Home Sweet Home, Old Kentucky Home, etc. Later my mom took me to the music store and I got a clarinet. I played with our gramophone records.

Starting at high school he went to the beginner's band practice, but it was only two weeks before he moved into the senior band.

One of his early jazz experiences was when he was in his teens. He recalls:

I met Jess Stacy and Bix Beiderbecke when the steamboat *Verne Swain* stopped at Evansville. The union called and said they needed a clarinet player for two cruises. I didn't play sax then. I had learned all the clarinet parts from records (Indiana Five, etc). The steward on the boat loaned me his C melody sax and the next night I played both sax and clarinet.

(This does not imply that Stacy and Beiderbecke played on the *Verne Swain*; there is no record that either did. However, George Snurpus says he received a write-up in the Evansville paper 'LOCAL CLARINETIST JAMS WITH CALLIOPE.' Does a reader have access to this paper, probably for the summer of 1922?)

Further experience came playing at the Colonial theatre in Indianapolis and at the Indianapolis Athletic Club.

In 1927 he was with the Landrey-Dorley orchestra at the Cinderella Roof in Los Angeles, then in 1928 with Howard Jackson at the Egyptian theatre in Hollywood. Later that year he was in Chicago, playing with pianist Walter Ford's orchestra at the Trianon. The personnel was: Johnny Bayersdorffer, first trumpet; Wingy Manone, second trumpet; Art Petersen, trombone; Rollie French, first sax; George Snurpus, tenor; Frank Teschemacher, alto/clarinet; Ford, piano; Joe Parks, bass/tuba; Bobby Conselman, drums.

It was during the Trianon engagement, which George recalls as lasting six months, that the Vocalion record was made. His memories of Teschemacher are that he was a jokester.

He'd put a penny in the barrel of my sax, and when I got up to play on the mike for a radio shot, it wouldn't blow. Then he'd put a small button in my tenor mouthpiece, so it would gurgle. There was Limburger cheese on the stand lights — what a stink! Yes, Tesch was a jokester.

George gradually moved away-from the jazz scene. He disliked the disreputable side of it, the dope and the bootleg drinking.

ORCHESTRA LEADER AND CRUISE DIRECTOR ON SALES INCENTIVE TRIPS AND
CRUISES: WEST INDIES * SOUTH AMERICA * MEXICO * HAWAII * MIAMI BEACH
NEW ORLEANS * N.Y. CITY * PALM SPRINGS * HOLLYWOOD * LAS VEGAS *
CHICAGO * ST. LOUIS * BOSTON * BUFFALO * DETROIT * R.C.A. * G.E. *
PHILCO * MOTOROLA * ZENITH * ADMIRAL * HOT POINT * INTERNATIONAL
HARVESTER * CADILLAC * OLDS * PONTIAC * BUICK * CHRYSLER * FORD *
CHEVE * DODGE * EUROPE 1953 - 1958 * AROUND THE WORLD 1961. *63 -71.— 5 Times

FOR AVAILABILITY CONSULT: *Ed Ganey man*

George M. Snurpus

Dear Derek! Thanks for your letter   Sept 8/93
an interest in an old Jazz man.   Born - June 27/190
I lost interest in the Jazz type of music + the
environment. most smoked pot + I never did. I
w-ingy Manone + I were playing at the TRIANON bar
room + Teschmacker played 3rd alto + clar. In
1928 when we made the record. I met Jess Stac.
+ Bix Biederbeck when the steam boat Verne
Swain stopped at Evansville Indiana (my birthpla
I was 16 + the union called + said they needed
a Clarinet player for 2 Cruises. I didn't pla
sax then. I learned all the clar parts from
records (Indiana 5 - Red Nichols, New Orleans
+ other Pathe records - The Stewart on the boat loan
me his c melody sax + the next night I played all
on sax + clar, The name Snurpus was too har
to remember so after playing with Chas agnew for
5 years I changed it to George Marshall. We
played at the Edgewater Beach hotel + did Lucky
strike shot, as well as the Lady Esther Radio show
+ many other gigs. We followed Paul Whiteman
Im into the hotel. Bix was with him then. I
played all the theatre + ballrooms in chgo. N.B.C
W. J.n - C.B.S. W.L.S. - I was an agent for entertainers + booked large productions everywhere.
I played the Sena for part with Gershwins On
American in Paris - Rhapsody in blue + other parts.
with chgo Symphony ___ I was playing in a theatre
when Stacey was here.
So you can see why I didn't follow
the Jazz route
                        Sincerely
                    George M Snurpus

1929 and 1930 found him with Jack Chapman at the Gold Coast room of the Drake Hotel in Chicago, and at the Wisconsin Hotel in Milwaukee, followed by a spell with the Joe Falvo orchestra in the Terrace Gardens of the Morrison Hotel in Chicago.

His longest employment was with trumpeter Charles Agnew's orchestra, from 1933 to 1936 - "we made many commercial records." He remembers the personnel for the Agnew band, when it replaced Paul Whiteman at the Edgewater Beach Hotel, as: Agnew, trumpet/marimba/sax; Jack Cavan, first trumpet; Ralph Pierce, second trumpet/mellophone; Jack Reid (Read?), trombone; Fred Holtz, George Snurpus, Stan Jacobson, reeds; Jack Wuerl, baritone/violin; Dave LeWinter, Hunter Kahlers, piano; Emil De Salvo, piano/accordion; Bobby Warner, guitar/vocal; Harlen Hassburgh, bass; Dusty Rhodes, drums/vocal; Marshall Sosson, violin artist. "We all sang and had a glee club."

Upon leaving Agnew, George Snurpus was involved in theatre, radio and ballroom work. During the war, between 1943 and 1945, he was in the service - "I was in the navy for two years. I played tenor, flute, piccolo and bass clarinet in the Great Lakes Orchestra."

After the war he joined the Henry Brandon orchestra in Chicago's Edgewater Beach Hotel. The following year, 1946, he had a spell with the orchestra of Jack Fulton, the ex-Paul Whiteman singer, and by 1950 he was on staff with Roy Shields at N.B.C.

Thereafter, until his retirement in 1973, he led his own band, using the name George Marshall, playing all types of popular music, as indicated by the flyer (reproduced here on pages 51/52) he sent to me.

During the last twenty years of his playing career he visited many of the major cities in Europe, went around the world three times, visiting Australia, New Zealand and Hawaii, and was cruise director for the ships *Rotterdam, Queen Of Bermuda,* and the *Ocean Monarch.* There was even a week's trip down the Ohio River, on the SS *Delta Queen,* with a five piece dixieland band. He appeared in performances by the Chicago Symphony Orchestra, and acted as a booking agent for bands and other entertainers.

The jazz world may have been left behind, but his musical career was a full one for this all-round and cosmopolitan musician. And for jazz buffs; the Wingy Mannone recording session will always seem that extra bit special because of the presence of George Snurpus, tenor sax.

He died in Evanston, Illinois, on 27 December 1996.

Maurice Bercov: Following Tesch

One of the many problems which discographers faced during the 1940s was accepting the quoted personnel for Jazz Me Blues and Sister Kate by Charles Pierce and his Orchestra on Paramount 12640. Cornetist Muggsy Spanier had said that he and clarinetist Frank Teschemacher had recorded these titles with Pierce, but apparently Maurie Bercov said he was the clarinetist. Not until Walter C Allen found a copy of the same Paramount record using different takes did it become clear that two sessions were involved, one with Spanier and Teschemacher, the other with Charlie Altiere on cornet and Maurie Bercov on clarinet. To quote Marty Grosz:

> Many collectors who had cherished the Altiere-Bercov versions, under the impression they were by Spanier and Teschemacher, later discarded these excellent jazz performances simply because they were not, after all, Tesch and Muggsy.

That Bercov should be mistaken for Teschemacher is not surprising. Dick Sudhalter wrote in *Lost Chords*: "Wade Foster ... sounds uncannily like Teschemacher ... So, too, do Bercov and Bud Jacobson." Pianist Tut Soper said: "Morrie *(sic)* Bercov could easily have been mistaken for Tesch." Frank Powers says that "Maurie Bercov was to become Teschemacher's most convincing imitator", while for Marty Grosz:

> Maurie Bercov ... seemed to have fabricated his hot style by pasting together Teschemacher's licks and runs and then reciting them in the form of a solo. He was such an apt mimic that for years some of his efforts were assumed by critics and musicians alike to be the genuine article. But by 1941 he had discarded the Teschemacher phrases and had shown himself to be no more than a competent journeyman.

Bercov's father, Samuel, was born in Russia on 5 October 1872, migrating to the U.S. in 1899. He married Sarah, who was born in Austria in 1880 and migrated to the U.S. in 1898. Samuel and Sarah had two children, Jacob and Maurice and the family spoke

Yiddish at home, confirming that they were Ashkenazi Jews. They resided at 404 East 33rd Street, in Chicago's 2nd Ward, where Samuel, a tailor by trade, operated his business.

Maurice L. Bercov was born on 25 January 1910. Christened Maurice, his name was shown on the 1920 U S Census as Morris and he continued to be shown as Morris Bercov in the AFM Local 47 Directory. His nickname was Maurie, though this has also been given in print as Morrie or Morry. Little is known of his education, musical or otherwise, but clearly he was precocious in his musical training and, as his later career indicated, became an excellent reader. Quoting Sudhalter again:

> After the Wolverines fell apart, the pianist Dick Voynow had gone to work for Brunswick, scouting talent and producing records. One of his first projects was an 'Original Wolverines' date featuring Jimmy McPartland and a few other youngsters around town, including seventeen-year-old Maurie Bercov on clarinet. Fresh out of Lindbloom High School, he'd heard Johnny Dodds and the rest on the South Side but worshiped Teschemacher and had subbed for him at the Midway, emulating his tone, attack, off-center figures. It's a small irony that, thanks to Voynow, he wound up recording two months before his idol.

Sudhalter must have had some biographical data on Bercov to be able to quote his age and school.

There are two Original Wolverines sessions which are shown with Bercov on clarinet, October 12, 1927 and May 24, 1928, the latter with perhaps an unknown cornetist replacing McPartland. These titles are on IAJRC CD 1007. (Note: writer Frank Powers suggests that it is Teschemacher on the two May titles, rather than Bercov.) The first recording by Teschemacher was the famous McKenzie and Condon's Chicagoans date of December 8, 1927.

Towards the end of 1928 Bercov was working with Joe Kayser's 13-piece band, which was definitely at the Merry Garden Ball Room for the week ending November 22nd. In October, also on the 22nd, Kayser's front-line soloists (Muggsy Spanier, cornet, John Carsella, trombone, Maurie Bercov, clarinet, Danny Altier, alto, Jess Stacy, piano) recorded two titles for Vocalion under Altier's name. It was more than a year later before Bercov's next known recording date, in February 1930 with trumpeter Louis Panico. Panico's was probably another of the bands which Sudhalter had in mind when he wrote: "Bercov jobbed around Chicago with dance bands until 1937, when he became a CBS staff musician."

In Chicago, when not working in the studios, it is likely that he participated in jam sessions. One such which has been reported was a Sunday afternoon affair at the Hamilton Hotel in August 1943, when Muggsy Spanier, cornet, Bud Wilson, trombone, Eddie Johnson, tenor, Robert Cram, piano, Henry Fort, bass, and Red Saunders, drums, were the other protagonists.

Down Beat correspondent George Hoefer, in the November 1, 1944 issue, reported:

Maurie Bercov's clarinet solos are a feature of Jimmy Hilliard broadcasts from WBBM [CBS, Chicago] at 11:30 pm (CWT) on Tuesdays. Hilliard's arrangements are in the jazz vein and there is some good jazz music to be heard.

Oro 'Tut' Soper, who played piano in Chicago for many years, recalled Bercov:

One hell of a clarinet player. I knew him before his marriage ... before he left Chicago for New York (sic). An extremely caustic, sarcastic and difficult man to get to know, let alone like. He made enemies so easily (but) he and I never had the smallest difficulty. For some reason or other we got along, yet it was not a close relationship at all. He was very unlikeable - tremendous ego, yet we never had a personality clash at all. He was extremely intelligent and may have been a very well educated person. Had a very light complexion, light, short beard; medium build and height, inclination to be stocky ... Morrie and I played different small affairs together.

To digress into a probable, but interesting, blind alley — the Howard Hawks film "Scarface" includes a night club sequence with a jazz band heard on the soundtrack. Many have considered the clarinet heard to have been Frank Teschemacher but it is evident that he was not in Hollywood in 1931, when the movie was made. For authenticity it is possible that the band was recorded in Chicago, the film's setting, in which case the musician could have been Teschemacher or an aspirer such as Bud Jacobson (his wife in fact claimed that he was, with Tut Soper on piano) or Maurie Bercov.

Allowing for the comparative briefness of his solos Bercov impresses on both clarinet and alto on the few recordings he made. With the Original Wolverines, on clarinet, he has pleasing low-register work on Royal Garden Blues and A Good Man Is Hard To Find. On Shimme-sha-wabble and The New Twister his alto solos are short but hot (DC) or run-of-the-mill and hot (BW). DC feels the clarinet playing on Limehouse Blues and the clarinet and alto work on Dear Old Southland are even closer to Teschemacher, leaving one to think that Frank Powers could be right to suggest that these really are by Tesch. But BW says it is not Tesch and may not even be Bercov! [Note that when Time-Life asked a panel of consultants to decide whether or not Teschemacher was present on a number of disputed recordings, the experts failed to reach any consensus.]

On the Danny Altier titles, Bercov's round-toned clarinet is heard only briefly at the beginning of I'm Sorry Sally, but he has a good Tesch-like solo on My Gal Sal. Leaving the best until last, we come to the two titles, Jazz Me Blues and Sister Kate, with Charles Pierce and his Orchestra. Bercov has clarinet solos on both which are Tesch-like, hot, spiky, and fluent, leaving one wanting more.

It would seem that Bercov moved west in the mid-1940s to further his career as a studio musician; he is listed in the accompanying personnel for a Hollywood session by Frank Sinatra, recorded October 31, 1946. Other Hollywood studio sessions in which his name has been noticed include Mel Henke (1950s for Warner Bros.); Frank Sinatra (January 7, 1952, for Columbia); the Bell Sisters (April 30 & July 30, 1953 for RCA Victor); Ray Anthony & Frank Sinatra (December 13, 1954, for Capitol); Red Nichols (March 6, 1956, for Capitol); the Stan Freberg Radio Show, with Billy May (July 14-October 20, 1957, some titles on Capitol); Maxwell Davis (December 1958, for Crown). There are certain to be many more such dates, though it is highly unlikely that any track features a hot clarinet solo by someone sounding like Frank Teschemacher. Neither has any report been traced of Bercov being involved in jazz events in the Los Angeles area, though his son, Brian, mentions sessions at Lou Singer's studio, with Singer, drums and vibes, and Jerry Rosen, the bandleader.

Bercov's wife, Sylvia, born 1914, predeceased him in 1973. They had two sons, Phillip and Brian. The latter, born circa 1943, used Brian Ross as a business name in the music business, playing piano and guitar, as well as working as a synthesizer programmer and record producer.

Maurie Bercov died in Los Angeles on 17 February 1977. So passed a splendidly free-wheeling and capricious clarinetist who for a few brief years contributed to the excitement that was Chicago jazz.

The Recordings

Original Wolverines

October 12, 1927

Shimme-Sha-Wabble / The New Twister (Brunswick 3707)
Royal Garden Blues / A Good Man Is Hard To Find (Brunswick 3708)

Original Wolverines

May 24, 1928

Limehouse Blues / Dear Old Southland (Vocalion 15708)
All six sides above reissued on CD: IAJRC CD 1007

Charles Pierce and his Orchestra

c. March 1928

Jazz Me Blues (take -3) / Sister Kate (take -4)
(Paramount 12640)
reissued on CD: Village VLCD001-2, Retrieval RTR7918

Danny Altier and his Orchestra

October 22, 1928

I'm Sorry Sally / My Gal Sal (Vocalion 15740),
reissued on CD: Village VILCD014-2, Timeless 1-041

Louis Panico and his Orchestra

c. February 10, 1930

Wabash Blues / Oh Doctor (Brunswick 4736)

Floyd O'Brien: He played Jazz Chicago Style

This biography of trombonist Floyd O'Brien is dedicated to the memory of his wife, Florence, and to his friend, Jim Gordon. Without their help this article would not have been written.

Floyd Walmer O'Brien was born in Chicago on May 7, 1904. After primary school he went to Hyde Park High School where he became interested in music. At the age of 14, he was playing tuba in the school band until, as he told his wife, the neighbors complained, which prompted him to switch to trombone.

At the request of a now unknown collector, Floyd O'Brien, shortly before his death, drafted some biographical notes. He wrote:

> I will try to put down in chronological order the bands I was with from the time I started playing. This will be a little difficult for me as I never kept a diary or anything of that sort. I just have some old newspaper clippings and a few pictures. Therefore, nearly everything I can tell you will be entirely from memory.

O'Brien said he had

> a picture of myself taken in 1919 with the Hyde Park High Church ROTC band. Also a picture taken in 1922 with a Masonic band (the Mountjoie Knights Templar Order of Masons) in New Orleans. I went there for the practice and because the whole trip was free - transportation, hotels, meals. They needed a trombone in the band so I got off school and took the trip. I hadn't played any jazz yet, at that time, but I went on the riverboats to listen to the music and I liked it very much. I heard a very good band there, Fate Marable, and also a white band. I think the name of it was Ward's jazz band. So then I started listening to and playing with bands around Chicago. Joe Oliver's band, in which Louis played second cornet, also Jimmie Noone's band -clarinet, piano and drums. I used to sit-in with them, taking my trombone along as there was none in the band.

After graduation in 1922, O'Brien became a professional musician and it was about this time he was "discovered" by drummer Dave Tough, who heard him at a University of Chicago

Floyd
O'Brien,
1930s.

Bob Crosby's Bobcats. Left to right: Muggsy Spanier, Floyd O'Brien,
Hank D'Amico, Eddie Miller, Bob Crosby.

fraternity dance and introduced him to the rest of the Austin High School Gang. So at the age of 18 he was already in the company of Jimmy and Dick McPartland. Bud Freeman, Mezz Mezzrow and Frank Teschemacher. Dave Tough has told of playing, as a teenager, at tea dances at the Lewis Institute in Chicago, with such musicians as Benny Goodman, Teschemacher, O'Brien, Freeman, etc. As Jimmy McPartland told Max Jones, speaking of The Wolverines:

> Finally we augmented with a trombone, Floyd O'Brien. We hadn't used a trombone much up to then and I've heard it said that the Chicagoans preferred a tenor sax in their groups. Believe me, the reason the Chicago bands used that kind of line-up - didn't have a trombone - was because there were no trombone players around! Outside of George Brunis, who blew real solid trombone, the first guy I heard play anything was Floyd. So we got him.

From June 1922, and for about the next 15 months, King Oliver's Creole Jazz Band was the hottest thing in Chicago. George Wettling and Bud Freeman have written of going with O'Brien and like-minded youngsters to hear King Oliver and Louis Armstrong at the Lincoln Gardens. Bud Freeman wrote: "Floyd, who became a fine trombonist, really loved and understood the music."

One date from around this period which O'Brien mentioned was with "Sugar Harold" [trumpet?] at the Friars Inn, perhaps opposite the New Orleans Rhythm Kings.

1923 was a special year: he became a member of the musicians union and he played with Bix Beiderbecke. In *Bix: Man and Legend*, Phil Evans reports that early in November 1923 Beiderbecke worked briefly in a St. Louis pit orchestra led by drummer Charles Cotterel. Also in the personnel were Frank Cotterel, trumpet; Floyd O'Brien, trombone; George Johnson, tenor; and Dick Voynow, piano.

It was probably during 1924 that he met his future wife. Florence O'Brien recalled that they met in a Chinese restaurant in Hyde Park."Floyd was playing in the band; I was with a date. Another friend of mine introduced me to Floyd and that was the beginning of a very full and happy life. We were only 17 and 19 years old."

Drummer Earl Wiley recalled one engagement from this period:

> One day I was talking to the boss of the Palace Gardens and he was asking, 'What shall I do for a little business?' I suggested a

Rupneck's Lounge, Chicago, 1949.
Bill Pfiefer, drums; Bill Tinkler, trumpet; Johnny Lane, clarinet; Floyd O'Brien, trombone. (Courtesy Bill Tinkler)

good Dixieland band. Just then Floyd O'Brien came in and said he had three good men—Ernie Prittikin, clarinet; Johnny Forton. piano - and he was really very good - and Charlie Curtis on trumpet. I said,'We've got a band!' and we got rid of the previous banjo-fiddle combination. In two weeks the place was packed. That particular band was only together a short time.

Early in 1926 O'Brien worked in the relief band led by Wingy Manone (or Mannone, as he was then) at the Merry Garden ballroom. Eddie Condon gave the personnel as Manone, trumpet; O'Brien, trombone; Bud Freeman, Frank Teschemacher, reeds; Art Grunwald, piano; Condon, banjo; Ralph Snyder drums. Possibly O'Brien was still there on March 15, the day that he and Florence were married.

A little later in the year he was with Husk O'Hare's Wolverines. In 1925. Jimmy McPartland had replaced Bix Beiderbecke in The Wolverines. As Bud Freeman recalled:

> Jimmy took the slot, but the band didn't have that much work and the original members kept dropping out. As they did Jimmy replaced them with members of our group. By the summer of 1926 most of the Austin High Gang were in the band. Husk O'Hare was our booking agent and we called ourselves Husk O'Hare's Wolverines. Jimmy led the group, which had Dave Tough, Tesch, Floyd O'Brien, Jim Lanigan, Dave North, Dick McPartland and me. We had two jobs. The first was for about a month at a dime-and-dance ballroom [in Riverview Park] in Des Moines, Iowa, where we played our regular numbers.

O'Brien mentioned this Des Moines booking, stating: "Tesch and I roomed together, then we came to the White City in Chicago."

This refers to the ballroom of the White City amusement park, with Mezz Mezzrow or Fud Livingston playing third sax on Saturdays. Mezz Mezzrow confirmed he joined "later on" as third saxophone. George Wettling was a replacement for Tough.

O'Brien also mentions playing with The Wolverines in Detroit's Graystone Ballroom, but this location is not mentioned by either Bud Freeman or Jimmy McPartland.

Charlie Pierce, butcher, alto player and part-time band leader, filled a booking at the Cinderella Chinese restaurant at Cottage Grove. Max Kaminsky remembered that Floyd O'Brien, Frank Teschemacher and George Wettling were in the band.

Writing of the 1926-1934 period, Florence O'Brien listed other musicians Floyd had played with: Phil Dooley, Bud Freeman, Gene Krupa, Floyd Town. Muggsy Spanier, Joe Kayser, etc. She continued:

> There used to be offices, MCA, Husk O'Hare, etc., where musicians would call and get jobs for the week, and also musicians would meet at the Union Hall and exchange their news and get jobs for one another. The better the musician, the more work they got. Floyd was always pretty busy. There were always a lot of jobs, as there were many dance halls, theaters, dining rooms and friends always helped each other so they could work together.

Bud Freeman also wrote of O'Brien's record collection and how the Austin High Gang would go over to Floyd's house and sit up all night playing records. Asked about this, Florence stated: "He once had a good size collection, but one night Frank Billings fell and broke three or four stacks of records. Floyd was really devastated."

O'Brien's notes include: "1927 Jan. to May, jobbed with Husk O'Hare with the guys, Tough, Tesch, McPartland, North, etc." This does appear to be separate from the Wolverine bookings.

As part of this constantly changing pattern of employment, Leonard Feather listed Earl Fuller, Jack Gardner, Henri Gendron and Phil Dooley as leaders for whom O'Brien played during the 1920s, in addition to studio work. O'Brien notes that he worked with Henri Gendron at the Golden Pump (presumably meaning the "Golden Pumpkin"). Jack Gardner's story in *Down Beat* reported that he led a band for nine months at the Commercial Theater, and that it included Floyd O'Brien, Bud Freeman, Eddie Condon, Dave Tough and others. No date was given for this gig, but Dave Tough's biographer, the late Harold S. Kaye, stated that during this spring of 1927, Dave Tough had been playing with Roy Peach, trumpet; Floyd O'Brien, trombone; Bud Freeman, tenor; Carl Kitti, violin; Jack Gardner, piano, leader; Eddie Condon, banjo, at the Commercial Theater in the 9500 block of South Chicago Avenue. It is this job which is reported to have ended when the band continued to play Clarinet Marmalade, oblivious to the fact that the newsreel showed Marshal Foch laying a wreath on the tomb of the unknown soldier.

In the summer of 1927 O'Brien worked in Bill Otto's band at Lake Delavan. His notes quote the period May to October. Florence O'Brien recalled Johnny Lane playing clarinet in the band.

Mezz Mezzrow wrote in *Really The Blues* of rounding up a band for Leo Schuken to play at the Rendezvous, "a gaudy high-class joint at Clark and Diversey Boulevard owned by Leo's uncle." The band was Leo Schuken, trumpet; Floyd O'Brien, trombone; Mezz Mezzrow, Frank Teschemacher, Phil Schuken, reeds; Joe Sullivan, piano; Herman Foster, guitar; Gene Krupa, drums. This was probably late 1927.

Mezzrow continued:

> In the beginning of 1928 I took a band into the Purple Grackle, a beautiful modernistic Spanish-patio kind of roadhouse, lousy with heavy purple drapes all over the joint. It was about 30 miles out of Chicago, between Aurora and Elgin. There was a big sign out front, reading 'Milton Mezzrow and his Purple Grackle Orchestra'.The job lasted for about three months...

In addition to himself on clarinet, he listed the personnel as Freddy Goodman, trumpet; Floyd O'Brien, trombone; Pete Viera, piano; Herman Foster, guitar; Gene Krupa, drums.

In his biographical jotting, O'Brien lists for March 1928 the Eagles Ballroom, Milwaukee, with Ding Bell, sax; Jack Ivett, trumpet; McCloud, bass. There is also a mention of "Sam Pick's nite".

Probably right after this O'Brien joined Floyd Town's band, which was opening at the Triangle Cafe in Forest Park. The personnel was Muggsy Spanier, cornet; Floyd O'Brien, trombone; Frank Teschemacher, Danny Altier, Floyd Town, reeds; Jess Stacy, piano; Pat Pattison, bass; and George Wettling, drums. Tesch left in June 1928, to be replaced by Rosy McHargue and then Rod Cless.

There was a lengthy engagement in 1928, recalled by Florence O'Brien, when Floyd played in a band led by Johnny Lane at the Leland Hotel in Aurora, while Floyd himself noted that in August he was in South Haven, with Sol Wagner. The Wagner personnel included Nate Bold, cornet; Floyd Hinkley, Charlie Spero, altos; Dave LeWinter, piano; George Wettling, drums.

Towards the end of 1928, Floyd Town took an engagement at the Cinderella Chinese restaurant at Cottage Grove and 64th, his personnel including Muggsy Spanier or Dick Fiege, cornet; O'Brien, trombone; Dave North, piano; Pattison, bass; Wettling, drums.

Pianist Art Hodes wrote that he first met Floyd O'Brien in the late 1920s. The location was the Pershing Ballroom, and the band was Ralph 'Doc' Rudder's, which included Muggsy Spanier, on a four-week sabbatical from Ted Lewis, and Frank Teschemacher, as well as Floyd O'Brien. [This would have been about late 1929.] For Doc Rudder, music was a hobby; he played saxophone, but by profession was an orthodontist. Perhaps it was about this time that Henri Lishon took over from Doc Rudder and Art Hodes walked out when Lishon started to tell Floyd O'Brien how to play trombone.

Other jobs of uncertain date were with Joe Kayser and Thelma Terry. Kayser organized a band to play at Merry Garden and Municipal Pier, which included Muggsy Spanier, O'Brien, Teschemacher, Marty Marsala, trumpet; George Wettling and Bud Jacobson, reeds. The same season The Golden Pumpkin featured Thelma Terry and Her Playboys, starring the bass-playing leader with Johnny Mendell, trumpet; O'Brien, trombone; Jacobson, reeds; Bill Otto, piano; and Gene Krupa, drums. Rust shows O'Brien recording with Thelma Terry for Columbia in March 1928, but Floyd told Jim Gordon this was incorrect. His first recording date was with Bud Freeman for OKeh on December 3,1928.

A further cryptic reference in O'Brien's notes is to the "Rainbow Gardens - Appleton Wisc[onsin] Si Freedheim (sax) Bill Paley (d)."

One job in 1929 was with the Gene Kerwin band at the Canton Tea Gardens, a Chinese chop suey restaurant at Van Buren and Wabash. Kerwin told John Steiner that the personnel was Marty Marsala, trumpet; Floyd O'Brien, trombone: Joe Marsala, Eddie Miller, Bud Hunter, reeds; Gene Kerwin, first piano; Eddie Condon, banjo, and Harry Goodman, bass. Dave Rose, then Jess Stacy and then Art Hodes played second piano, while Gene Krupa, Dave Tough and George Wettling followed each other as the drummer. [Tough's presence might be doubtful. Harold Kaye's researches indicate that Tough was in Europe and then New York during most of 1929.]

Another Joe Kayser group mentioned in O'Brien's jottings was at Carlins Park, Baltimore, May to September [1931]. Names shown are Johnny Mendell, trumpet; Ches Bay, unknown; Dave Tough, drums.

O'Brien gives September 1929 for an engagement at the Pershing Ballroom with Charlie Pierce, alongside Max Kaminsky trumpet; Ralph Rudder, tenor; Paul Kettler, drum? and others unknown.

Perhaps this is the same engagement as that mentioned by Florence, when she wrote: "The marathon dances were at several dance halls. Another was the Pershing Ballroom - Floyd played there with several different bands, Charlie Pierce for one."

Much of the period 1930-31 was spent in the pit band of the Paramount Theatre in Des Moines, but by January 1932 he was with the Don Hugo band. Playing at the Chateau LaMar in Janesville, Wisconsin, and broadcasting over WCLG, the personnel was: Johnny Mendell, Leo Schuken, Cliff Goman, trumpets; Floyd O'Brien, Ted Goss, trombones; Doc DeHaven, Peewee Kelly, Norris Johnson, reeds; Tut Soper, piano; Frank Salerno, guitar; Herb Campbell, bass; and Rollo Laylan, drums. Laylan was later replaced by Wally Gordon, while Tut Soper thought perhaps Norris Johnson was actually Stan Norris, whom he remembered as a very good first alto man.

Later in the year he was back in Des Moines, playing with Cato and his Vagabonds at Lake Okoboji. For this engagement O'Brien listed the following names: Les Rhodes, leader; Cootie W., cornet; Bud Berkshire, tenor; Glen Ensfelder, sax: Gus Fuhrman, piano; Shorty, bass.

Florence O'Brien commented that "In the pre-summer most of the musicians would go to play at summer resorts or towns close by, like Milwaukee, Wisconsin." She also mentioned that Floyd played at the World's Fair.

About May/June 1933 O'Brien was back with Floyd Town, appearing at the Casino Moderne on 63rd Street, playing for dancing and accompanying an all-girl floor show. The personnel was Dick Fiege, Graham, trumpets; O'Brien, trombone; Rod Cless, Cal Green, Floyd Town, reeds; Jess Stacy, piano; Dick McPartland, guitar; Pat Pattison, bass; George Wettling. drums.

Around August of 1933 he and Bud Freeman were tempted to New York by Mezz Mezzrow, who was eager to form a big band. Max Kaminsky came from Boston and in his biography wrote: "While Mezz was trying to find work for us, we were all so broke that three or four of us had to stay at Mezz's apartment up in the Bronx, and it was awful." Those three or four included Floyd and Florence O'Brien.

The band featured Max Kaminsky, trumpet; Floyd O'Brien, trombone; Pee Wee Russell, Bud Freeman, Mezz Mezzrow, reeds; Joe Sullivan, piano; Eddie Condon, banjo; Alex Hill, arranger, and "some others." To use Mezzrow's words, "I rounded out the brass section with some good guys I picked up downtown." The band rehearsed a lot and then played a Long Island cafe, substituting for Guy Lombardo. PR man Ernie Anderson has written of Mezzrow leading a "twelve piece thoroughly mixed band" at The Downtown Uproar House. The personnel included Max Kaminsky, Frankie Newton, tpt; Floyd O'Brien, J.C. Higginbotham, tb; Mezzrow, Benny Carter, rds; Willie 'The Lion' Smith, p.; Chick Webb, dr. Kaminsky recalled: "Mezzrow tried very hard with this band, but although we had a few little jobs, nothing much happened, except for a record date in the spring of 1934." [Kaminsky was overlooking a November 1933 session.]

To keep the wolf from the door during the stay in New York, O'Brien found occasional work with leaders Joe Venuti, Mal Hallett, Smith Ballew and Mike Durso. O'Brien's notes infer that he played with both Venuti and Durso at Del Monico's. He may even have been one of the Mezzrow band members who rehearsed for Cass Hagan without Mezz knowing. There were also recording sessions with Fats Waller (Mezz was hired for this date, so he mentioned Floyd, and Fats said, "Sure, bring him along too."), Eddie Condon, The Chocolate Dandies and Wingy Manone. Rust also shows O'Brien as possibly recording with the Johnnie Davis orchestra in October 1934, but on aural and other evidence this is most unlikely. Davis told 'Bozy' White he thought the trombonist was Spanky Davis.

To summarize these New York recording sessions:
October 10, 1933   The Chocolate Dandies.
October 21, 1933   Eddie Condon and his Orchestra.
November 6, 1933 Mezz Mezzrow and his Orchestra.
November 17, 1933 Eddie Condon and his Orchestra.
May 7, 1934   Mezz Mezzrow and his Orchestra.
June 28, 1934   Wingy Manone/New Orleans Rhythm Kings.
September 28, 1934 Fats Waller and his Rhythm.

Of the May 1934 recording session for Victor, Mezz Mezzrow wrote:

In fact, just about everybody on that session won the fame they deserved but Floyd O'Brien, who I consider studied harder and got closer to the New Orleans trombone style than any white man that ever lived.

In October 1934 Mezzrow moved to Jackson Heights on Long Island and he recalled Fats Waller, Ben Webster, Buck Clayton, Floyd O'Brien, among others, playing in the jam sessions there.

Very early in 1935, O'Brien joined the Phil Harris band. *Down Beat* for March 1935 reported that Harris had reorganized his band, starting with four weeks at a Buffalo theatre. The trombonists were Floyd O'Brien and Ward Silloway. Thus, it would seem that Floyd did not return directly to Chicago from New York, as has been suggested, though he may have played there as the band worked its way across the country, back to its base in Los Angeles.

The first dance organized by the Chicago Rhythm Club that year featured a pick-up band of Chicago veterans - Jimmy McPartland, Johnny Mendell, trumpet; Floyd O'Brien, trombone; Boyce Brown, alto; Bud Jacobson, clarinet, tenor; Dave Rose, piano; Jack Goss, guitar; Pat Pattison, bass; George Wettiing, drums. It was reported in *Down Beat* for October, 1935, so may have been held in late August.

An undated clipping from O'Brien's scrapbook may refer to this period: "Phil Harris opened at the Chez Paree [Chicago] the first of the month with a new band."

About this time Harris had joined Jack Benny's radio show, on which he acted as a foil to Benny, as well as providing musical interludes. The show and its rehearsals were on Sundays, avoiding conflict with O'Brien's other commitments. Florence O'Brien believed that Floyd was on the Benny show, which was broadcast from September to June, between 1935 and 1938.

Harris made annual tours during the summer months but played only the Los Angeles area during the winter season when Jack Benny's "Jello Show" was on the air. Among these Los Angeles venues were the Palomar Ballroom and the Wilshire Bowl. The band was featured in the film "Turn Off The Moon," with Charles Ruggles. Pinky Tomlin and Bill Robinson. [There is a still of Jack Benny, with O'Brien in the background, identified as from "The Horn Blows At midnight." However, this film was made in 1945. O'Brien may have been hired by Harris just for this movie or, more likely perhaps, the photograph was incorrectly identified. Perhaps the film was Jack Benny's "Man About Town" from 1939.]

Florence O'Brien said that her husband made "a couple of movies with Ozzie Nelson and Harriett Hilliard" and she also refers to a

Phil Harris movie, 1936 or 1937, with possibly Judy Canova. None of these films can be pinpointed, nor is there any reason why Floyd should appear with Ozzie Nelson.

There were also four recording sessions with Phil Harris in Los Angeles for Vocalion between December. 1936, and March, 1937. These featured such popular Harris material as Woodman, Spare That Tree, That's What I Like About the South and You Can Tell She Comes From Dixieland, so any instrumental solo space is probably very limited. One of O'Brien's companions in the trombone section at this time was Irvin Verret.

O'Brien also found regular work during the winter season as a freelance studio musician, playing such radio shows as Al Jolson's, the Kraft Cheese Program and Ballentine Ale. It was in 1938, on August 31, that Floyd's daughter. Susan, was born.

Florence O'Brien's collection included a copy of the script for a Jack Benny show on June 12, 1938. confirming Floyd's continued employment with Phil Harris. In fact, he was with Harris until April, 1939, when he left to join Gene Krupa in Chicago, replacing Bruce Squires, who in turn was joining Benny Goodman. The stay with Krupa lasted about 13 months, until the end of May 1940. and seems to have been uneventful; just the usual swing band touring, playing ball-rooms and theatres. At this time, the Krupa band was a competent but undistinguished outfit. It took part in 14 recording sessions with O'Brien present, the titles being issued on Brunswick, Columbia and OKeh, but the trombonist was not well featured.

Fortunately, he was chosen to be part of George Wettling's Chicago Rhythm Kings for the Decca Chicago Jazz 78 rpm album, playing alongside Charlie Teagarden, trumpet; Danny Polo, clarinet; Joe Marsala, tenor; Jess Stacy, piano; Jack Bland, guitar; Art Shapiro, bass, and George Wettling, drums. Four titles were recorded in New York on January 16, 1940, and the results were excellent. Critic Charles Fox commented: "O'Brien, gruff but agile, plays a splendidly teasing muted solo on Sister Kate, taken at a slow bluesy tempo."

O'Brien joined the Bob Crosby Orchestra on June 1, 1940, the same day as cornetist Muggsy Spanier. This band was anything but undistinguished. Its personnel at the time included Hank D'Amico, clarinet; Matty Matlock, alto, clarinet; Eddie Miller, tenor; Jess Stacy, piano; Bob Haggart, bass, and Ray Bauduc, drums, and its story is well enough known not to bear repeating here. Suffice to say that O'Brien was happy within its ranks, he and Florence enjoying the family-like atmosphere. What is surprising is that he was allocated few solo spaces with the full orchestra, an unexpected failing on the part of the band's chief arrangers, Bob Haggart and Matty Matlock. So it is fortunate he was a member of the Bob Cats, the small group within the band. Critic George Avakian was unhappy over the mis-use of Floyd's abilities and wrote a piece for *Jazz Information* entitled, "Why Bury O'Brien?" in which he complained about the trombonist being confined to playing tailgate in the "super-commercial Crosby band."

The Crosby band disbanded in December 1942, the final booking being a week, 11-17, at the RKO theatre in Boston. Many of the members, including Floyd, returned to Los Angeles, where they became the basis of the orchestra under the name of tenor-star Eddie Miller.

The 30 months with Bob Crosby had one other side effect. *Down Beat* for January 1, 1943, listed Floyd O'Brien in sixth position in the trombone section of its 1942 readers' poll.

A listing in *Down Beat* indicated that about May 1943 the Eddie Miller personnel was: Hal Barnet, Burt Moncrief, Kenny Apperson, trumpets; Floyd O'Brien, Harry Uhlman, Bob Logan, trombones; Eddie Miller, Matty Matlock, Doc Rando, Vic Carver, Rosy McHargue, reeds; Lew Qualding, piano; Nappy Lamare, guitar; Hank Wayland, bass; Nick Fatool, drums. This personnel was to appear in a film tentatively entitled, "Oh Say, Can You Swing?" [Was this a working title later changed to "You Can't Ration Love"? And then to the title known to have been used, "Mr. Big," with Donald O'Connor and Ray Eberle? To confuse matters further, "Mr Big" was also titled "School for Jive"!]

A corrected personnel given by Jim Gordon for a Golden Era album (LP-15023) by the Miller orchestra was Barnet, Ralph Harden, John Kee, trumpets; O'Brien, Irvin Verret, trombones; Miller, Matlock, Rando, McHargue, Clyde Rogers, reeds; Stan Wrightsman, piano; Lamare, guitar; Wayland, bass; Fatool, drums. The band sounds unimpressive and there are only a few bars of poor trombone. The same personnel possibly applies to the titles from a One Night Stand (AFRS ON56) Palladium Ballroom broadcast on September 13, 1943, for which Mickie Roy, Eddie

Miller and Clyde Rogers are the vocalists. During live appearances, a Dixieland group was featured: Barnet, O'Brien, Matlock, Miller, Lamare and Fatool, plus piano and bass. On AFRS ON56 there is nothing to identify O'Brien, even on the one title (Who's Sorry Now?) by the sextet. On the basis of probabilities, the Miller band was an "evenings-only" unit, with most of the musicians working in the film studios during the day.

It would have been about this time that the O'Briens opened a photographic shop - "a portrait studio". Florence helped decorate the shop, kept it tidy and gave a hand with the printing. As she said, "Sorry to say it wasn't a success. It was a lot of work, too. It was in Glendale and was a beautiful studio. Floyd always liked photography, but in Los Angeles there was usually a depression."

Florence mentions Floyd working five or six nights a week at the club Virginia in addition to running the shop, but this may have been later in 1944. An entry in her scrapbook refers to a Virginia Club in Pasadena and a five-piece band with Benny Strickler, a young traditionalist trumpeter who died in 1946.

O'Brien joined Jack Teagarden's orchestra towards the end of 1943. This is confirmed by the December 26, 1943, concert at the CLI Hall, in San Francisco, when Teagarden, Joe Sullivan and O'Brien sat in with Bunk Johnson at his regular Sunday session. Sullivan was playing just the one week with Teagarden's orchestra at the Golden Gate theater. Teagarden's band was undergoing a period of rapidly fluctuating personnel, caused, as Howard Waters ("Jack Teagarden's Music") put it, by the usual wartime problems. Florence O'Brien thought the stay with Teagarden was as long as six months. "They played a lot of one-nighters up and down the coast - one or two radio jobs." There was also movie work for the band in Universal shorts. In his jottings. Floyd surprisingly wrote: "Played with Jack Teagarden with his big band for about a year", listing the trombone section as Joe Gutierrez, Jack Teagarden Jr ('Little Jack') and himself. O'Brien probably left Teagarden when the latter set out on tour in March 1944.

For the rest of the year, he worked with Duke Shaffer, Hal Grayson and Freddy Slack. He also recorded with Manone, Bunk Johnson, Charlie LaVere and Red Nichols. There may have been some one-nighters with Wingy Manone, but these have not been confirmed. Mention has also been made of movie studio work, by

Leonard Feather for one, but again no details have been traced. The Charlie LaVere session was for the new Jump label and features some of O'Brien's best work.

In July 1944, after 18 months in San Francisco. Bunk Johnson was returning to New Orleans by train. En route he stopped in Los Angeles to record for World Transcriptions on Tuesday, July 11th. Originally scheduled to record with Kid Ory's band, he found himself with an impromptu group that included Floyd O'Brien and part-time clarinetist Wade Whaley. This session was issued complete (false starts, alternatives, etc) on G.H.B. GHB-lOl. Bunk researcher Paul Larsen believed that O'Brien was playing with either Duke Shaffer or Hal Grayson at this time. In a letter to Barry Martyn, printed in *Bunk Johnson: Song Of The Wanderer* (Jazzology Press) by Mike Hazeldine and Martyn, Floyd O'Brien said he was called to make the date with no notice whatsoever. "It was the most unrehearsed session I was ever on in my whole life".

An undated flyer lists Duke Shaffer and his Orchestra at the Aragon, Lick Pier, Ocean Park, featuring Bobby Hutton. Dolores Ellison, Frankie Darrington, Ernie Mathias and Floyd O'Brien. Asked about Shaffer, Florence O'Brien said: "Floyd played quite a while with him, down at the beach, at the Trianon, at Ocean Beach."

O'Brien's stay in the early part of 1945 with trumpeter Shorty Sherock's orchestra was probably as short-lived as were his sojourns with Shaffer and Grayson. Of the Sherock band, Florence only recalled that "they played down at the beach - dance halls." In addition, there may have been gigs with Red Nichols and his Five Pennies.

At least during 1945, on February 24, he was able to share another Jump recording session with Charlie LaVere, with two titles (Carolina In the Morning/Royal Reserve Blues) appearing under the name of Floyd O'Brien's State Street Seven.

It may have been the following year that he had short stays with Max Baer, Frankie Masters, Horace Heidt and Spike Jones. Florence O'Brien recalled that "Spike Jones used to play 'special shows'. I remember taking our daughter to see them in different arenas and halls. He (Floyd) played about five or six shows." Of Max Baer, ex-heavyweight world champion, Florence said that she never heard the band. "They played on Wilshire Boulevard near

Vermont. Floyd was with him about two or three months - wasn't too thrilled but the pay was there." And Frankie Masters, whose hit number was Scatterbrain? "Floyd played with Masters a couple of different times, maybe a couple of months each time. Frankie liked him, but his band was not really Floyd's style. I heard the band. Not bad."

Floyd's own notes do not tie in exactly with the above, which merely confirms there is no certainty about the times when he played with any of these particular bands. He wrote: "Also about this time, I was with Freddie Slack, Ted Fiorito, and Frankie Masters, I think six weeks with each, one right after the other."

There was a further session for Jump Records on March 11. 1946, this time with a band led by Chuck Mackey on trumpet and with Matty Matlock on clarinet. (Jump owner, Clive Acker, mentioned to Wayne Jones that there was an unissued session that included O'Brien, Matlock, Eddie Miller, Stan Wrightsman and drummer Richie Cornell. No other details arc known.)

Down Beat for April 22, 1946, carried a report: "Floyd O'Brien, whose trombone helped to create many a collectors' item, is planning to open a collectors' platter shop." Florence was not queried about this, but one suspects the shop would have been mentioned if it had been opened. Or was this one idea which then changed into the photographic studio?

There are no specific mentions of 1947 and the first nine months of 1948, which might indicate this was the period when the O'Briens were endeavoring to make a success of their photographic studio. Even if this is so, it seems reasonable to assume that O'Brien would have kept his lip in shape by playing whenever possible.

Towards the end of 1948, the O'Briens returned to Chicago. In fact, Florence could pinpoint the day they returned as October 30. She wrote: "There wasn't too much work in L.A. and my mother wasn't too well, so we decided Chicago would be best for work and family life. Both our parents were alive and we thought it best to be near them. We were glad we made that decision. It worked out to be good for us."

Floyd was soon back in action. He was in the Bud Freeman band that played for the New Year's Eve dance at the Sherman Hotel, alongside Bill Dohler, alto; Charlie Spero, clarinet; Sheldon Robbins, piano; Jim Barnes, drums, and, of course, Bud Freeman on tenor.

Early in January 1949, he joined the Johnny Lane band, with Bill Tinkler, trumpet; Ray Dixon, piano; and Bill Pfeiffer, drums, at Rupneck's, but the job folded on February 20.

Shortly after, he was in The Dixieland All Stars at the Argyle, playing with Don Slattery, trumpet; Wally Wender, clarinet; Little Brother Montgomery, piano, and Stanley Williams, drums. That gig ended late April/early May, then there was a short-lived job, until the end of June, at Isbell's restaurant, where the Dixielanders included Jack Ivett, trumpet; Charlie Morrell, clarinet; Floyd Bean, piano; Eddie Meusel, drums. In July, Ivett and Morrell's Dixielanders had found a new home at the Zebra, with Floyd still on trombone, Jack Condon on piano and Joe Pepp, drums. Other dates during this period included at least two Sunday afternoon concerts at the Hunt Club, with players like Bill Tinkler or Jack Ivett, trumpet; Johnny Lane or Bud Jacobson, clarinet; Chet Roble, piano. In late June there was a moonlight cruise on the *SS City*, featuring Carl Rinker, cornet; Floyd O'Brien, trombone; Bud Jacobson, clarinet; Bud Freeman, tenor, and others.

Writing in *Down Beat* for October 21, 1949, that most energetic and dedicated journalist, Pat Harris, reported: "Floyd O'Brien, with Jack Ivett's band, is, like the band, at liberty. O'Brien recently has been showing what a generally poor unit can do to a top instrumentalist, which is nothing good."

At the end of November John Schenck's promotion at the Bee Hive club featured a battle of trombones, with O'Brien, Don Thompson, Jimmy James and Miff Mole.

On December 11, Johnny Lane opened at the 11-11 Club with O'Brien on trombone, Jimmy Ille, trumpet; Roy Wasson, piano; Orville Searcy, drums, but O'Brien soon left to join Art Hodes for an eight-week engagement at the Blue Note, where Sarah Vaughan was the headliner. With Hodes were Lee Collins, trumpet; Pee Wee Russell, clarinet; Freddy Moore, drums, and Chippie Hill, vocal. However, O'Brien was replaced by George Brunis before the eight weeks were over, as Hodes' agent tried, unsuccessfully, to build an all-star band. Hodes tells the full story in his autobiography, "Hot Man." O'Brien returned to the Johnny Lane band at the 11-11.

On June 13, Art Hodes began a stint at Rupneck's and both Floyd O'Brien and Jimmy Ille left the Lane band to work with him. One highlight of the year was when the band (Ille, O'Brien, Jimmy

Granato, clarinet; Hodes; Bill Moore, bass; Bill Pfeiffer, drums) featured on a Treasury Department television show.

Hodes was still at Rupneck's as 1951 began. During January, Bill Price replaced Jimmy Ille as the trumpet player and then, in March, Price was replaced by the 21-year-old Muggsy Dawson. After 13 months at Rupneck's, Hodes left on July 15 for a short tour with the same personnel, O'Brien included.

A concert, which would seem to date from 1951, was held at the Grand Theatre in Oshkosh, Wisconsin, on Monday, June 18. It featured Lee Collins, trumpet; O'Brien, trombone; Granato, clarinet; Don Ewell, piano; and Booker T. Washington, drums, plus five local guest musicians. And on June 7, 1951, a John Schenck promotion at Gaffer's club had also featured Lee Collins, Floyd O'Brien and Jimmy Granato, but this time with Art Hodes, Earl Murphy on bass, and Danny Alvin on drums.

There exists a tape of six titles recorded at Gaffer's and dated April 7, 1951, with Dawson, O'Brien, Granato, Ewell and Booker T. Washington, namely the Hodes band but with Ewell on piano. It is not clear how this fits in with Hodes' engagement at Rupneck's.

The band was back in Chicago in time for an August 24th opening at Helsing's nightclub at 4361 N. Sheridan. During this booking, Whitey Myrick replaced Dawson on trumpet, no doubt when the latter had to undertake military service. Hodes remained at Helsing's until the end of 1951, then went on tour again. It is assumed that O'Brien was with Hodes throughout this period, though perhaps there were some gaps in the employment. John Dengler recalled playing cornet at Jazz, Ltd. on Christmas Eve, 1951, stating: "It was a lonely time. Fightin' Floyd O'Brien was on the job. The nickname must have come from some boxer, as Floyd was a gentle man in every way. Drank a bit, but why not?"

One date for the Hodes band during 1952 was April 14-19 at the Colonial Tavern in Toronto. British fan T.P. Stanton recalled O'Brien's kindness at this time, letting him sleep on the floor of his hotel bedroom for two nights, even feeding him. "The rest of the time he preferred to talk about baseball and piano tuning!"

Perhaps Hodes was short of bookings in the summer of 1952, for in July O'Brien was playing, yet again, in Johnny Lane's band, this time at the Preview with Don Ewell on piano.

Hodes was back at Rupneck's by September 1952 for a shorter stay before going on tour once more. When Hodes played one week at the Flame Club in St. Paul, about November, 1952 the personnel of the band was Whitey Myrick, trumpet; Floyd O'Brien, trombone; Jimmy Granato, clarinet: Art Hodes, piano; Ken White, bass, and Buddy Smith, drums.

As Hodes put it,"Work ran out around 1953, so that I couldn't say no to an offer to go into Jazz, Ltd." Of this 1950-1952 group Hodes wrote: "We had a good band (I wouldn't say it was a great band); it swung and it held the people."

By January 1953, O'Brien was back with the Johnny Lane band, which was playing at the Famous Tap. Both O'Brien and drummer Doc Cenardo were with Lane when he moved to the Normandy in June of that year.

During 1954, Floyd O'Brien was featured on two recording sessions. One was with a Natty Dominque group, the trumpeter leading O'Brien, Frank Chace, clarinet; Lil Armstrong, piano; Israel Crosby, bass; and Baby Dodds, drums, for Windin' Ball Records. The second was held on April 19, when Art Hodes recreated his band for EmArcy, with Muggsy Dawson, cornet: Floyd O'Brien, trombone; Jimmy Granato, clarinet; Earl Murphy, bass, and Hap Gormley, drums. Hodes continued to be at ease with this front line. For a concert in Park Forest on May 1, 1955, he worked again with Dawson, O'Brien and Granato. Another job during 1955 was a Saturday-only effort, which lasted for about a year, at the Copacabana in Chicago Heights. Led by trumpeter Bill Tinkler, the personnel was O'Brien, trombone; Mac McBee, clarinet; Andy Johnson, piano, and Don King, drums.

Three months later, about August 1955, O'Brien appeared at a Firehouse concert that featured Jimmy, Marian and Dick McPartland. Jim Lanigan and Baby Dodds, while Thomas Gilmore recalls Muggsy Dawson, O'Brien and Frank Chace playing in late 1954 at a short-lived bar.

These were probably the years when O'Brien was in and out of music more than ever, the years when Art Hodes recalled: "From time to time, I'd hear of him taking some sort of a day job. One time it was photography. Floyd got very excited ... 'That's the coming thing'. Then, a couple of years later, here's Floyd making duplicate keys at some big shopping store. That didn't last either. Finally, he turned to piano tuning. Took a couple of years for him to complete the course. But whatever, it never kept him away from music. If I had a job, he'd be there. Through all his gyrations, Florence went along. Financially, I never did figure out how they made it but I do know he had a two-story brick building (a two-flat) where he lived, so there was always a roof over his head."

It may have been late 1956 when O'Brien joined the band at Club Basin Street. O'Brien's own comment on this was: "Also with Danny Alvin for about a year, making one record session with him." Led by drummer Alvin, who was also owner of the club, the band personnel was Norman Murphy, followed by Del Lincoln, trumpet; Floyd O'Brien, trombone; Ray Daniel, clarinet, and Andy Johnson, followed by Joe Johnson, piano. In the summer of 1957 Jug Berger was the clarinetist and Chuck Folds the pianist, with Lincoln and O'Brien still there. Probably O'Brien remained at Basin Street until Danny Alvin's death in December 1958.

For the album recorded for Stephany (MF4002). the personnel was Del Lincoln, trumpet: Floyd O'Brien, trombone; Ray Daniel, clarinet; Andy Johnson, piano: Joe Johnson, bass, Danny Alvin, drums. An anomaly here is that the recording sessions are dated February 17 and 21, 1959, but if the date of Alvin's death has been correctly reported the sessions would presumably have been held in 1958.

Jim Beebe reports a Floyd O'Brien incident that happened during a Smokey Stover tour. The band was well served between sets, Floyd went outside for some air and suddenly had to relieve himself. According to other band members, he did so against the front tire of a car parked right in front of the club. There were two guys in this car and they were both cops. Floyd was locked up, courtesy of the city, and spent the night in jail.

Few other gigs during 1957 are known. On June 30, a benefit concert for Lee Collins was held at Lombard Firehouse in Lombard and O'Brien was one of "all my good friends from local 10," as Collins put it. *Down Beat* for June 27, 1957, also reported that the Monday night jam sessions at Jazz, Ltd. were featuring various local musicians, including Floyd O'Brien.

At the end of July 1959, Bob Koester held a recording session for his Delmark label (DL209) to take advantage of Albert Nicholas' presence in Chicago. The band assembled was Nap Trottier, trumpet; Floyd O'Brien, trombone: Albert Nicholas, clarinet; Art Hodes, piano; Marty Grosz, guitar Mike Walbridge, tuba, Fred

Kohlman, drums. Remembering the date, Bob Koester wrote: "I believe Floyd was tuning pianos at the time of the Hodes-Nicholas sessions. Later he worked in Sears as a key-maker." Marty Grosz recalls little about the session, except that "Floyd said he had consumed a lot of gin playing cards the night before" and that after the first number Albert Nicholas lifted Fred Kohlman's large cymbal off the stand and let it drop on the floor, saying something like, "That's enough of that damn cymbal". Kohlman demurred without a word.

The next engagement we have is listed in *Down Beat,* September 3, 1959, which reports O'Brien "fronting the Dixieland group at the Preview on Mondays and Tuesday." It was not long after this that O'Brien became a regular member of the Robert "Smokey" Stover band.

On September 1 and 2, he recorded with Stover's Original Firemen. Stover was a young trumpet player (he was 44 when he died in December 1975) who had begun making a name for himself with his Dixieland band ("It was a sort of Firehouse Five group," remembered Jack Tracy, one-time *Down Beat* editor). O'Brien's comment here was "Then I was with a traveling band for two or three years (Smokey Stover) and one record date was made with them." [Actually two dates, one in 1959 and a second in 1960.]

As one of the band's itineraries shows, he was with Stover throughout 1960, while a report in *Down Beat* for April 12, 1962, would seem to confirm throughout 1961 also. The report stated:"Trombonist Floyd O'Brien, lately of the Smokey Stover Dixie group, has decided to quit the road and will gig around town. He will also teach." Jim Beebe remembers him going into business with a photo shop. "Fans and friends tried to help him and take their photos to him to be developed. You might say that Floyd was not a hustler and didn't want to do anything, and he would look sheepishly over his glasses and say, 'Oh, why don't you take these to Walgreens?'"

In 1961, Floyd's Conn trombone, which he had played for 38 years, was stolen. Trombonist Beebe even says,

> I swear that I sounded like Floyd when I played his old Conn trombone. It seemed to have that dark but warm bluesy sound built right into it. Jack Teagarden tried to buy it from him. Floyd wouldn't part with it and of course the inevitable happened ... it

was stolen from him. And his mouthpiece that had been made especially for him was stolen with it. Floyd got a new Conn but he was never really comfortable with it and his playing was never quite the same.

For a time during 1962 Floyd O'Brien helped out The Gold Coast Jazz Band when it was short a trombonist. In *Jazz Report* for August 1962, Bob Koester wrote:"The Gold Coast Jazz Band has broken up again. They played their last job at the Red Arrow Saturday, June 23, with Ted Butterman, cornet: Floyd O'Brien, trombone; Kim Cusack, Bob Gordon, clarinets: John Cooper, piano; Bob Sundstrom, banjo; Mike Walbridge. tuba, Wayne Jones, drums. The band never sounded so good and Floyd O'Brien was better than I have heard him play for several years, particularly when he did extra choruses."

The following month O'Brien was a member of the Freddie Masters group, which was booked by MCA for Westover Air Force Base, Mass., July 13-26, 1962.The flyer for this engagement lists the personnel without identifying instruments: Gordon Anderson, Don English, Brenda Nelson, Freddie Masters and Chuck Spear.

Towards the end of 1962 it was reported that pianist Little Brother Montgomery's trio was working Sundays through Tuesdays at The Plugged Nickel on Wells Street and that frequent Monday night sitters-in had been clarinetists Joe Marsala and Frank Chace and trombonist Floyd O'Brien. *(Down Beat,* October 25, 1962).

A November 1963 "40 Years of Jazz In Chicago" concert featured two bands, one of which was the Frank Chace Sextet, with Johnny Mendell, trumpet; O'Brien, trombone; Chace, clarinet: Marty Grosz, guitar; Jim Lanigan, bass; Wayne Jones, drums. The same personnel, with Tut Soper on piano and Bob Skiver, tenor, was featured in a Chicago Historical Society concert on April 19, 1964. Wayne Jones recalled: "Gene Krupa dropped in and played Nobody's Sweetheart on my spare-parts drum kit!" Marty Grosz also remembered Krupa sitting in: "He had been appearing at the London House with his quartet and dropped by to see his buddies. (He) added marvelous touches and plenty of pepperoni."

Jan Scobey and Her Dixie-Cats were featured May 11-23, 1964, at the Colonial Inn in Toronto, the personnel including Rostelle Reese, trumpet; Floyd O'Brien, trombone, and Jug Berger, clarinet.

Another Austin High School Reunion took place on August 14 1964 at the *Down Beat* Jazz Festival, held at Chicago's Soldier's

Field. The personnel was Jimmy McPartland, cornet; Floyd O'Brien, trombone; Pee Wee Russell, clarinet; Bud Freeman, tenor; Art Hodes, piano; Jim Lanigan, bass, George Wettling, drums.

In 1966, O'Brien suffered a fall in a motel in Kalamazoo, Mich. He hit his head, causing a blood clot on the brain, and under-went surgery in August to have the clot removed. After that, his wife recalled,

> he didn't play much. Did rehearse with the S.W. Symphony Orchestra a few times, because it was close to home. Played maybe two concerts. Didn't play after that, except out at Jim Lanigan's house, maybe three or four times a year. The Lanigans lived in a coach house on about two acres of ground, no one near for a couple of miles, so the boys could play to their hearts content. There would be maybe seven or eight musicians and they would play for a crowd of about 35 or so, and we'd have a buffet dinner. Whenever Marian McPartland or Jim (Jimmy McPartland, who was Jim Lanigan's brother-in-law) were in town we'd be out there with Bud Freeman, Floyd Town, etc.

Floyd O'Brien died at the Little Company of Mary Hospital, Evergreen Park, Ill., on Tuesday, November 26, 1968, and was buried on the 29th.

Towards the end of her life Florence O'Brien worked two or three days a week as a guide at The Museum of Science and Industry in Chicago. She died, I believe, in 1995, leaving a daughter, Susan, and two granddaughters.

What Musicians and Critics thought of Floyd O'Brien

Writing in *The Mississippi Rag,* Thomas Gilmore wrote of seeing Floyd O'Brien at Danny Alvin's Basin Street:

> He was a slight, pale man with thinning brown hair and large, sad, attractive brown eyes like a basset hound's; in manner he was reserved and shy. Perhaps for this reason Alvin seemed to feel constrained occasionally to exhort him to play a little more or a little longer. O'Brien's playing was really unique and satisfying. His tone is hard to define, but I would call it pleasantly dark.

This reference to O'Brien's unwillingness to put himself forward assumed something of mythic stature in his later Chicago years. Bob Koester's mild comment was that O'Brien "was a very laid-back guy".

Marty Grosz told Shirley Klett that O'Brien was the world's laziest trombone player. "You'd say, 'Take a chorus' on something like Basin Street Blues or something, and he'd say, 'I'll take a half'." One suspects exaggeration here for the benefit of a good story. Perhaps a more considered assessment by Marty Grosz was the one he gave to Bert Whyatt, writing about a 1964 concert:

> Floyd O'Brien was his laconic self, except that over the years some of the 'hot' had gone out of his playing. Those years in pit bands and in Phil Harris and Bob Crosby trombone sections made his sound a bit more bland than in the early years. Or were the causes booze and age? Probably a mixture of all the above. But then many players swap hot for bland as they grow older.

Drummer Wayne Jones, also present at the 1964 concert, was in the Gold Coast Jazz Band when O'Brien deputized on trombone:

> Floyd picked up what he could of the simpler arrangements on the stand with only a minimum of in-progress coaching. He never seemed to mind playing, but of course the Lazy Floyd anecdotes colored our view of him. I wish I'd known him as a young man. Despite his 'lazy' style, which seemed to reflect his personality - slow-paced, easy-going - he worked hard as a sub. Took his choruses, followed directions, didn't demur or slack.

Among writers of an earlier period, concentrating on his 1930s recordings, he was rated very highly. In *Really The Blues* Mezz Mezzrow wrote: "More than any other white, Floyd O'Brien mastered the real solid tailgate style of Kid Ory and growl of Tricky Sam Nanton, the greatest trombone player who ever lived." Similarly, Hugues Panassie said: "Inspired by Kid Ory, he is one of the few white musicians who has assimilated the New Orleans style on trombone. He is a remarkable ensemble player, as well as a good soloist." In The *Real Jazz*, Panassie went as far as saying. "I am persuaded that the best white trombone player is neither Teagarden nor Tommy Dorsey, but is Floyd O'Brien."

The 1960 edition of *Jazz On Record* stated: "A remarkably distinctive white musician who achieves a unique effect with an absolute economy of notes and an acute rhythmic sense. All his solos are interesting..." Historian Richard Hadlock linked him with Bix Beiderbecke, Pee Wee Russell and Jess Stacy in having a "gift nestled in the realm of the artfully understated melodic phrase."

William H. Miller, the Australian critic, wrote in his booklet entitled "Three Brass":

The sobriety of Floyd Brien's character is reflected in his work, which is a constant reminder that a good musician can play a thing straight and still make it hot. It is exceptional for him to depart very far from the melody - he usually merely adds an occasional unobtrusive twist, relying for effect on his intensely hot tone and the atmosphere created by his attack, sometimes employing a mute with beautiful results.

His obituary in *Down Beat* commented:

O'Brien was a remarkable and original musician who absorbed much of the classic New Orleans style in his youth and added it to his own inventiveness. He was particularly adept with a plunger mute. ... During the 1950s he recorded ... but rarely reached his former heights.

That may have been written by Gil Erskine who, in 1964, devoted half of his review of the Albert Nicholas album on Delmark to telling O'Brien's story .and praising his work. He wrote: "O'Brien brings a full measure of musicianship to these tracks, showing an exquisite Bix-like sense for the warm sound." After referring to O'Brien's rustiness, Erskine continues: "He uses restraint, as well as power and punch, in building ensemble stresses, and he uses mechanisms of time and space that give an Oliver-like swing to the band."

And in *The Trouble with Cinderella*, Artie Shaw devoted a paragraph to his impression of O'Brien's playing after hearing him about 1926 (?), including such comments as: "There was one trombone player, Floyd O'Brien, who had one of the most peculiar, lazy, deliberately mistaken-sounding styles I've ever heard," and "after a while you began to get the idea that this guy not only wasn't making any mistakes at all, but had complete control over his horn.

Jack Tracy recalled the Smokey Stover sessions:

(Floyd) did play on a Dixie album I recorded on Argo. What I remember about Floyd was that he was short, sturdy, wore thick glasses, was extremely quiet and self-effacing and was a fine trombonist with a big, pretty tone who played ballads excellently but secretly (I felt) was not too comfortable playing in Dixie bands, but there was no other work to be had for him. One of the things that I do flash on is Floyd's solo on Smoke Rings, which he played just as pretty as you please.

Another *Down Beat* staff member, Chuck Sweningsen remembered that O'Brien was

... gentle, polite, extremely self-effacing and colorless. He had an electrical repair business in Chicago that put bread on the table when music didn't. He had one of the loveliest trombone sounds ever - big, full tone and nice, sort of sneaky ideas that never called attention to themselves.

Trumpeter Bill Tinkler: "Floyd was a great person... was not a fast note player, but had a good ear and put in the right notes in a Dixie band."

British trombonist Campbell Burnap, who was aware only of O'Brien as a musician, proved to be accurate in matching O'Brien's playing with his personality. On the plus side, he agreed that Floyd had an engaging, warm and burry sound. He was effective with mutes, understood the tailgate role, not too busy and not wandering into the trumpeter's lead. He had a thorough knowledge of the tunes, which he played with a warm legato, and he was a reliable, solid reader. He had a good feel for the blues, with nice bent notes. But he was reticent, adhered to the middle register, played safe, never passionately. He was not too adventurous, not someone really telling a story.

Jim Beebe, veteran Chicago trombonist, remembered: "Floyd O'Brien was one of my first idols on trombone and remains so to this day. Years after I heard him live for the first time we became good friends." Writing of the Jump records he said: "I immediately fell in love with his bluesy solo and ensemble style." Beebe continued:

Floyd had such a pleasant, easy going personality and demeanor you wondered where his very deep and powerful blues feeling came from. Floyd's solo style was very basic... no excess and everything just right, logical and executed with a great sense of time and swing. He had a way of expressing a blues feeling by bending and twisting a minor note in his own special way. His solos would stay right in the middle register and on a blues number he would sometimes take a delightful excursion into the lower register. He had a big sound with a dark but at the same time warm tone quality ... a distinctive sound immediately recognizable, which is the mark of a true jazzman. It was his ensemble style that enthralled me. Very few trombonists can play good ensemble in the New Orleans-Dixieland-counterpoint style of jazz ... Floyd was one who could. He had just the right combination of a good bass-harmonic line, playing off the trumpet-cornet and clarinet and punched out in such a way to give the band a lilting forward movement. He would use the middle and lower register of the trombone to great effect.

Floyd O'Brien's story confirms that he was a pioneer Chicagoan and the comments of his peers indicate that he was one of the very best trombonists of his period and style. Now, put Home Cooking or The Eel by Eddie Condon, Tin Roof Blues by Bob Crosby, I've Found A New Baby by George Wettling, or Baby, Won't You Please Come Home by Charlie La Vere onto the record or CD player and see if you agree that here is the individual voice of a hot jazz trombonist who does not deserve to be forgotten.

Floyd O'Brien On Record

On Floyd's first recordings, by Bud Freeman, Craze-O-logy is a feature for the leader, with a few bars of trombone, while Can't Help Lovin' That Man has a trombone solo which stays close to the melody and is slightly hesitant. His ensemble playing is strong on this title, especially on the C take.

The sides which brought him to the attention of jazz fans were those with Eddie Condon, recorded in 1933. On these he plays mainly muted, with a particularly effective blues solo on Home Cooking. The Eel reveals a dirty sound and rhythmic flair, while his lazy, muted solo on Tennessee Twilight is styled to suit the wistful melody by Alex Hill. Geoff Cole, trombonist with Muggsy Remembered, says of Home Cooking, "he used a kind of bucket mute, I guess, which sounds quite like Glenn Miller on the Hello Lola session, while on Tennessee Twilight he plays a superb moody, muted solo which is immediately followed by a two-bar break, apparently played with a totally different mute (rubber plunger?). I have no idea how he did this!" Campbell Burnap suggests that the plunger mute is tightly inserted initially and then slightly loosened for the last two bars.

The Chocolate Dandies titles of October 1933 are filled with fine playing by such as Benny Carter and Teddy Wilson but contain only two short muted solos by O'Brien either side of a Carter alto chorus on I Never Knew.

Neither is he given a lot to do on the Mezz Mezzrow and Fats Waller records. With Mezzrow he has a typical muted solo on Dissonance and plays the introduction for Love, You're Not the One for Me. He is heard on each of the four titles recorded at the second Mezzrow session, his best solo probably being that on 35th and Calumet, for which he also receives an arranging credit. With Waller, he has a nice, brief solo on Let's Pretend There's a Moon and effectively contributes to the rocking final ensemble on Sweetie Pie. To a cry from Fats Waller of "Dirty dog" he plays melody on How Can You Face Me? and on Serenade to A Wealthy Widow there is an interesting but too short a trade between O'Brien and Herman Autrey.

The New Orleans Rhythm Kings titles, June 28, 1934, with Wingy Manone and Eddie Miller, were unknown until issued by Jerry Valburn on a Meritt LP, though they have recently appeared on a Classics CD. O'Brien solos on both Panama and Tin Roof Blues, that on the latter being a nice variation on the Brunis solo.

With the Gene Krupa orchestra Floyd O'Brien was singularly neglected. I have not heard all of the titles issued on Brunswick, OKeh and Columbia, but from a sampling of many of them, only the short solo on No Name Jive sounds like O'Brien. He probably also has a spot on Ta-Ra-Ra-Boom-Der-E on Joyce, taken from a One-Night-Stand air shot.

During the year with Krupa there was just one outside session, the well-known George Wettling's Chicago Rhythm Kings date, organised by George Avakian in January 1940, with Charlie Teagarden, Danny Polo, Joe Marsala, Jess Stacy, etc. The trombonist takes solos on all four titles and is in excellent form throughout, as are the rest of the musicians on this beautifully relaxed session. In addition to his solo on Bugle Call Rag O'Brien takes a good break at the end.

With the Bob Crosby orchestra he recorded few solos and some of those are in doubt! Whether this was due to a lack of interest by the band's arrangers or to O'Brien self-effacing attitude we will never know. There are two short, neat breaks on Original Dixieland One Step, and another on Chain Gang, which is in keeping with this mood piece. There is what seems to be a typical solo on Vultee Special, though both John Chilton and Ian Crosbie prefer Buddy Morrow.

They also opt for Morrow on part two of Brass Boogie though I prefer O'Brien, unless it is Morrow copying him! On air shots O'Brien can be heard on Jimtown Blues (Sunbeam), Vultee Special again (VJC), Panama (Blu-Disc), and Diga Diga Do (Alamac). There is a fine tightly-muted solo on Soft Jive (Hindsight) but is it O'Brien?

Fortunately. O'Brien was a member of the Bob Cats, whose recordings offer more opportunities to hear his work, though he was still not strongly featured. Among the titles worth sampling are I'll Come Back to You, Sweethearts On Parade, and particularly Tin Roof Blues and Juke Box Judy. Commenting on these titles. Geoff Cole mentions O'Brien's "wonderful ending phrase on Don't Call Me Boy and his excellent solo on Tin Roof Blues, on which he not only plays a fine 12 bar solo, not unlike Kid Ory in approach, but also takes a good break to lead into the last chorus." Geoff also refers to Floyd's short solos on the cowboy songs Tears On My Pillow and I'll Be True to the One I Love.

It was a surprise to find him on the 1944 Bunk Johnson session for World Transcriptions, reissued on GHB, but he had little to do. He plays a subdued ensemble part, while his only solo, on Ballin' the Jack, is sophisticated in the context of this session.

It is with the Jump sessions that O'Brien comes more into his own. That label's very first session in 1944. by Charlie La Vere, has the trombonist in top form, particularly on I'm Comin' Virginia and on Baby Won't You Please Come Home, where he introduces and closes the record, as well as contributing apt ensemble work. The 1945 session had two titles credited to La Vere and two to Floyd O'Brien. He does not solo on the La Vere titles but plays two fine solos on Royal Reserve Blues. He is not as assured on Carolina In the Morning but his playing is in keeping with the arrangement. Trumpeter Chuck Mackey was the nominal leader of the 1946 session for Jump and again O'Brien is in good form. He solos on each of the four titles, mainly staying close to the melody, but his few bars on Happy Blues include a Kid Ory-like burst.

Also in 1944, O'Brien was part of a three trombone section on a Wingy Manone session for Capitol, but there are no solos. Also for Capitol he recorded as a member of Red Nichols Five Pennies, but the two titles have not been heard by this writer.

Eight years were to pass before O'Brien's next recording session, with Art Hodes and his Hi-Fives for EmArcy. This was the regular band with Muggsy Dawson on trumpet and Jimmy Granato on clarinet. Hodes, naturally, is well featured, but Floyd makes a full contribution to the overall sound. It is a good, tight unit, not an "old warhorse" band. As Hodes said."It had spirit and it had musicianship." Blues Keep Callin' is a typical example of O'Brien's blues playing, economical with notes, yet very effective.

That same year he recorded four titles for Windin' Ball with Natty Dominique and his New Orleans Hot Six, which also included Frank Chace, clarinet: Lil Armstrong, piano; Israel Crosby, bass, and Baby Dodds, drums. Though not a well-recorded session. O'Brien plays a good, tightly-muted solo on Touching Blues and is forceful on the final ensembles of Someday Sweetheart and You Rascal You. (Geoff Cole feels that Floyd is blowing out hard in a failed attempt to get the turgid session off the ground.)

Danny Alvin's regular band from his Basin Street club recorded an album for the Stephany label in 1958, while in 1959 and 1960 O'Brien appeared on two sessions by Smokey Stover's Original Firemen on the Chess subsidiary, Argo. Both the Alvin and Stover bands were competent but undistinguished Dixieland bands, with O'Brien as the only individual voice.

Generally, he solos close to the melody but still sounds hotter than his more verbose colleagues. Stover's Smoke Rings is a feature for O'Brien. He plays the theme with a fruity tone and characteristic economy of notes, as he does on Alvin's After You've Gone. But his best solo with Alvin is on Riverside Blues. As Geoff Cole points out. the arrangement for this follows the one recorded by Muggsy Spanier in 1944 for Commodore.

In 1959, prior to the Smokey Stover sessions, O'Brien recorded with the Albert Nicholas All-Star Stompers for Delmark. Clarinetist Nicholas was visiting Chicago and Bob Koester took the opportunity to record him with a band that also included Art Hodes, Nap Trottier and Marty Grosz. Now on CD (Delmark DE-209), the success of these titles owes much to Trottier's excellent lead trumpet but O'Brien too is in fine form, both solo and ensemble.

As Geoff Cole put it, if that overworked cliche "unsung hero" applied to anyone, it applied to Floyd O'Brien.

Addenda

Chilton gives Johnny Mendel, but Wayne Jones advised that his autograph shows Johnny Mendell. Similarly, Volly De Faut's autograph shows "Volley".

Jim Lanigan (as per Chilton) is often spelt Lannigan.

Smokey Stover's band wore fireman clothes and played "fire tunes" but there was no musical similarity to the Firehouse Five Plus 2. (Wayne Jones).

September 1952: Chuck Sweningsen did not recall a Flame Club in St. Paul, but there was one of some notoriety by that name in Minneapolis.

June 23, 1962: this was the only date which O'Brien played with the Gold Coast Jazz Band.

July 1962: Freddie Masters was a commercial reed player who tried to keep a dixieland band on the road. Don English was a drummer in his youth. (Wayne Jones).

Oro 'Tut' Soper, Chicago pianist

Of the few white jazz pianists associated with Chicago who gained some measure of fame, very many remain almost unknown, some not even recorded. Reasons for near-obscurity are probably as numerous as the men themselves. Oro "Tut" Soper was one such pianist, and that which follows will, amongst other things, explain why he remains an almost shadowy figure to many jazz buffs and even entirely unknown to some.

He was born in Chicago on April 9, 1910. Both parents were descendants of immigrants from the southwestern county of Devon in England. Jesse Soper, Tut's father, was a professional musician playing cornet in various bands in the city. Jesse encouraged the boy to take an interest in music, and this was aided by lessons at school - and it was at school that an archaeologist involved in the discovery in Egypt of Tutankhamun's tomb in 1922 gave a talk as part of a lecture tour. A few days later, Oro was daydreaming in the outfield during a baseball game when a fly ball was struck his way. The pitcher yelled, "Wake up, King Tut!" and the nickname stuck for the rest of his days. He liked to remark that both his given and nicknames were three-letter palindromes.

Several of Tut's school friends were interested in music; the father of one of them was Elmer Feam, a senior executive of the OKeh Phonograph Corporation. On November 21, 1923, Tut made his first recording. Arthur Roth and Bob Feam played violins, Howard Snyder played the lead on C-melody saxophone, Arthur Ellefson was on drums, and Tut was on piano, of course. They called themselves the Five Baby Sheiks, and they recorded Meet Me Tonight in Dreamland and Our Boys March. These were just test recordings, and Tut kept the two single-side discs all his life. They had nothing to do with jazz. Tut recalled that

> ...it took us a good three months before we could hear them and four or five before we got copies. We were there at 2:30, but they didn't call us until about 4:50. Sophie Tucker had preceded us and she needed the time. We were tired of waiting and also apprehensive. No second takes.

The following year, Tut went to Florida where he played piano at the Royal Danieli Hotel in a forgotten location. His first job there was as a bellhop! But his real beginning as a professional musician came in Chicago when he attended a dance. The pianist in the band failed to turn up, so Tut took his place. Not long after this, a band led by guitarist Harvey Brown and Boyce Brown on reeds attracted Tut because it played jazz and he played many gigs, including one at the Garden of Allah, a roadhouse.

Soper said, however, that his first real job came before he was in the union.

> I started at 16 … I was the musical director at radio station WHFC. I was the staff pianist. Didn't know tunes or anything - could read but I couldn't transpose, but I was getting by OK. A friend of mine had built the station, so I had an in. Then the Union found out that I wasn't a member, and they forced the owner to fire me.

Late in 1927 he was in a band led by Wingy Manone at a place known as the Three Deuces because of its address, but the name over the door was My Cellar. One night, at 222 North State St., Bix Beiderbecke and the Dorseys, along with Hoagy Carmichael, stopped in after the Whiteman show at the Chicago Theatre. Tut told Phil Evans,

> It was a madhouse with at least a hundred musicians present and all seemingly wanting to sit in and play … Jess Stacy and Eddie Condon showed up, as did George Wettling, Gene Krupa, Don Carter and Joe Sullivan. The music … went on until five or six in the morning.

He then was in a band for a while at a place called Prehn's; others present included Boyce Brown on alto, Buck Ram, tenor, and Maurie Rose at the drums. This was an evening gig, so he attended classes at the University of Illinois during the day, and, during this period, he met Bunny Berigan, who was in a band in Champaign, Illinois. By 1929 Berigan was in a band known as the Castle Farm Serenaders and, when the pianist gave notice, Berigan asked Tut to replace him. That summer, the band moved to Lexington, Kentucky, and Tut's wife of a few months, Irene, joined him there. In July of that year, Berigan and Soper were in a band led by Joe Shor (or Shoer) at a ballroom known as Joyland in Lexington. The drummer was Harry Haberkorn and there was another trumpeter,

Tut Soper.

Benny Woodworth. "He was the most foul-mouthed bandleader I ever worked for and that includes Wingy," said Soper. "A year or two later, he was shot and killed while trying to repeat a robbery of a store on the seedy side of Madison Street."

Tut was back at My Cellar with Wingy for the winter of 1929-30, along with Buzzy Knudsen on clarinet and Dash Berkis *(sic)* on drums. The pianist said, "It was a middle-class joint downstairs on Clark just north of Lake - ...with food, a small dance floor and stage. Wingy literally blew the roof off many a night." Once again, Bix stopped by one night, this time with Art Hodes, and sat in, as well as played some piano solos.

Probably late in 1930, Soper became accompanist to a mimic who appeared as Jerome. His real name was Jerry Mann.

> I joined him in Chicago, and we played the State Theatre for a week. A guy by the name of Verne Buck was the bandleader. After that, Denver, where we played the RKO-Palace - also played the RKO-Palace in downtown Los Angeles. I stayed at the Werner Kelton Hotel in Hollywood where Joe Sullivan was playing piano for his meals. This was around January of 1931.

Subsequent engagements with Jerome took Tut to San Francisco, Chicago, New York and Baltimore.

Wild Bill Davison spent much time and effort organizing a big band around this period, and Soper was the pianist at least some of the time. Chronology is not really clear; this may have been in the fall of 1931. The personnel changed considerably, perhaps due to lack of work and therefore earnings, but at various times the band included Harold Moeller, John Whitehead and Davison, trumpets; Mort Croy and Tommy Miller, trombones; Frank Teschemacher, clarinet and alto; Joe Schneider, alto; Ray Evans, tenor; George Anders (spelling?) or Tut Soper, piano; Jack Goss, banjo and guitar; Basile Dupre, tuba and bass; Don Carter or Wally Gordon, drums.

This orchestra rehearsed for hours six days a week at the Brunswick studio in the Furniture Mart at 600 Lakeshore Drive and, later, in a studio run by Ted Arkin at Leland and Sheridan, The men had to work for other leaders to make a living, but the band did get an engagement at Guyon's Paradise. This was immediately before Tesch's death in a car accident (March 1, 1932). His place was taken by Kensel C. Paul, known as Toasty Paul. Tut was the pianist except for the Guyon's job when

... Pete Viera, a much older man, took my place. After Carter and I left and Tesch was killed, the band lost its integrity and was doomed. I was there every night the band worked even though I wasn't in it. They were my friends, musically speaking, and I wanted to be around. Things were tough for Bill and he didn't finish the gig as leader - ... Toasty might have.

Despite the foregoing, Soper was in a band led by Don Hugo in a ballroom known as Chateau LaMar in Janesville, Wisconsin, during at least January of 1932. This was another big band with Johnny Mendell, Leo Schuken and Cliff Goman, trumpets; Floyd O'Brien and Ted Goss, trombones; Doc DeHaven, Pee Wee Kelly and Norris Johnson, reeds; Soper, piano; Frank Salerno, guitar; Herb Campbell, bass; Rollo Laylan or, later, Wally Gordon, drums. Norris Johnson may be confused with Stan Norris whom Tut remembered as a very good first alto man and who appears in Rust's *Jazz Records* in the personnel of the Midnight Ramblers who recorded for Paramount during 1928 in Chicago.

There followed another period of scuffling and starvation, broken during 1933 by Tut succeeding Art Hodes at the Brown Derby and, later in the year, when Tut's own band, which he called the Avatars, obtained a gig at the Variety Club. This was the year in which Irene and Tut's son, Jesse, was born, so things were tough and not helped by so many out-of-town bands being booked for the Chicago World's Fair.

Many different pianists played in bands led by Floyd Town [see DC's article] and Tut was one of them. He remembers the time when the leader purchased

... a brand-new baby grand. Suddenly the whole pedal attachment fell off. You can imagine the consternation! But I didn't deliberately damage the instrument.

In October of 1934, Soper replaced Jess Stacy in the band billed as Frank Snyder's Rythm *(sic)* Kings at the Subway Cafe, located at 507 North Wabash Avenue. Here there was dancing and entertainment, plus a seven-course dinner for a dollar. The place was open 24 hours a day. Apart from Tut on piano and Snyder on drums, there was Carl Rinker, trumpet, George Lugg, trombone, Bud Jacobson, clarinet. It was claimed that the joint had the longest bar in the world. It certainly must have been spacious, as Tut remembered that

> ... there were five pianos going at one time, all about 50 feet apart. Each player had his own girl singer. We in the band would start work at 11 p.m. and finish at 7 a.m. We lived in the same building as Frank Snyder, so I always got a ride home from work. We would work hard from start to about 1:30 or 2:00 a.m., then business would mostly go to the bar.

Some reports say that the Subway closed in July of 1935, but Tut always claimed that this didn't happen until January 5, 1936, and this does seem to be correct. John Steiner spoke of Bud Jacobson playing a place called the Ball of Fire "on the far North Side with drummer Don Carter and Tut Soper" in 1935. Just how this fits in with the Subway job remains a mystery.

There followed a spell of work with Floyd Town and then in a band at Liberty Inn with Earl Wiley on drums and Boyce Brown on alto. All the pressures and responsibilities worked havoc on Tut's health and he had a nervous breakdown. As he got better, he was able to take on solo piano gigs and he spent much time studying so that he embraced work other than with jam session bands. One result of this effort was to become an accompanist to singers, including Anita O'Day. In her autobiography, *High Times, Hard Times,* she recalled being at the Vanity Fair as a dancer when she was asked to sing.

> Oro Tut Soper worked out two or three tunes with me...and I became convinced that I had a real shot at becoming a singer... most nights he walked me to Mom's apartment after work. The very fact that he wasn't trying to get me in bed was enough to separate him from most of the other guys around the taverns.

That apart, Tut set Miss O'Day on her singing career, which is really something when we learn that the pair of them knew only one tune, I Can't Give You Anything But Love, in the same key on the night she sang in public for the first time.

During the year which followed, Soper worked many jobs in such places as the Brass Rail and Liberty Inn, both as soloist or as pianist-singer and also in many bands, including Bud Freeman's Summa Cum Laude crew in the Sherman Hotel's Panther Room during 1942. He did a tour with Phil Levant the following year.

Except for the schoolboy session in 1923, it was 1944 before Tut Soper took part in a recording session. On January 31st, Tut and Baby Dodds cut sides for John Steiner and Hugh Davis which they issued on their own label In July the *Down Beat* reviewer was ecstatic:

> ... they constitute some of the finest jazz piano waxed in years. This little-known Chicago pianist ranks with the best. *Oronics* is a marvelous original, played magnificently. Stardust is the first stomp version of this number to be cut in the '40s and how fine. Thou Swell gets a thorough going-over. It's a Ramble; another excellent Soper composition, really moves on down. Soper is super...

At the same date, Tut accompanied Dodds in drumming interpretations which eventually appeared on an American Music LP.

Then, that March, Bob Thiele cut four sides for his Signature label with Johnny Mendell, trumpet; Bud Jacobson, clarinet; Pud Brown, tenor; Soper, piano; Dick McPartland, guitar; Pat Pattison, bass, Earl Wiley, drums. Muskrat Ramble, After You've Gone, I Found A New Baby, and a Jacobson original, Bluesiana, were made but never issued. This session was by Jacobson's Jungle Kings as was yet another unissued batch of sides recorded on March 6, 1945, for Phil Featheringhill's Session label. This time, it was Bill Stapleton, cornet; Warren Smith, trombone; Volly De Faut, clarinet; Jacobson, tenor; Soper, piano; Pattison, bass, and Lew Finnerty, drums. Curiously, the tune titles are not known, but it *is* known that the blow was at the Zanzibar Cafe on State Street.

The next month, yet another variant of the Jungle Kings played at the University of Chicago's Burton Hall: Mendell back on trumpet, Smith still on trombone, De Faut and Jacobson both on clarinet and the latter also tenor, Tut at the piano while the guitar was handled by Jack Goss. Drummer Hey Hey Humphrey completed the line-up. The same gang, plus Jim Lanigan on bass, played a concert staged by Catherine Jacobson on July 8th at the Uptown Players Theatre on North LaSalle. Don Haynes reports, "Outstanding was the work of pianist Tut Soper, one of the finest in the country."

Still in 1945 and at the same venue as the last, a Jimmie Noone Memorial Concert was held on the afternoon of Sunday, the 5th of August. The promoter was John Steiner, who presented Darnell

Howard, clarinet; Boyce Brown, alto, Gideon Honore and Tut Soper, piano; Jack Goss, guitar; Pat Pattison, bass, and Baby Dodds, drums. During the course of the show, Soper and Goss formed a trio with Josh Billings who did his suitcase and clothes brushes act. The *Down Beat* report said, "(The) clever routine, nostalgic of innumerable sessions the same three sat in on many years back, brought down the house."

The mid-40s was a marvelous period for Soper; he was wonderful pianistically and working very steadily. John "Jax" Lucas, writing in *Down Beat* in October '45 said, "The Chicagoans deserving a great deal more praise and publicity than they've received so far are Jack Gardner, Floyd Bean and Tut Soper ... Tut has still to break into big time. I consider Sullivan, Stacy, Hodes, Gardner, Bean and Soper the six best pianists in white jazz today."

At that time, few would have disagreed. There's no doubt that the period of the 1940s was a heyday for jazz piano in the city; Esquire's *1946 Jazz Book*, while noting that drummer Earl Wiley had been resident for 11 years at the Liberty Inn, listed Soper, Melrose, Hodes and Zurke among the men who had played the place.

September 30, 1946, gave John Steiner a successful recording session. Jack Gardner and Tut Soper shared the piano duties and the latter accompanied altoist Bill Dohler on Blue Lou and tenor man Bud Freeman on The Man I Love. Lanigan was on bass and Jim Barnes was the drummer. The sides appeared on SD 505, a 78, and later on a now rare Paramount LP with a different take used on the second tune.

During the later 1940s, Tut worked many of the Chicago clubs such as the Bee Hive on 55th Street where he replaced Mel Grant (September '48), the Riviera (October '48 to about May '49) with Eddie Higgins on alto and Jimmy Kileran on drums, then on to the HiNote as intermission pianist. By the end of the year, he was doing a single at the Minuet on Rush Street. Before this last, however, he was in a band led by drummer Danny Alvin at Rupneck's, a restaurant on Thorndale Avenue. This job lasted at least a couple of months, and it may well be the one that trumpeter Bill Tinkler remembers:

> I worked many times with Tut. The steady gig was at Rupneck's about 1948-49,... the band was Johnny Lane's. I also played

North Shore private parties with Tut... (and) some club dates with him in the Bill Reinhardt Jazz, Ltd. band. The Lane band had four piano players. Tut played most of the time when we were there. However, due to a drinking problem, not so much Tut but the other three, we changed piano players from time to time. The other three were Art Gronwall, George Zack and Jack Gardner. We always had someone ready.

In April of 1950, Soper was with Muggsy Spanier at the Hangover in San Francisco, Tut and Muggsy apart, the band had Julian Laine, trombone; Darnell Howard, clarinet; Pat Patton, bass, and Eddie Lightfoot, drums. For various reasons, there were many problems: "The drummer dragged the tempo, which got Muggsy mad. He showed him how to play and then fired him," according to Soper. A local man filled the spot for a while. Then the AFM local gave trouble over the bassist who was replaced by Earl Murphy and also the trombonist who was succeeded by Harry Graves. Added to all this, Tut fell out with Muggsy's wife, Ruth (she'd married the cornetist just a couple of months prior to this), and this created an unpleasant atmosphere.

Despite all this, the four-week booking was so successful that it was extended by another couple of weeks. By mid-May, the band was back in Chicago, this time at the Silhouette, when Truck Parham came in on bass and Doc Cenardo on drums.

We finished May the 31st and opened the Chicago Railroad World Fair on June the 2nd. We played at the Dixieland Showboat in that .section of the Fair that was called the Dixieland Village. Two weeks later, my association with Muggsy ended, I never saw him again although he called me twice after that to rejoin him

Tut had a couple of weeks with Eddie Condon's band in October '50. Soper recalled only Pee Wee Russell who

... did not touch a drop of any kind of alcoholic beverage whereas Eddie could hardly lift a shot glass of gin with both hands because of shaky nerves. Pee Wee surprised me so very pleasantly by his friendly, gentlemanly and cultured expressions towards me. Eddie was superb.

The beginning of 1951 saw Soper leading Don Slattery, trumpet; Ralph Hutchinson, trombone; Wally Wender, clarinet, and Ken Krause, drums, at the New Apex Club in Chicago. Business was only fair, so the pianist accepted a job with Hot Lips Page in San Francisco, only to have it canceled when Hangover owner Doc Daugherty wouldn't pay Page another hundred on top of the $300 he'd originally agreed to pay.

Denny Roche, trumpet; Paul Severson, trombone; Frank Chace, clarinet, and Jim Barnes, drums, were in a Soper-led band that June at the Vanity Fair. A little later, Tut was back with Wingy Manone at the Silhouette with George Lugg, trombone; Bob McCracken, clarinet, and probably Doc Cenardo, drums.

Tut's health was very variable now and there were long periods when he was able to work very little. So, in the late summer of 1953, he and Irene decided to take a vacation by driving their Phantom II Rolls Royce to San Francisco. The journey took six days before they "... finally made it to the Pattons' (bass player Pat and his wife Patsy). We lolled around for a couple of weeks". Then Tut remembered that Doc Daugherty had said that if he brought the Rolls over to show to him, the drinks would be on the house. So, he drove down to the Hangover.

> Almost immediately Ralph Sutton came over and said would I take over for him as he had to get to New York. I made the mistake of going to the union and depositing my card as a transferee. The second night they pulled me off the job because a transferee cannot work a steady job until six months go by. But I didn't care as I was vacationing.

Oddly enough and despite this, an October *Down Beat* listed Soper as being intermission pianist!

By early 1956, Tut was in Jazz, Ltd. in Chicago with Nappy Trottier, trumpet; Jack Reid, trombone; club owner Bill Reinhardt, clarinet, and Walt Gifford, drums. Then, toward the end of 1957, Tut took a phone call.

> I had never even heard of Marty Grosz until he called me and asked if I'd be interested in taking part in a recording session ... mutual friends' names were mentioned ... I felt at ease and made the commitment. Many weeks and much partying and travel were involved and although I did receive $100, I had to regard this as a token payment. I figured at least $500 but never got it.

Present on the date were Carl Halen, cornet; Bud Wilson, trombone; Frank Chace, clarinet and baritone; Bob Skiver, clarinet and tenor; Chuck Neilson, bass; Bob Saltmarsh, drums, and, of course, Tut at the piano and Grosz playing guitar and doing a couple of vocals. Bill Priestley played additional cornet and guitar on three tunes and eight tracks were issued on a 10" Empirical LP, EM10761. Later and plus another four tracks, these appeared on Riverside RLP12-268 with some pseudonyms used on the liner in the personnel details. Years later, ten titles from different takes appeared on a British LP, Collectors Items 008 (also known as Ristic SAH) with another five, non-Soper, Grosz tracks. Tut wasn't too pleased with his own work here, and Wayne Jones doesn't think of it as his best either.

Jim Beebe is a little hazy about the date but thinks it may have been 1959 when Tut was in Bob Scobey's band. With the leader on trumpet and Beebe on trombone were Brian Shanley on clarinet, Clancy Hayes on banjo and vocals, Rich Madison on helicon (a brass bass), a drummer and Soper at the piano. Beebe recalls,

Both Tut and George Zack worked with Scobey's band for several months each, but I can't remember which was first. The piano chair was demanding because of the wide range of material. We did a lot of early jazz classics and Clancy Hayes did a wide range of vocal material. We had a female vocalist, Toni Lee Scott, who had some fancy arrangements on stuff like Ten Cents A Dance. Neither Zack nor Tut were show pianists, and they had trouble with those arrangements. There was grumbling in the rhythm section and it became apparent that they wanted to get rid of Tut. I asked Clancy what the trouble was. He said that Tut was rushing the beat and it was driving everyone in the rhythm section nuts. Well, he was right. Tut was committing the worst sin that a pianist can do. It happens to a lot who single piano too much; they lose the sense of timing necessary to play in a band. So, Scobey finally let Soper go but hired him to play intermission piano at the Cafe Continental in Chicago. He had Tut out there in the middle of the room with a sort of piano bar and, when we were off, Tut would play.

During 1960, Tut played various gigs including a tour with Eddie Condon and was in a band led by George Brunis at the 11-11 Club in Chicago. The following year came another crisis. Soper was booked to play with a band led by Dave Remington at a restaurant but that evening the place caught fire. No one was injured and the firemen quelled the blaze, but Tut, standing there outside, reflected on his situation. He had little to show for his career to date and not even a single booking forthcoming. Back home he checked the job ads and got work selling insurance for the Chicago Motor Club. Although his health continued to decline during the next few years, he managed to keep this going. Just the same, he undertook an occasional gig. Like one on the 19th of April, 1964, at the Chicago Historical Society at Clark and North Avenue. Apart from the leader, Johnny Mendell, on trumpet and Tut at the piano, present were Floyd O'Brien on trombone, Frank Chace on clarinet, Bob Skiver on tenor, Marty Grosz on guitar and Wayne Jones at the drums. Gene Krupa stopped by and sat in for one number, and Tut had a solo piece in the program.

The International Association of Jazz Record Collectors held its annual get-together in 1980 in Chicago. Responsible for hiring a band for the Friday night session were Warren Plath and Jim Gordon. Gordon recalled

I approached both Art Hodes and Tut Soper. Tut said that he wasn't in practice and hadn't been on a gig for something like ten years. I knew he would be the correct choice if I worked on him to practice. He finally reluctantly agreed that maybe he would do it. He kept telling me no and then I'd talk him into a yes, and Warren all the time was asking if I was sure he would come. The band began to materialize: Tom Pletcher on cornet, Don Ingle on valve trombone, Frank Powers on clarinet and tenor, Spencer Clark, bass sax, and Bill Priestley, guitar. Then we got Truck Parham for bass and Don DeMichael and Wayne Jones to split the drum chair. As Spence and Priestley were old buddies of Tut, he began to warm up a little bit to doing it after all, and told me he would do it. Wheee! We're in. I thought... On to Wednesday I thought I had him in the bag. On calling, I found him hesitant and, I believe, scared to death that he'd be terrible. I finally got another OK from him - Friday night I drove up to Addison and there he was waiting, ready to go. I was taken aback to see that he could only walk 10 or 12 steps at a time due to his severe emphysema. I never until that moment realized how very fragile he was. I began to have visions of his not making it through the evening and my not being able to get him home still alive.

Well, the first tune was Big Butter and Egg Man and Warren and I sat there frozen with fear that it would come to Tut's solo and everything would fall apart. A bit hesitant, he came through with a slightly restrained solo. From then, we needn't have worried. He played his ass off the rest of the night, and everyone was delighted. Tut went home happy and refreshed, so glad so many came up and asked to meet him, plus he saw his friends from times gone by.

Bob Hilbert remembers the event clearly.

I heard Tut play at the IAJRC convention, and he was superb. I wanted to record him for Pumpkin, and Jerry Valburn wanted him for Aviva, but Tut told us he wasn't ready.

The Association has issued one selection, Four or Five Times (IAJRC 40), from the evening; it would be a real service for collectors and a memorial to Tut Soper if a whole LP could be produced from the best of the session.

That was about it, really. Tut's wife, Irene, had died in October 1980 and in March of '81, he underwent a prostate operation, closely followed by severe vision problems. The Jazz Institute of Chicago mounted what it termed a Piano Orgy at the Blackstone Hotel on South Michigan, and Tut took part (billed as Soaper!).

Tut recalled:

Buddy Charles was really great - good friends from back in 1950 when I was with Muggsy. The pedals kept falling off the rented Kimball grand piano. I never felt so uncomfortable playing, yet the audience was really fine to Buddy and me. The rest of them were avant garde players - no beat, no theme, no beauty, no swing ...

Although health problems continued to cause difficulties, Tut kept active with interests such as CB radio. In September 1983, when Wayne Jones and Warren Plath spent a few hours in his apartment interviewing for the Jazz Institute, Tut was (said Wayne)

... in pretty bad shape, but sharp and wound up; couldn't keep him on a jazz or chronological track... so, after a while, we stopped trying and just talked. Not what the Institute wanted but interesting, nonetheless, in a more personal way. He always remembered my name, and I was flattered by that.

Just a year later, Tut said that he'd " ... lost the vision of the left eye and we are fighting to maintain that which I have in the other ... glaucoma set in pretty strongly. I've had three laser-beam operations."

He was also suffering from emphysema and diabetes, but, even so, the following summer he traded his car for a new Audi and also passed his driver's license test - "good for another four years."

Oro "Tut" Soper died March 20, 1987, in St. Francis Hospital, Evanston, Illinois. Jim Gordon was at the funeral:

> With 40 minutes left of the wake, only three musicians — Iver Buerk, Bill Dohler and Wayne Jones — had shown to pay their respects to this great musician. How sad. I was last in touch with Tut at Christmas. My understanding is that his health plummeted after the first of the year. The big guy weighed only 127 pounds when he passed away....

Soper's views on jazz might be considered conservative.

> The '20s and '30s were the best years, as I determine them. If the jazz musicians of that period had expanded their repertoire instead of falling into the rut of constant repetition of the same titles, things might have been better for the real jazz. [...]
> However, the war and its attendant horrors changed the flow of the forces. Suddenly things had to be exciting: tempos accelerated, drummers taking command - bang, bang, banging. Violent dissonance, erratic tempos, no more of that fine steady beat with its flexibility of feelings because the percussionist listened; he knew how to inspire the ensemble and the soloists. I feel that in jazz the energy and expression of the players is best accomplished when a recognizable theme is traceable and that the tempos selected are most important

He was completely convinced that Chicago's part in the music was of the highest importance, saying,

> It is the center of gravity as far as jazz is concerned. True jazz expresses enthusiasm and carried terrific kicks for the players as well as their listeners. Is it any wonder, therefore, that Chicago, being the sort of city it is and so centrally located, was really the cradle of jazz? Not the exact birthplace, to be sure, but the mother and father of the child, jazz. Chicago gave the world jazz, nurtured and developed it until its fledglings were able to leave

their nest and go forth to conquer, a conquest that was world-proportioned. Chicago with its myriads of opportunities has offered the greatest of opportunities for the greatest number of jazz men.

Tut Soper was a religious man and also a great believer in astrology. He consulted the stars assiduously as a day-to-day guide to behaviour and activities. This gave him a reputation for eccentricity. Don DeMichael said that Tut would go through periods when he would not walk through a doorway except backwards. Jim Beebe commented

He walked, dressed, ate and even tried to play backwards. He was interested in and involved with an assortment of mystic pursuits... astrology and an array of occult movements.

When Anita O'Day first knew Tut, he explained that he was delving into the occult and belonged to a group known as the Mystic Brotherhood of Tampa, Florida. One of their tenets prohibited sexual relationships. Not just outside marriage. Prohibited them period. Tut said he was having a hard time living with that rule.

Bill Tinkler remembers

.... Tut would come to work in his Rolls Royce with a neighbor as chauffeur in uniform and in the open with Tut in the enclosed glass area. He would be well-dressed in black with a high, silk hat. Guests at Rupneck's would always look forward to his arrival. When Soper was intermission pianist with Bob Scobey's band, he seized the opportunity to get some practicing in and soon drove everyone crazy. He brought in piles of music and never only played a piece completely through. You could hear this tune going along and all of a sudden he would stop and go back a few bars and commence again or go back to the beginning.

Jim Beebe recalled another time when he, Brian Shanley and George Zack were in a five-piece band at the Clarite Lounge on Clark St. They were having a rehearsal when Soper arrived.

He announced that he would book this band as Tut Soper's Chicago Jazz Band as six pieces, and he would get the money for the sixth member because we would be using his name. I'll never forget the look on Zack's face. He said, 'No, Tut, you got it wrong.

We'll book the band as mine and I'll take the money and you play the piano' and let off a marvelously profane blast. Tut retreated and we didn't see him again for some time.

Tut Soper's other problem was his lack of confidence. He just considered that his playing wasn't good. "Tut jobbed a lot in his latter years," says Bill Tinkler, "and he did not seem to want to play. He always thought he didn't play well, but I liked it and so did most of the musicians I knew."

Phil Pitt, an enthusiast from London, spent time with Tut in 1971 and tells of visiting John Steiner, who persuaded Soper to use the grand piano "... although he seemed embarrassed about playing."

On another occasion, Tut and Pitt went to the Happy Medium on Rush Street, where the band included Norm Murphy, trumpet; Jim Beebe, trombone; Bobby Wright, piano; Truck Parham, bass, Don DeMichael, vibes, plus others. "Tut sat in and apologized for playing so badly (as he put it)."

But Wild Bill Davison, in conversation with Phil Pitt, said,

You knew how good Tut was? Quickness of mind ... he seemed to know all the requirements of a song - tempo, key and he liked to play fast songs as ballads and the other way round. Wish I had him now. He never realized how great he was.

Tut Soper knew many of the musicians on the Chicago scene from the later 1920s and onwards. Some comments on a few of them:

Frank Teschemacher was light-complexioned, clean and always well dressed. Wore a homburg mostly but liked caps, had average type mustache, about 5'10", partial to brown and gray suits. A rather shy and soft-spoken man - never saw him angry or impolite to anyone. He was one of my favorite people. He played for a while with Joe Kayser at the Merry Garden ballroom. Dave Rose was on piano, and Danny Alvin on drums. Tesch had such a magical command of the band and his playing forced them to heights that I've never heard equalled before or since. He used to wail on the clarinet and effected pure enchantment on the dancers and listeners. It was an awesome thing to behold and hear. We played a few small gigs together and I will always thank God for having known him.

Maurie Bercov was one helluva clarinet player. I knew him before he left Chicago for New York. He was an extremely caustic, sarcastic and difficult man to get to know, let alone like. He made enemies so easily. Maurie could easily have been mistaken for Tesch; their approach to jazz was identical. Tesch was more on the ball and more liked and better known because of his naturalness.

As might be expected, Tut Soper liked to talk about pianists:

Charles LaVere (Lavere Johnson) was quite an intellectual, a clean-cut and likable guy. Good piano player. With Clyde McCoy for a long while, then went to the West Coast and did great at movie studio work as well as accompanying Bing Crosby. My memory of the way he played jazz is not in the Stacy-Hines tradition. He played a full piano, sort of rolling style. Not Bix-ian though he'd have liked it to be. Didn't play strident octaves. He put in all the fill-ins and created his own style. Kind of high-class guy.

Dave Rose (David Rosenberg): a close and personal friend I tremendously admire and love. Writes music arrangements with the speed of a man writing a letter and what delicate and beautiful notes he makes.

Mel Grant I knew almost as long as I've known Art Hodes. He was a truly great pianist and a fair composer. Mel was 6'3" and 235 pounds, so a good-sized man. Had a good-sized temper, too, but under control most always. His playing as he matured got to be fabulous.

Art Gronwall was one of my most beloved friends. He did an awful lot. I subbed for him twice with the Ray Miller band. He was a real great Bixian pianist and used to play Hoagy Carmichael stuff - full, great harmony and rhythm and his arrangements were masterful.

Frank Melrose I knew well enough to be able to discuss this and that. He was quite a drinking man. He could play early jazz and ragtime and boogie and blues as well as they ever could be played, and he only used his ear. He was murdered after a drunken argument over nothing. It was a very hot morning when he got it on his way home.

But Soper's main man was **Earl Hines**:

There was only one jazz musician and pianist whom I heard and who taught me, mentally and spiritually, about the great conceptions and victories over the mundane. He not only taught me, but he taught Sullivan and Stacy and countless others. His rhythmic freedom, expressed so freely and so free of carnality was unbelievable. We heard him at his peak, consistently great. I heard him once a week when he played with Jimmie Noone's Apex Club Orchestra. He and I were very close, and he had me play for him at the Apex and also had me sit in with his Grand Terrace orchestra. He always insisted, when I arrived at the Apex, that I stood next to him; the set-up made this possible. Hines had a small Howard baby grand. He pressed me to find myself in my playing and not to try to copy him or anyone else. He wanted me to be able to fly and not drag my jazz. No one ever before or since flew like Mr. Earl Hines.

Tut Soper at home, Chicago, October 21, 1979.

Tut Soper's memories of Chicago

In the course of a US jaunt in 1979 Derek Coller and I spent a few days in Chicago. There, thanks to collector Jim Gordon, we were able to visit long-established pianist Oro 'Tut' Soper at his home on Addison Street on the near-North Side. He was very friendly and entertaining and later I had a great deal of correspondence which eventually added much to my biography of Muggsy Spanier, published in 1995.

[Tut Soper's memories of Chicago pianists are also quoted, in little more detail, in the next chapter.]

In some of my letters I asked him to talk about the Chicago clubs and bars and something of the musicians, particularly pianists. The following are carefully edited transcriptions of Tut's comments. I started by asking him about a prominent jazz venue in the Windy City.

The Panther Room at the Sherman Hotel

Well, let's say a high class joint. There were middle class joints and low class joints. The Liberty Inn was a low class joint, located at Clark and Erie Street on the near-north [side of Chicago. In my memory there were four pianists who worked the back room or cafe part of the Liberty. They were Morrie Krumbein, Art Hodes, Clayton Ritchie, and myself. The last took my place when I left working there the last time. The Liberty Inn was originally the 70 Club [and] I played this too. Joints were usually called [that] if they had a bar and were very flexible as to locations and connections. A restaurant might be next door with a sliding panel and you could order food with your drinks. [Others] had a small dance floor or some kind of stage where people could either dance or watch a floor show. The type of neighborhood generally classified joints as being low-down, or middle.

Floyd Towne and his Men About Town band was a wonderful seven-piecer with John Italiane (Lane) on clarinet and alto. Bill Dohler played first alto and Floyd on tenor and Dick Donahue was on trumpet and the arranger. Art Hodes was pianist and Van Hook the bass man. They played about a block south of us by the

Wabash Avenue Bridge, a place called Harry's New York Bar. I was working at the Subway at this time (about 1935?) and then I joined and stayed for about a year and a half doing local and one-nighters around the bordering states.

I first played with Wingy [Manone] when he arrived in Chicago, from New Orleans around 1928. That was the 70 Club and Liberty Inn. I played many gigs, too many to remember, with him and also worked steadily with him as the leader at a place called My Cellar at Clark Street, just north of Lake Street on the east side, and it was a downstairs middle-class joint, food, small dance floor and level stage. He literally blew the roof off on many a night to a capacity filled dance floor. It was a cozy room, fairly large and had red and white table cloths accompanied by candlelight. The My Cellar band was only four pieces. Piano, me, Wingy trumpet and leader, Buzzy Knudsen clarinet and Dash Berkus [sic: Burkis] drums who was a great time drummer. A few years later Louis Armstrong played there with a fairly large band. The name had been changed to the Liberty Club. I won't forget that because I met Louis for the first there and with a group of three or four other guys, smoked a bit of stuff called marijuana. It was fun and Louis was waxing philosophical too. Wingy left Chicago. I think in 1951 or 1952 he came back and I worked an enjoyable couple of weeks at the Silhouette Club. I'm pretty sure that Doc Cenardo was on drums for this job [with] Bob McCracken on clarinet, originally from Texas, eventually went back there and died there. We didn't have a bass and the trombone man's last name I can't remember - George - played very well and was quite a soloist.

Fellow Pianists:

Charlie (LaVere) Johnson was quite an intellectual, clean-cut, likeable, kind of high class. A good piano player. Played with Clyde McCoy for quite a long while then went to the West Coast and did great at movie studio work. My recollection of the way he played is certainly not in the Jess Stacy - Earl Hines tradition. LaVere played a full piano, sort of rolling style. Not Bixian, though he'd have liked it to be. He did not play strident octaves. David Rose, his real name was Dave Rosenberg, was a close and personal friend who I tremendously admire and a wonderful gentle man who writes arrangements with the speed of someone writing a letter and what beautiful notes he makes. He decided not to be too deeply involved with the jazz clique but he knows his jazz.

I knew Mel Grant almost as long as I know Art Hodes. Mel was a truly great pianist and a fair composer although I don't have any great idea how much he composed. I have a score on a ditty of his entitled In a Quaint Gypsy Tea-Room; very Mozartian. As Mel was a 6'3" 235 pounds man, he was a good size. He had a good sized temper too but under control most always. His playing as he matured got to be fabulous only he developed very painful arthritis and marital difficulties started him drinking. For about six months we worked a job alternating shifts in the middle 50s at The Backstage, a strip-tease joint; a good job for a piano player and you always got your pay. He quit playing and opened a restaurant specialising in barbecue in a town called Rockton in Illinois. I played there for a week with trumpeter Bob Scobey.

I knew Frank Melrose well enough to be able to discuss this and that. He was quite a drinking man. He could play early jazz and ragtime, boogie and blues as well as it ever could be played and he only used his ear. He didn't develop his music reading ability at all. Very friendly, social guy, loved the blacks and loved to mingle with them. He was murdered by one of them after a drunken argument over nothing. Pete Daily, trumpet player, was with him in some black and tan restaurant earlier.

Floyd Bean and I were were quite close friends. After he left Muggsy (exactly when I don't know) he joined George Brunies at the 11-11 (Eleven Eleven Club) on West Bryn Mawr in Chicago. He stayed on year after year and played on a piano in such horrible condition (I know; I sat in on a set which was quite enough for me) that it's a true wonder to me that he could have held on to his sanity. Floyd, as I knew him, was not a very happy man. His wife was a bundle of negativity and after he married her I seldom saw him unless it was professionally. A good musician and a fine arranger. Played with the progressive jazz band of Boyd Raeburn during the war years at the *Down Beat* Room. I played next door but never caught that band.

George Zack and I were friends. He knew I loved and respected him and he in turn returned the muted feeling. He was a huge man, about 6'3" and solidly built. His piano hands were the largest ever, I think he could stretch a twelfth. His father was a Chicago symphony clarinettist and George's musical education was very well based. A really great jazz pianist who also liked to sing Hoagy's Snowball.

You would have liked Joe Sullivan. Not only was he one of the greatest but he was an easy going friendly guy; very intelligent and always learning.

At various times Soper wrote anecdotally on several musicians including one Stanley Norris who played alto on a Paramount Chicago record of mid-1928:

I knew and played with Stan with the Midnight Serenaders. A very good alto man standing six foot-six.

Floyd O'Brien, John Mendell and Rollo Laylan (later Wally) on drums and I worked a job in Janesville, Wisconson's Chateau LaMar, around 1930 or 1931. There was a magazine called Jazz of which twelve issues were published. Catherine Jacobson did a story on me in one of the issues and a picture of the band is shown along with a shot of me.

Fazola and Pee Wee Russell are still considered the best of jazz clarinettists. Charles Russell - can you imagine - I played with him in Eddie Condon's band in the first two weeks of October 1950. He did not touch a drop of any kind of alcoholic beverage whereas Eddie could hardly lift a shot glass with both hands because of shaky nerves. Pee Wee surprised me very pleasantly by his friendly, gentlemanly manner and Eddie was superb.

Morrie Bercov, a hell of a clarinet player. I knew him before he left Chicago for New York and whatever fame he garnered. I knew him before his marriage, an extremely caustic, sarcastic and difficult man to know, let alone like. He made enemies so easily. But he and I had never had the slightest difficulty. For some reason or other we got along yet it was never close at all. He was extremely intelligent and may have been a very well educated person. Yes, Morrie could easily have been mistaken for Teschemacher; their approach to jazz was identical. They were contemporaries, of course, but Tesch had more on the ball, was more liked and better known because of his naturalness. I was playing in a three piece jazz group in a Chinese restaurant on West Madison Street. We had sax, drums and piano.

Tesch would come and sit in with us night after night when he wasn't working. He was such a guy to know. He was a light-complexioned man, clean, well-dressed, wore a Homburg but mostly liked caps. He played for a while at the Merry Garden ballroom with Joe Kayser only five blocks from my home and at that time Dave Rose was on piano and Danny Alvin on drums. Tesch had such a magical command of the entire band and his playing forced it to heights that I'd never ever heard equalled before or since. We played a few small gigs together and I will always thank God for having known him.

[Clarinettist] Bud Jacobson I've worked with for over a year at the Subway Cafè. Bud was a practical musician; he could make small arrangements [and] could play the piano and did so towards the end. His talents were very mediocre but he was a literate and knew his jazz. His instruments were a disgrace, pads always leaking, keys held together with rubber bands. Bud was a real friendly guy and most everyone liked him.

Tut's influences:

There was only one jazz musician and pianist who I heard and who taught me mentally and spiritually about the great conceptions and victories over the mundane. Earl Hines not only taught me but he taught Sullivan and Stacy and countless others. His rhythmic freedom, expressed so freely and free of carnality, was unbelievable. We heard him at his peak, consistently great.

I heard him once a week for a full year when he played with Jimmie Noone's Apex Club orchestra. He and I were very close mentally. He had me play for him at the Apex and he had me sit in with his Grand Terrace orchestra and he always insisted when I arrived to stand next to him. The way the set-up existed made this possible; he had a small baby-grand to play. He always insisted for me to try to find myself in my playing and not try to copy him nor anyone else. He philosophised and made this open-sesame possible for me. He wanted me to be able to fly and not drag my jazz. Hines could play 24 choruses and keep that marvellous pulsation going and swing as Louie swung the trumpet. Earl certainly swung the piano. All through 1927 and 1928 every Monday night I was at the Apex and as great as Earl played so also was Jimmie Noone great. It's too bad in a way that Earl's star was on the rise but Jimmie's never came up.

Now when I sit down to play I don't consciously think of sounding like anyone, but jazz - true jazz - is a combination of energies that are released through the idiom of jazz. I hope to contact these energies that are automatically captured in the form of the music we're playing and, according to the individual, the success or failure depends on himself and possibly on his audience.

Lee Wiley

Lee Wiley was a good personal friend and although we only played together as professionals through the years, we'd spend a lot of hours - she singing and me playing - at the home of Bill and Crickie Priestley here in suburban Lake Forest, Illinois.

She may have been a "real bitch', I can see the possibilities, however, under some of the most trying musical circumstances, wherein I was involved, she was tops. I liked and respected her very much, loved her style of singing, I first met her in the 1940s here in Chicago. She was with Jess Stacy and Jess had just broken up his band when they came to town. They played a place called The Band Box [56 West Randolph] and I played the Brass Rail directly above them. I think if one was a friend of a friend of Lee's one would be completely accepted regardless of what might transpire. Those who knew her certainly loved her and were rewarded the best of Lee.

Our correspondence had several unavoidable lapses and again later as Soper's health declined. His words on Lee Wiley were in his last letter in August 1986. He died the following March, at the age of 76, and just three musicians turned up at the wake, plus the collector Jim Gordon, who'd joined the IAJRC back in 1968.

Postscript

I asked Tut Soper to tell something of his recording experiences so he spoke of the Marty Grosz session(s):

Many weeks and much partying were involved and although I did receive $100 I had to regard that as a token part payment. I figured at least $500 - never got it. You asked me to expand on this type of happening. Well, in the course of human events mysterious forces are working. I had never even heard of Marty Grosz until he called me and asked if I'd be interested. Because of mutual friends that had their names mentioned I felt at ease, I accepted and made the full commitments. In the case of the John Steiner recordings there was no pay either - but got lots of fame - and because unions and union contracts are so obnoxious to our freedom we do not exhibit a business judgement and trust our leaders and the people whom we deal with to be fair and honest. They usually aren't.

Tut Soper Discography

This compilation is based on Lord with various notes made down the years and mostly no longer traceable except those from Jim Gordon (the IAJRC 1980 Convention), Wayne Jones (corrections to data on Ristic SAH) and from Tut Soper.

Tut Soper and Baby Dodds:
Tut Soper, p/v; Baby Dodds, d/v,

Chicago, Jan 31, 1944

13144-1 Oronics #1	
13144-2 Big Butter And Egg Man #1 TS-BDv	
13144-3 Big Butter And Egg Man #2 TS-BDv	
13144-4 That's A Plenty	33: Baby Dodds 2
13144-5 Oronics	#2
13144-6 It's A Ramble	78: Steiner Davis 5001
13144-7 Right Kind Of Love TSv	
13144-8 Thou Swell	78: Steiner Davis 5001
13144-9 Keepin' Myself For You	
13144-10 Stardust Stomp	78: Steiner Davis 5000
13144-1 1 Oronics #	3
13144-12 Tea For Two	33: Baby Dodds 2
13144-6	also33:DanVC4013,VC7015.
13144-12	also 33: American Music LP2.
13144-4/6/8/1 0/11	also CD: Document DOCD5662.
13144-1/2/3/5/7/9	unissued.

The SD records have master nos. 9135/9133/9134/9132 respectively.

Bud Jacobson:
Johnny Mendell, t; Bud Jacobson, cl; Pud Brown, ts; Tut Soper, p; Dick McPartland, g; Pat Pattison, b; Earl Wiley, d;

Chicago, March, 1944;

Signature   unissued:
Bluesiana/Muskrat Ramble/After You've Gone/I Found A New Baby

Bud Jacobson's Jungle Kings:
Bill Stapleton, c; Warren Smith, tb; Volly De Faut, cl; Bud Jacobson, ts; Tut Soper, p; Pat Pattison, b; Lew Finnerty, d;

Chicago, March 4, 1945

Unknown titles recorded for Session but unissued.

Bud Jacobson's Jungle Kings:

Johnny Mendell, t; Warren Smith, tb; Volly De Faut, cl; Bud Jacobson, ts; Tut Soper, p; Jack Goss, g; Jim Lanigan, b; Claude Humphrey, d;

Chicago, July 1, 1945

NOS6OI Diga Diga Doo   78: white label 17040

A continuous performance edited to two sides of disc.

Bill Dohler Four / Bud Freeman Four:

Bill Dohler, as or Bud Freeman, ts; Tut Soper, p; Jim Lanigan, b; Jim Barnes, d;

Chicago, September 30, 1946

SD93046 Blue Lou BDas   78: Paramount CJS105
SD93046-11-1 The Man I Love   Bft 78: Steiner Davis 505
SD93046-1 8-1 Ontario Barrel House   BFt 78: Steiner Davis 506
CD (all): Classics 975. Another take of SD93046 issued on
Paramount CJS105.

The third title has Jack Gardner, p, added and also issued on 33: I Giganti del Jazz GJ34, Europa Jazz EJ1027. Other titles without Soper.

Marty Grosz and his Honoris Causa Jazz Band:

Carl Halen, t; Bill Priestley, c/g; Bud Wilson, tb; Frank Chace, cl/bar; Bob Shriver, cl/ts; Tut Soper, p; Marty Grosz, g/v; Chuck Neilson, b; Bob Saltmarsh, d;

Lake Forest, Chicago, October/December, 1957

Changes MGv	33: Riverside RLP12-268
Cry in' All Day Lonely Melody (rehearsal)	33: Ristic SAH
Lonely Melody	
Lonely Melody	33: Riverside RLP12-268
I'm Gonna Meet My Sweetie Now (rehearsal)	33: Ristic SAH
I'm Gonna Meet My Sweetie Now	-
I'm Gonna Meet My Sweetie Now	33: Riverside RLP12-268
Sorry	-
My Pet MGv BPc	-
The Love Nest (rehearsal)	33: Ristic SAH
The Love Nest -	
The Love Nest	33: Riverside RLP12-268
Clementine (From New Orleans)	-
Oh Miss Hannah BPg	
Wa Da Da -1 (rehearsal)	33: Ristic SAH
Wa Da Da -2	(rehearsal)
Wa Da Da	33: Riverside RLP12-268
For No Reason At All In C	33: Ristic SAH

For No Reason At All In C	33: Riverside RLP12-268
Because My Baby Don't Mean "Maybe" Now BPc	-
High Up On A Hill Top	33: Ristic SAH
I'd Climb The Highest Mountain	(unissued)

Riverside also CD: Good Time Jazz GTJ1 0065-2; Ristic also 33: Collectors Items 008; For No Reason At All In C (Riverside) also 33 Franklin Mint GJR068. The Riverside sleeve has pseudonyms for non-AFM members: Priestley as "Turk Santos" (he plays only on the three titles marked BPc or BPg); Bud Wilson as "Harry Budd"; Bob Saltmarsh as "Pepper Boggs". The repeated titles are, of course, from different takes and the Ristic labels have them as shown above. Other titles on the Ristic and Collectors Items issues do not include Soper.

Tut Soper:
piano solos -

Chicago, early 1960s

I Need Some Pettin'/ I'm Sorry Sally / After I Say I'm Sorry (unissued)

IAJRC 1980 Convention:
Tom Pletcher, c; Don Ingle, vtb; Frank Powers, cl; Spencer Clark, bss; Tut Soper, p; Bill Priestley, g; Don DeMichael, d;

Chicago, August 8, 1980

Big Butter And Egg Man / Song Of The Wanderer / Cherry / China Boy / I Found A New Baby

Add Truck Parham, b:

| Four Or Five Times | 33: IAJRC 40 |

Sugar / Hindustan / Coquette / Indiana

Sub Wayne Jones, d:
Oh Baby / I'm Coming Virginia/ Rose Room / Lonesome Road / Thou Swell / Struttin' With Some Barbecue

(Discography compiled by Bert Whyatt)

Floyd Town: His Story

Husk O'Hare, Maurice Sherman, Doc Rudder, Art Kassel, Joe Kayser, Charles Pierce and Sig Meyer were just a few of the Chicago band leaders during the 1920s who gave employment to the young white musicians aspiring to become jazz players. These leaders - opportunists, semi-professionals and career musicians alike - were providing dance music, playing the commercial songs of the day, decorating them with vocals and novelties. Other leaders were jazz players themselves. Not at the highest level perhaps, but they had the ability to lead and the personality to sell themselves to saloon owners and dance hall managers. Drummer Frank Snyder was one, trumpeters Louis Panico and Al Turk were others. Then there was Floyd Town, who for a time led one of the finest groups in Chicago, a formidable combination which included Muggsy Spanier, Floyd O'Brien, Frank Teschemacher, Jess Stacy and George Wettling.

A native Chicagoan, born October 20, 1899, Floyd Town had an elder brother; both were educated at Lane Technical College, where their father was a teacher. Music was not a tradition in the family, but Floyd became interested in the piano. Later, he mastered the saxophone and clarinet, though it was surprising that he ever found the time. As his widow, Iris Town, comments, "Most of his young life was spent swimming. Floyd was an outstanding swimmer."

He was a member of the Illinois Athletic Club, joining it shortly before Johnny Weismuller. "Unlike Weismuller, Floyd's love was water polo and eventually he became captain of the water polo team," says Mrs. Town. These endeavors were to lead to the 1932 Olympic Games.

"Floyd was married to Ardell Arnum when he was quite young," says Mrs. Town. "They had a son, Floyd Jr., before Ardell died from T.B."

The late Floyd Jr., who was an amateur cornet player, married Joyce Flindt. Her father was Emil Flindt, violinist and band leader, whose first job was probably the one he had playing with Fate Marable in 1907 on the *S.S. J.S.* Flindt was also the composer of Wayne King's theme, The Waltz You Saved For Me.

Floyd Town, early '30s. (Courtesy Iris Town)

Town's first musical job was alongside his old friend, trombonist Clarence (Slim) Freitag, who later played with Wayne King for many years. His next known engagement was in the ballroom of the White City amusement park, probably around 1924/25, with violinist Sig Meyer and his Druids. A photograph of this band shows a personnel of Muggsy Spanier, cornet; Bob Pacelli, trombone; Volly De Faut, clarinet, tenor; Floyd Town, clarinet, alto; Horace (Shorty) Williamson, piano; Marvin Saxbe, banjo; Arnold Loyacano, bass; George Petroni, drums.

Iris Town did not meet her husband until 1928, and details of his engagements before this time are sketchy. He did play at the Wilshore Ballroom on the Lake Front on Wilson Avenue prior to the lengthy Midway Gardens job, but with whom is not known.

In late 1926, Town obtained an engagement leading one of the bands at the Midway Gardens "pleasure palace," the enormous ballroom at 60th and Cottage Grove. There are two known photographs of this band, the presumed earlier one showing nine pieces, with Muggsy Spanier, cornet; Cy Simadel, trombone; Frank Teschemacher, clarinet, alto; Floyd Town, tenor; Danny Altier, alto; Jess Stacy, piano; Earl Wright, banjo, guitar; George Tupper, tuba; Al Waller, drums. For the second photograph, an unknown cornet player is added.

Jazzmen tells how Jess Stacy came to join the band, but little else has been written of this engagement, although it lasted into 1928. It would seem that the personnel was generally stable until about the time that it moved to the Triangle Cafe. Although unable to remember the exact chronology, Iris Town says, "David Rose played piano for a while, and I remember John Carsella playing the trombone for a while. I know Floyd O'Brien had replaced Simadel at the Midway, but then he came back at the Triangle."

Esquire's *1946 Jazz Book* says that

In 1927 and 1928 the Midway Gardens Ballroom booked a series of dates featuring 'battles.' One night Floyd Town, Husk O'Hare, Charlie Pierce, Louis Armstrong, Del Delbridge, Verne Buck, Herbie Mintz, Elmer Kaiser and Doc Cook were on hand.

By early 1928, the band had settled at the Triangle Cafe. The personnel was Muggsy Spanier, cornet; Floyd O'Brien, trombone; Teschemacher, Altier, Town, reeds; Stacy, piano; Pat Pattison, bass; George Wettling, drums. Of this group, George Wettling said, "We had the best band, and conditions were very good."

Floyd Town and the Midway Garden Orchestra, Chicago, 1927.
Left to right: Muggsy Spanier, cornet; Al Waller, drums; Danny Altier,
reeds; Cy Simadel, trombone; Jess Stacy, piano; Frank Teschemacher,
reeds; Earl Wright, banjo, guitar; George Tupper, tuba; Unknown,
cornet; Floyd Town, reeds, leader. (Courtesy Iris Town)

The presence of Louis Armstrong in Chicago in these years was, of course, a considerable additional benefit. In a 1939 *Down Beat* Muggsy Spanier is quoted as saying, "The best band I ever played in was the one we had at the Triangle in Chicago... there's never been a band as good since."

Eddie Condon, in *We Called It Music*, tells the story of the Triangle Cafe's owner, Mickey Rafferty, having a dispute with Spanier and Wettling and exploding a tear-gas gun in their car. Iris Town is not convinced by this account.

> Mickey never had any problem with the band. Floyd was the leader and all the sidemen were his friends. They worked very well together; they had great respect for each other and their talents.

The Towns knew Rafferty and his wife, Irene, very well and even after the band left the Triangle they kept in touch.

> Floyd and I loved to play golf and quite often we would stop on our way home. Mickey always seemed glad to see us. We would have a glass of beer and Mickey would bring us something to eat, so we would stay and talk.

Iris Town also recalls that

> Whenever the Triangle is mentioned, everyone remembers the name, Ray Reynolds (Renolds?). He was master of ceremonies for the floor show, a very funny man. He stayed until the very end. Years later Mickey and Irene moved to California; this was the last we heard.

Frank Teschemacher left the band in June 1928 to go to New York with Eddie Condon to play for Bee Palmer. Condon has written, "Towne (sic) was as amiable as (Louis) Panico; he agreed to let Tesch go without notice." The replacement was Rosy McHargue and, later, possibly Rod Cless.

The confusion over the spelling of Floyd Town's surname is explained:

> Mickey Rafferty had a belief that having five letters in both your first name and your last name was lucky. Being the gambler that he was, he insisted on putting an 'E' on Town on all the posters.

Both spellings are used in this story, depending upon period and quotations. All quotations used, unless otherwise attributed, are by Iris Town.

It is a cause for regret that no records by this band were issued. George Wettling did suggest that a recording session took place, but if it did, then the resultant masters have no doubt long since been destroyed. The nearest we can get now are the two titles (I'm Sorry Sally/My Gal Sal) recorded for Vocalion on October 22, 1928, as Danny Altier and his Orchestra. Spanier, Stacy, Pattison, Wettling and Altier are present, augmented by John Carsella, trombone; Maurie Bercov, clarinet, alto; Phil Robinson, tenor; Ray Biondi, guitar; and Frank Sylvano, vocal on the first title. These recordings, with good solos by Spanier, Carsella, Altier, Bercov and Stacy, go a little way towards giving us an indication of the sound of the Floyd Town band.

Iris Town was born in Sweden, coming to the U.S.A. as a three-year-old.

I eventually became a freelance commercial artist. I think I worked for all the commercial photographers in Chicago, retouching negatives.

In May of 1928, a girl friend took her to the Triangle to meet George Wettling, and the evening ended with a nervous young lady being taken by strangers (Floyd Town and Helen and Frank Teschemacher) on her first visit to a black club - to hear Earl Hines at the Apex Club! This first date with Floyd Town eventually led to 36 years of marriage.

Towards the end of 1928, Floyd thought they needed a change. He accepted an offer from the Cinderella Restaurant (Chinese) at Cottage Grove and 64th Street. Floyd was well known on the south side. In between the Triangle and the Cinderella the band had a week off.

It was during that week that Mickey Rafferty was shot by a hoodlum and not expected to survive. Here, too, it seems that George Wettling was over-dramatizing when he said, "At the Triangle Club, the boss was shot in the stomach one night, but we kept working. After that, he walked sort of bent over."

For the Cinderella personnel, Iris Town gives Muggsy Spanier, Floyd O'Brien, Pat Pattison, George Wettling, and Dave North on piano, but it should be noted that Spanier said that he and Stacy

Floyd Town's Men About Town, Harry's New York Cabaret, Chicago, 1935. Left to right: (standing) Floyd Town, Jimmy Barnes, Norman Van Hook, Johnny Lane, Art Hodes; (sitting) Dick Donahue, Bill Dohler. (Courtesy Iris Town)

EDDIE NEIBAUR
and his
SEATTLE HARMONY KINGS
Alternating With
FLOYD TOWNE
and his
Casino Moderne Orchestra
Thursday Sept., 6th

GRAND OPENING
of the
Casino Moderne
913 East 63rd St.
40c Per Person   DANCING 3 Till A.M.

left Town together to join Joe Kayser. Iris also remembers that "Dick Fiege, cornet, comes in here somewhere."

It was towards the end of 1929 that Town forsook the role of band leader for a few years. He became a side-man with Art Kassel.

"Floyd and Art Kassel had been friends through the years. Art was forming a new band; he wanted Floyd to join him," says Iris Town. "It would be a rest for Floyd; he would have time to do other things. Art opened at the Club Metropole in one of Al Capone's hotels on South Michigan Boulevard. The early band had many good musicians. When Floyd went with the band, Jack Reid, a great trombonist, came along."

An early photograph shows Jimmy Awad (?), cornet; Ponzie Crunz, trombone; Cal Green, alto: Floyd Town, clarinet, tenor; Elmer Schoebel, piano; Pat Pattison, bass; Jimmy Blank, drums; and one unidentified musician.

Schoebel, Reid and Town are in the personnel which recorded in Chicago as Elmer Schoebel's Friars Society Orchestra. This was Town's only jazz recording session, made with Dick Fiege, cornet; Jack Reid, trombone; Frank Teschemacher, clarinet; Elmer Schoebel, piano; Charles Berger, guitar; John Kuhn, tuba; George Wettling, drums. Copenhagen and Prince of Walls were first made at a rejected session on September 20, 1929, followed by the issued date of October 18. Writing in the Time-Life Teschemacher booklet, Marty Grosz comments on the "brisk tenor solo" on Copenhagen and says that "Floyd Town's tenor croons 12 bars of blues with a degree of viscosity not usually encountered among Chicago reed men.

Art Kassel's "wasn't a jazz band, but it was alright," recalls Iris Town.

> The salary was good (and) the band travelled to cities all over the United States, always first-class. Floyd stayed for four years. Most of the wives travelled with the band. In Chicago, on Saturday nights, we used to go in the Grand Terrace to hear Earl Hines' Band.

Floyd was a good arranger, he also had a great singing voice. He was featured in a vocal trio with the other reed players, Ralph Morris and Ding Johnson. Rust lists four sessions (14 titles) recorded by Art Kassel and his Kassels in the Air for Columbia in New York between March 1932 and January 1933. All but two of the titles have vocals, with the vocal trio on some. Those titles heard show a strictly commercial approach, with no hint of jazz, except for a brief spot of growl trumpet by Jack Davis on Hell's Bells. The two unheard instrumentals are the Century of Progress March and the potentially interesting Chant of the Swamp.

It was in the middle of his stay with Kassel that Floyd Town's swimming interest took precedence again. As Iris Town recalls it,

> In 1932 Floyd was asked to be a member of the U.S. Olympic Water Polo team at Los Angeles. He took a month's leave from music and went back into training. I don't remember how this came out; I know he brought back a special medal. This was to go to his son when he grew up.

The 1932 Olympics were held from July 31 to August 7, with Hungary winning the water polo gold, and the U.S.A. in third place. United States Water Polo Inc. do not have Town's name on record, so his exact status at the L.A. Olympics is not known. But perhaps the major event during his stay with Art Kassel had already taken place when he and Iris were married on March 28, 1932.

According to Iris, "Floyd was itching to get back to jazz," and he gave Art Kassel his notice. His last date with the band was in the Walnut Room of the Bismark Hotel in Chicago. Shortly after, early in 1933, Town was appearing at the Casino Moderne, a ballroom on 63rd Street in Chicago, owned by Herb Shutter, George Wettlings's brother-in-law, playing for dancing and accompanying an all-girl floor show. The personnel was Dick Fiege, - Graham, cornets; Floyd O'Brien, trombone; Rod Cless, Cal Green, Floyd Town, reeds; Jess Stacy, piano; Dick McPartland, guitar; Pat Pattison, bass; George Wettling, drums. This engagement seems to have been around May and June.

On July 1st, at Mickey Rafferty's request, a return engagement began at the Triangle Cafe. Bill Dohler recalls himself and Johnny Lane on altos; Town on tenor; Johnny Mendell on trumpet; Pat Pattison on bass; Don Carter on drums; and, almost certainly, Paul Jordan on piano.

The next known job was in the spring of 1934 at the Tin Pan Alley at 114 N. Dearborn. Then, on September 6th, Town returned to a completely refurbished Casino Moderne, playing alongside Eddie Neubar's (sic) orchestra on the opening night. This engagement seems to have lasted until the end of the year.

Early in 1935, Paul Mares' small band closed at Harry's New York Cabaret (or CaBARet!) in Chicago, to be replaced by Floyd Town's "Men About Town," with Dick Donahue, cornet; Bill Dohler, alto; Johnny Lane, clarinet, sax; Floyd Town, tenor; Art Hodes, piano; Norman Van Hook, bass; Jimmy Barnes, drums. Broadcasts took place over station WBBM and the CBS network. The Esquire Jazz Book recalled that "their local broadcasts were in the best jazz traditions." Queried recently, Art Hodes said that he had liked Floyd Town, he was a good leader, a good man to work for.

Entertainers at Harry's New York Cabaret were backed by pianist Elmer Schoebel, as well as the Men About Town. *Pittsburgh Courier* columnist Earl Morris, with a Chicago dateline for April 11, wrote:

Many Chicagoans are wild about the orchestra of Floyd Towne ... broadcasting from the swank ofay Harry's New York cabaret, downtown. This ofay band plays strictly Harlemese. Sez us!

In similar vein, an unidentified newspaper columnist wrote:

... For the benefit of Chicago radio listeners of the late hour dance music, Floyd Town and band who broadcast over WBBM are NOT colored but are a group of white musicians who play the music the way you like it and also appreciate it...

Iris Town remembers

When the band left Harry's (late 1935?), Floyd had booked the band into a ballroom in Madison, Wisconsin. This was a six week engagement and we rented a lovely home on Lake Mendota. Art Hodes didn't want to leave Chicago at this time, and Tut Soper took his place. The rest of the band was intact. It was a great relaxing time; we played golf every day on the course across the road.

Next came the Chez Paree, where Town also played for dancing and broadcasts.

Henry Busse played all the acts. I think the next stop was the Via Lago, a beautiful place with a glass dance floor with lights underneath, with every colour coming through. Here they also had a floor show.

A publicity postcard for the Via Lago Café calls it "The Beauty Spot of America – 837 Wilson Ave. By the lake. Uptown Chicago's Famous Illuminated Glass Dance Floor". Reference is also made to "Good Food – Good Service. Refined Atmosphere for the Discriminating."! Town played here from March to July of 1936.

It was here that Don Carter came into the band; Jimmy Barnes had not been feeling well. Tut Soper was not asked to join. Tut had many problems; he could be very difficult. He was a great believer in horoscopes. If it said that he should take it easy that day, he would come to work, sit down at the piano and fold his arms. Floyd used to lose his mind.

So, Tut Soper was out and Paul Jordan was the new pianist, though many years later, in a letter to Bert Whyatt, Tut Soper was to remember the Men About Town as "a wonderful seven piece".

Anita O'Day, in her autobiography, *High Times, Hard Times*, remembers the Via Lago:

...one night this man came in and asked me how I'd like to sing at the Vialago *(sic)* with Floyd Towne's band. How would I like it? Towne's band had seven pieces, we had four. Towne would provide a lot of harmony ... there were some other sharp cats in the band. But the one who caught my eyes was a tall drummer [Don Carter] ... he played ... drums, vibes, cymbals, tympanis, bells, the whole bit!

It would seem that O'Day was not employed solely at the Via Lago, but would go there when her first engagement was over for the night. Contrary to Miss O'Day's references, which would suggest that this was in 1937, Iris Town's recollections place it in 1936.

Publicity material for the Men About Town refers to

The Biggest Little Band in the Country – were featured recently for a period of one year over the C.B.S. network, from coast to coast, playing from Harry's New York Cabaret, Chicago – has just finished a six month's engagement, ending August 1st, at the famous Via Lago Restaurant, Chicago. At present playing a series of hotels, banquets and parties until August 28th, when they leave for the West Coast and luminous (sic) offers. They will be available for a limited number of dates en route.

No details are known of this tour.

In 1937 Floyd Town opened the Midway Café for a Mr. Dietrick, who had been the boss at the Midway Gardens. The Café "was located across the street from the old Midway Gardens. It was a small night club (on 61st and Cottage Grove), but very nice."

Another unidentified newspaper cutting dated January 5, 1938 gives the Men About Town personnel as Dick Donahue, trumpet, Al Gold, clarinet, Bill Dohler, "saxophone and lyric tenor"!, Paul Jordan, piano, Norman Van Hook, bass, Don Carter, drums; and says that "the band recently closed a several months engagement at the Storke Club located on the north side of Chicago." This was in the course of announcing an "indefinite stay" at Hotel LaFontaine in Huntingdon beginning December 31, 1937.

By September, the band was opening another Mickey Rafferty enterprise. Rafferty had bought the old Golden Pumpkin restaurant on West Madison and renamed it the Pla-Mor Café. "Floyd stayed there quite a while."

This ended yet another era. The depression was starting to hit; many night clubs were closing. Floyd and Richard McPartland decided to try a small entertaining group, with Floyd, tenor sax, clarinet, Dick McPartland, guitar, Dean Whitaker, trumpet, Rennie Collins, bass." Whitaker told Iris Town that "they started to get the band together in 1938.

It must have been the right thing to do; they were very successful. They all had good singing voices and they called themselves The Embassy Boys. Rennie Collins had a beautiful voice and they also did a lot of comedy skits. They played in the Balinese Room of the Blackstone Hotel on Michigan Avenue.

This was a long residency with coast to coast broadcasts.

Cornetist Jimmy McPartland has recalled playing with his brother, Dick, around 1935 in a group called The Embassy Four.

"Then the travelling started again – the Atlanta Biltmore Hotel, the Gibson Hotel in Cincinatti, and on and on." To quote Dean Whitaker again: "The Embassy Boys were together until 1943."

While playing in Fort Wayne, Indiana, it snowed and Floyd took a very bad fall on the ice. He suffered a Potts fracture of his ankle and he was on crutches for months. This was when he took up wood carving. He surprised everyone and some of his carvings were displayed in Chicago. One large company made molds of the carvings and they came out in metal.

During the war Floyd's brother owned a tool and die company. With all the work he had, he asked Floyd to work for him as general manager. So this came to pass and life became very different. We moved from Austin, out to Villa Park (but) this did not stop Floyd from playing. He worked many Saturday nights. All the musicians still around got together for jam sessions.

The Embassy Boys were reformed in 1945 and continued touring until 1948, ending with a job at a Dakota corn festival. Town continued in the music business until he retired. "He was constantly getting work from different music agencies," Iris recalled.

In one of her Piano Jazz radio shows, Marian McPartland comments: "I actually played with Baby Dodds in Chicago in the 1950s, with Jimmy McPartland and Floyd Town ... in a concert."

During the 1960s, certainly between 1966 and 1968, there were sessions almost every Sunday at the home of bassist Jim Lanigan. He had moved to a large house in Elburn and any musician was welcome. In addition to Lanigan himself and his son, Jimmy Junior on clarinet, other musicians who appeared were Dean Whitaker, trumpet, George Kenyon, mellophone, Floyd O'Brien, Harry Graves, trombones, Floyd Town, tenor, Hayden McPartland (Dick's son), guitar, Rags Ragland (not the comedian), piano, Wayne Jones and Freddie King, drums.

Wayne Jones recalls one session at the Lanigan home in Villa Park, before the move to Elburn, which included himself on cornet, Floyd O'Brien, Floyd Town, Jim Lanigan Sr and Jr, Bill Priestley on guitar and Doug Kassel (Jimmy McPartland's grandson) on drums. Jones also remembers one session at Elburn. His memories of Floyd from those two occasions are that "by the '60s, of course, he was rusty, as are all of those who don't keep up with their playing for whatever reason. I remember him as being warm and genial. Floyd looked even then in fine shape, with a great chest development, quite athletic looking."

Iris Town quotes Jim Lanigan Sr. as always saying that Floyd "had such great intonation."

Another Chicago collector, Jim Gordon, remembers:

Floyd Town was very nice to me. Would always call us when he would be having a Sunday afternoon jam session in Villa Park at the local VFW (Veterans of Foreign Wars) Hall. Some nice times. He played nice clarinet ... I always thought he had a little of Tesch in him, or vice versa.

Midway Garden Orchestra.
Left to right: Earl Wright, banjo, guitar; George Tupper, tuba; Cy
Simadel, trombone; Al Waller, drums; Muggsy Spanier, cornet; Jess
Stacy, piano; Danny Altier, reeds; Frank Teschemacher, reeds; Floyd
Town, reeds, leader. (Courtesy Iris Town)

The Villa Park VFW Hall is recalled by Iris Town as

a lovely building, with a large ballroom upstairs, a dining room and a large bar downstairs. We had friends who were members and they always welcomed us. Floyd played a lot of their dances, including New Year's Eve. They had a very good organist and Floyd would play along with him.

One Saturday night Town was playing a set with the organist when he felt unwell and Iris drove him home. The following day he was in the hospital, dying of heart failure that night. The date was March 4, 1968.

Today, Iris Town still lives in Villa Park, still interested in jazz and still taking in local jazz sessions. She is content, happy in her friendships and in her memories of her husband's achievements. As she says, "He lived a good life and had his music."

*

This article appeared in *The Mississippi Rag* for February 1990. It is believed that Iris Town, who helped so much with this article, died in the early 1990s.

A dance card shows Floyd Towne and his Orchestra playing at the Casino Moderne on April 28, 1933 for a sorority dance. The location is given as 913 E. 63rd St. and confirms that Town had left Art Kassel by early 1933.

An unidentified cutting, probably a radio listing, shows Floyd Towne and his Memphis Melody Boys working at Tin Pan Alley on Dearborn Street, with dates of Saturday, March 10 and Tuesday, April 3 indicating 1934.

A letter to Floyd Town date-stamped September 6, 1935, confirms that he was still working at Harry's New York Bar at that time.

An undated note states that "When Paul Whiteman appeared at The Drake Hotel in May (1936 or 1937?), he chose Floyd Town and his Men About Town to play on his rhythm contest, along with the Lew Diamond unit. Floyd Town won this contest." An undated radio listing gives: 11:30 Paul Whiteman Swing Concert, battle of swing between the orchestras of Paul Whiteman, Lou Diamond and Floyd Town.

From news items gathered by the late John Miner from issues of *Down Beat*, we now know that there was an Embassy Four prior to the Embassy Boys. Around October 1936 The Embassy Four consisted of Jimmy McPartland, cornet, Dick McPartland, guitar, Joe Peters, probably reeds, and Connie Webster. And they were appearing in the Blue Room in New Orleans. In December they were still in New Orleans, but on the Fountain Terrace of the Roosevelt Hotel.

Jimmy McPartland himself told Max Jones ("Talking Jazz"),

I got a wire from my brother inviting me to Chicago. He had a little outfit called the Embassy Four, and I joined them at the Palmer House Hotel. ... then went to St. Louis, Kansas City, New Orleans, and down around there. I did this for a year and a half before deciding to have a change.

An unknown source lists Dick McPartland's Embassy Four, with Jimmy McPartland, at the Palmer House in Chicago, 1936 into 1937. The December 15, 1941 issue of *Down Beat* shows Dick McPartland and his Embassy Boys (Whitaker, trumpet, Town, reeds, Pat Pattison, bass, Dick McPartland, guitar) at the Sky Club in Chicago.

Johnny Lane: "Played with gusto"

Johnny Lane was a clarinet player and a band leader. He was not an outstanding performer, but led dixieland groups for thirty or more years. He was a hustler, yet never recorded commercially. His personal claims were often exaggerated, but his bands included many of the best jazzmen available in Chicago and Los Angeles. He was considered a wimp by some, a kind, sweet man by others. In short, he was one of the many intriguing minor figures in the story of jazz.

Born in Palazzo Adriano, a small town near Palermo in Sicily, on 18 October 1900, his family name was Italiane. When he was aged two his family emigrated to the U.S.A., settling in Chicago. Musical appreciation began with his father, who was a keen follower of street bands and an enthusiast for operatic and symphonic music, particularly Verdi and Puccini.

As a youngster Lane was apprenticed to a barber. He has said, "Every Italian barber shop in those days had a guitar and mandolin. They used to have concerts between haircuts and shaves." He learned to play the mandolin and worked jobs with a trio. "I never did become a barber, but I did get a job in a bank as a messenger boy."

The mandolin was forgotten sometime in his teens when he heard a Ted Lewis record.

> His music was my first inspiration, and found that I would rather practice than eat. I traded my mandolin for a clarinet and before I went to bed that night I was playing Home Sweet Home. I could imitate him (Lewis) better than anybody in the neighborhood.

To learn music he went to Tony Quitsell [spelling?], who played clarinet at the Majestic Theatre. Lane also lays claim to have had lessons from Jimmie Noone: "We played those trills and things together ... in his bedroom on 33rd Place and Cottage Grove." These lessons were during the Apex Club period, but presumably did not last for long, as he then went to Clifford King. Although Jimmie Noone was his main influence, there was also an early association

Johnny Lane, Rupneck's, Chicago, December 1948. (Courtesy Bill Tinkler)

with Leon Roppolo. At one afternoon session Lane told Roppolo, "You know, I like you better than Ted Lewis"!

He visited Roppolo, who called him 'Kid Lewis'. Both Roppolo and Noone told him it was all "just practice".

He credited Roppolo with teaching him the dixieland standards. Lane's early jobs are not known, but George Hoefer, in a *Down Beat* article on Muggsy Spanier, wrote of the Sig Meyer band: "When this band played the old Columbia dance hall on N. Clark street, other members included Dale Skinner, sax; Marvin Saxbe, banjo; Volly De Faut and Johnny Lane, clarinets; and Mel Stitzel, piano." This engagement may have been in 1924.

Lane's recollections continue: "I rehearsed a five piece band and auditioned for Frank McGuire, owner of Chicago's northside Columbia Ballroom, where we played four seasons (1924 to 1928)." Joe Marsala, who was to study under Lane, has recalled standing outside the Columbia Hall

> ... where Muggsy played, Johnny Lane was clarinet and had an orchestra there. I liked that kind of music. The others would go to dance, but my brother, Marty, and I used to listen to the band, and hear them jam.
>
> Four years I worked the Columbia in the winter and Lake Delavan in Wisconsin in the summer," said Lane, though on occasions he was inclined to over-emphasise his own part in a band. Florence O'Brien recalls her husband, the trombonist Floyd O'Brien, working with Lane in 1927 at Lake Delavan in another's band, probably Bill Otto's. At this time Lane was, in Florence O'Brien's words, "married to an Italian girl, Yolande, a beautiful blonde. We had a cottage and Johnny and Yolande had the one next door. She had a temper you wouldn't believe. You've seen cartoons of people running after their husbands with the frying pan! She'd get after him screaming Italian. He didn't stay married to Yolande very long.

John Steiner has written that Lane and Bill Dohler married sisters, but no other details are known.

There was a lengthy engagement in 1928, Florence O'Brien recalls, when Floyd O'Brien played in a band led by Lane at the Leland Hotel in Aurora.

With Joe Marsala, Lane went on a tour with an Ernie Young Road Show, and then came work in various speakeasys.

Red Arrow Show Lounge, 1955. Jim Cunningham, co; Sid Dawson, tb; Johnny Lane, cl; Art Hodes, p; Hap Gormley, d. (Courtesy John Miner)

Louis Armstrong, Johnny Lane, Lee Collins, Chicago, June, 1952. (Courtesy Bill Campbell)

One of the best known was the Breakfast Club, on North Clark St. where we had a long and successful run. At different times I had Bud Freeman, Wingy Manone, Bob Zurke, Dave Tough, Art Hodes, and Miff Mole in my band. With prohibition and the depression still in effect, jobs became scarce, so I broke up the band and jobbed around as a sideman.

In 1932 he was a member of a ten-piece orchestra which Herb Karlin attempted to keep together, playing dates in places like Champaign, Peoria, and La Salle. Saxist Buzz Knudsen told Jim Gordon that the personnel included Wingy Manone, trumpet; Lane, Knudsen, Mike Piatt, reeds; George Finlay, [?]; and Gene Krupa, drums; later replaced by Jim Barnes. The band recorded for Brunswick.

It has been reported, by Warren Vaché, Sr, that "a sax player called Johnny Lane was with the Charlie Eckel band in New York City in 1933." Could this be the same Lane?

The source is uncertain, but John Miner has a note that a group which played at Liberty Inn circa 1933/34 included Fritz Wleckie (or Wlecke), trumpet; John Bothwell, alto; Lane, clarinet; Clayton Ritchie, piano; Earl Wiley, drums. (If this was 1933, as seem likely, and if Bothwell was present, he would have been fourteen years old!) It has also been suggested that Lane played with Art Hodes at Liberty Inn.

On 1 July 1933, Floyd Town started an engagement at the Triangle Cafe. He had recently returned to bandleading after a long spell with Art Kassel. His band at the Triangle was Johnny Mendell, trumpet; Bill Dohler, alto; Lane, alto, clarinet; Town, tenor; probably Paul Jordan, piano; Pat Pattison, bass; Don Carter, drums.

Further engagements at the Tin Pan Alley and the Casino Moderne are known, and by the time Floyd Town's Men About Town replaced the Paul Mares band at Harry's New York Bar early in 1935, the personnel was Dick Donahue, trumpet; Dohler, Lane, Town, reeds; Art Hodes, piano; Norman Van Hook, bass; Jim Barnes, drums. The band left Harry's New York Bar towards the end of 1935, and began a six week engagement in Madison, Wisconsin, with Tut Soper replacing Hodes as pianist. At some point before the end of 1937 Johnny Lane was replaced by clarinetist Al Gold, and it seems likely that at this time Lane left the music business. As

New Orleans Jazz Band, Los Angees, 1976.
Left to right: Johnny Lane, Bill Stumpp, Bill Campbell, Nick Fatool, Abe Lincoln, Harry Babasin, Nappy Lamare. (Courtesy Bill Campbell)

he said "I was lucky enough to get a position in the bank (Federal Reserve) again and eventually became Teller and Auditor."

He played the occasional gig, one of which was the Jimmie Noone Memorial Concert. Organiser John Steiner says: "I had asked Boyce Brown to play clarinet ... and he said, "No, you want to get Johnny Lane." He wasn't as good a representative of Jimmie Noone's style as, say, Joe Marsala. I didn't know anything about Johnny Lane, but when he performed it wasn't so bad."

The following was recorded by John Steiner:

JOSH BILLINGS and his Suitcase Busters
Johnny Lane, cl; Gideon Honore, p-1; Tut Soper, p-2; Jack Goss, g; Pat Pattison, b; Josh Billings, brushes, vocal.

Chicago, Illinois - 5 August 1945

Three Little Words -1	unissued
Mean To Me -2	unissued

Wingy Manone came to town, probably in late 1947, and he used Johnny Lane in his band. This job, plus the burgeoning dixieland business in Chicago, prompted Lane to leave the bank and return to music and, for the next eight years, he was active in clubs all over the Chicago area. They included the Bee Hive, the Sky Club, Rupneck's, the 11-11, and the Preview Lounge. There were occasions when the band was led by Danny Alvin or Georg Brunis, but generally Lane was the leader. Musicians who played in these groups included Lee Collins, Floyd O'Brien, Georg Brunis, Tut Soper, Jack Gardner, Floyd Bean, Don Ewell and Jasper Taylor. In addition most of the second and third division names on the Chicago scene worked for him at one time or the other. An attempt at listing the clubs and personnels involved is appended to this article.

Bill Reinhardt remembered Johnny Lane as "an old-timey clarinet player." When Reinhardt was planning to open Jazz, Ltd. in Chicago in 1947 he had not originally intended to play, and Lane was one of those auditioned for the clarinet spot. Then it was planned that Lane would have the food concession, po-boy sandwiches and suchlike, but this didn't materialise either.

Lane had spent a total of six months during 1948 at Rupneck's. *Down Beat* quoted a bartender as saying that business "was pretty sad until ... Johnny opened." The same report referred to the common faults with this type of band: "While the band has first-rate ensemble power and drive where it's needed, it overdoes this steam roller quality... For a while we doubted if they did anything softly or with much restraint. One night, however, we heard Stars Fell On Alabama polished up in a nice quiet manner. But this is one of the too few." Another John Steiner recording in this period was:

JOHNNY LANE
Lane, cl; Jack Gardner, p; Jack Goss, g.

Uptown Players Theatre, Chicago, Illinois - 21 March 1949

St. Louis Blues	unissued
Cherry	unissued
Embraceable You	unissued

About June 1949 Danny Alvin led the band at Rupneck's, with Bill Tinkler, trumpet; Jimmy James, trombone; Lane, clarinet; and Art Gronwall, later replaced by Tut Soper, on piano. Lane left after a few weeks to take a band into the Sky Club.

The opening personnel at the Sky Club was Lee Collins, trumpet; Bill Johnson, trombone; Lane, clarinet; Floyd Bean, piano; Bill Pfeiffer, drums. Collins is quoted in his biography: "I left the Victory Club for a while in 1949 because Johnny Lane ... was at the Sky Club and asked me to join his band there. He also had Georg Brunis with him. I stayed there for some time, but the place was too far for me to travel, so I went back to the Victory Club."

By the fall of 1949 the band was down to a quintet, but with trumpeter Jimmy Ille added on Saturdays,

It was in this period that John Steiner recorded Lane again.:

JOHNNY LANE BAND
Jimmy Ille, tp; Georg Brunis, tb; Lane, cl; Boyce Brown, as; Art Gronwall, p; Andrew Saucier, d.

Sky Club, Chicago, Illinois - circa October 1949

Clarinet Marmalade	unissued
Struttin' With Some Barbecue	unissued

Some points to note here. Most bands in Chicago at this time worked without a bassist. Sometimes it was claimed that the bandstands were too small, but generally it was a cost-cutting arrangement. Georg Brunis had a tendency to take over bands with which he played and that may have happened here. Andrew Saucier is the New Orleans drummer Anderson Saucier. Jimmy Ille said: "He was loud."

Early in 1950 Lane began an engagement at the 11-11 Club (on Bryn Mawr at the El). Rupneck's was next to an El. stop too. This gig lasted two-and-a-half years, until Georg Brunis took the band over. Thomas Gilmore, in the August 1992 issue of *The Mississippi Rag*, wrote:

> Johnny Lane enjoyed some brief fame as a band leader at the 11-11 and before then, I believe, at the Preview Lounge on Randolph Street in the Loop. Aside from a rotund geniality and a willingness to work hard, what made him a leader was a mystery. He was an indifferent clarinetist ... Brunis was the major drawing card and at the height of his powers.

Towards the end of 1951 the 11-11 Club was the likely location for some titles put on tape by the Magnacorder company, which was recording various kinds of music with which to demonstrate their machines. The following titles were given to John Steiner by a Magnacorder representative.

JOHNNY LANE BAND
Benny Woodworth, tp; George Winn, tb; Lane, cl; Roy Wasson, p; Hey Hey Humphrey, d.
probably 11-11 Club, Chicago, Illinois c. December 1951
Royal Garden Blues/At The Jazz Band Ball/High Society/Royal Garden Blues/ Basin Street Blues/High Society (#2)/Weary Blues/ Jazz Me Blues/Clarinet Marmalade/Black And Blue (incomplete ?)

Claude 'Hey Hey' Humphrey was so called because of a speech impediment. His surname is sometimes spelt Humphries, but is correct as shown.

Sometime in early 1954 Lane was a member of the Georg Brunis band playing at The Red Arrow in Stickney, another Chicago suburb. He was at this location for about two years, in this case becoming the leader when Brunis left early in 1955. The following private tape is a further example of the repertoire and tempos aimed at the visiting firemen.

GEORG BRUNIS BAND

'Muggsy' Dawson, c; Brunis, tb/v-1; Lane, cl; Roy Wasson, p; Don King, d:
The Red Arrow, Stickney, Illinois - 23 May 1954
At The Jazz Band Ball/Royal Garden Blues/Ja Da/Ugly Child -1/1 Found A
New Baby/ Lady Be Good/Panama/Riverside Blues/Basin Street Blues/I Found
A New Baby #2 -1/Sweet Georgia Brown/South/When The Saints Go Marching
In/Darktown Strutters' Ball/Ballin' The Jack/Sister Kate -1/Jazz Me Blues

Other titles played but not taped were Original Dixieland One-Step
and Grandpas Spells. Theme played at end of each set was Tin Roof
Blues.

Jack Tracy, at the time an editor with *Down Beat*, summarises
Lane's Chicago activities in the 1940s and 1950s:

> Although Johnny Lane played around Chicago a lot with various
> Dixie bands, many of them his own, he was actually a lot better
> promoter than player. He was dogged and persistent in going to
> club owners to seek a gig and would not hesitate to ask the best
> guys in town to play with him when he got one, even though he
> was not in their class as a jazz player. His style, as I best recall,
> was notey and florid with a tone that was principally legitimate
> and lacking in personality.

Collector Jim Gordon remembers him as

> a plump little man with hair combed like General MacArthur.
> A sweet guy, always amiable and willing to talk. We enjoyed
> his sweet clarinet work, where he would sound very much like
> Jimmie Noone. He would play the pretty things that Noone had
> done.

1955 and 1956 have both been quoted as the year in which Lane
moved to Los Angeles, but his Chicago engagements would suggest
that he actually moved late in 1956. He went to work as a bookkeeper
at North American Aviation, apparently asking a manager he met
in a club for a job. His first gigs seem to have been in 1957 with
the Knights of Jazz. Trumpeter Don Kinch recalls that when he
was in the band there were, in addition to Johnny Lane, "Minor
Hall on drums, K.O. Eckland on piano, and I think Roy Brewer on
trombone." Elsewhere Roy Brewer has been listed as leader.

In September 1957 clarinetist Joe Darensbourg recorded his
slap-tongue version of Yellow Dog Blues. This became a hit on the

Lark label, and Darensbourg has recounted how he went on a four day trip to publicise his record, putting Johnny Lane in his place at The Lark club.

The band-list at the end of this story will give some indication of the clubs, bars and other establishments at which Lane played during his Californian stay, and of the musicians he employed, the 'names' including Wild Bill Davison, Irving Goodman, Al Jenkins, Warren Smith, Marvin Ash, Dick Cary, Nappy Lamare, Doc Cenardo, and Nick Fatool.

Chuck Sweningsen recalls: "After Lane went to California, he stayed in touch with me, telling what great little bands he had out there and all the work he had. From other sources, I learned that much of this was either illusory or overstated. "At other times Lane said: "I was responsible for reviving Dixieland music in Chicago" and "I'm an aeronautics engineer", the first statement being debatable, and the second untrue. He suggested to Jim Gordon that he had almost joined Louis Armstrong's All Stars, which could have been true, but one wonders .

Trumpeter Bob Higgins tells a story about an evening at the Downey Wonderbowl when the band was Higgins, trumpet; Warren Smith, trombone; Lane, clarinet; Bill Campbell, piano; Doc Cenardo, drums; (a line-up of some merit). Lane commented, "I'm not as good a player as I was," to which Warren Smith replied, "You never were!"

Joe Marsala moved to California, and drummer Bill French remembers that Lane employed Marsala on a lot of jobs when he moved to Los Angeles and was having difficulty finding work.

In addition to shopping malls, another Los Angeles specialty place for bands to play was the bowling alley. One of these, the Wonderbowl, was situated on Firestone Boulevard in Downey, and pianist Arthur Schutt worked there for many years. The music room was Jim's Roarin' '20s, and Lane was there for a total of five years or so, working anything from two to five days per week. Bill French began working with Lane in May 1963, initially as a sub. He recalls the Wonderbowl as a large bowling alley, with a lunch counter,

> and a good-sized room where we played. Probably seated 75-100, and a small dance floor, as with so many places like that, here was a beautiful long bar, and along with the booze there was always tons of free popcorn! It was a jumping place for quite a while. We played mostly jazz.

Another Saturday night was in the Gay Nineties room of the Compton Bowl bowling alley. Johnny Lane said of this gig, "Me and 64 other lanes."

In the 1960s Lane was working in the purchasing department of Autonetics, part of the aircraft business. A column by Jerry De Muth said, "After eleven years, advancing to position of senior planner, Lane retired from his day-to-day job at the aircraft plant." All those years Lane had been combining his playing activities with the full-time day job.

Bill French says, "It should be mentioned that Johnny never did have a set band; that is, the personnel changed frequently, often from gig to gig. During the last few years of his life we played scads of senior citizen and singles dances where there was no chance to play jazz. A real drag, but we sure were busy."

Leona Lane died in 1975. Bill French believes, as does Chuck Sweningsen, that her death was the beginning of the end for her husband. As Bill French says. "They were inseparable. Yet he played on until a week before his death. The last date was 19 July 1980. The piano player got lost going to the job and was quite late, and old Andy Blakeney, the fine trumpet player, never did show up!"

In his last years Lane suffered from arthritis in his hands, yet he continued playing until his death, officially of a stroke, on 26 July 1980.

In conclusion, a few more quotations about Johnny Lane as a man and a musician.

Bill French: Johnny was a kindly gent, always easy to get along with, on and off the bandstand.

Don Kinch: I remember Johnny as a pleasant, quiet man who took his music seriously. I also remember him being one of the fellows it was easy to work with.

Bill Bacin: That he was a hustler, there is no doubt.

John Lucas: He aimed for that Noone vibrato but like many others who imitate, sounded quaint at best. I think he tried for a mystique of coming from Chicago in the "good old days", but folks in Los Angeles had a whole colony of vintage New Orleans cats to enjoy. In his favour, he had a good tone - if you could discern it through that quaint vibrato.

Al Jenkins: He was always getting on the phone, talking to somebody. I'd say he got some jobs I don't know how the hell he come up with them.

Buzz Knudsen: He always had an ace in the hole.

Bill Tinkler: He was the old style type of player. Loved to play. Nice person.

Jimmy Ille: He knew how to talk.

Chuck Sweningsen: Lane was ebullient - the eternal optimist. He worked for work and some considered him a pest on this account. He would always try to ingratiate himself, hoping it would do him some good. Withal, I liked the guy and his playing, though today I have to admit it was quite limited - he did do a lovely *Apex* a la Noone.

Bill Campbell: I always got along well with him because I let him throw the bullshit, which he did well, without comment or contradiction. He was similar to Wingy Manone in the b.s. department. John didn't have a regular job (I met him in the 1950s) although I believe we worked a week or two here and there through the years. He would walk down the street into any tavern and sell a man a band for a nite - below scale - and would start calling musicians. He also knew someone in the Veterans' Administration; we did quite a few for them, especially the Long Beach Veterans' Hospital every Christmas Eve.

Art Hodes: I'd say Johnny Lane sometimes played like he'd studied Ted Lewis's style. He should have been recorded, but here in the U.S. should doesn't mean will be — a shame. He kept promoting work for the handful he employed. Played with gusto.

John Steiner: (Lane had a) timid, retiring nature. Might be described by a woman as a sweet man. He would make concessions on the price, and work an extra half-hour, and do a whole lot of things. So the boss knew he was the boss. It wasn't like Georg Brunis come in and become the boss. Brunis did take jobs away from Lane.

So that is Johnny Lane's story. It is unfortunate that his playing and his use of the fine musicians he employed seem to have lacked imagination, but it must be said that the climate in which he worked was not conducive to sensitivity or experimentation. Even a more forceful character might have despaired.

Regardless, Johnny Lane deserves his tiny niche in jazz history for finding work for so many of the excellent players with whom he was associated.

JOHNNY LANE BAND LISTING
Compiled by John Miner, with additions by Derek Coller

Dates shown for these engagements are estimated, except where a precise date is given. Source of this information was mainly *Down Beat* magazine (date in right hand column), plus three issues of International Musician (also indicated in right hand column). Johnny Lane's presence is indicated by his initials.

1948

Mar	Bill Tinkler, tp; Jimmy James, tb; JL; Art Gronwall, p; Eddie Meusel, b; (5 week engagement) Rupneck's		(21apr48)
Apr	Bill Indelli, tb; for James. Bee Hive (19may48)		
May	Tinkler; James; JL; Gronwall; Danny Alvin, d. Bee Hive		
Aug	Bill Pfeiffer, d; for Alvin. Bee Hive		(25aug48)
Sep 10	Tinkler; James; JL; Gronwall; Pfeiffer. Rupneck's		(02oct48)
Nov	Jack Gardner, p; for Gronwall Rupneck's		(15dec48)

1949

Jan	Floyd O'Brien, tb; for James; Ray Dixon, p (Fri/Sat only for a time) Rupneck's(28jan49)
Feb 20	Rupneck's engagement ended
Mar 16	Opened at the Silhouette, with Art Gronwall, p. (08apr49)
Aug	Lee Collins, tp; Bill Johnson, tb; JL; Floyd Bean, p; Bill Pfeiffer, d. Sky Club (09sep49)
fall	Collins out
Oct	Georg Brunis, tb; JL; Art Gronwall, p; Anderson Saucier, d. Jimmy Ille, tp; on Saturdays. Sky Club (18nov49)
Dec 11	Opened at 1111 Club Jimmy Ille, tp; Floyd O'Brien, tb; JL; Roy Wasson, p; Orville Searcy, d.
?	Claude 'Hey Hey' Humphrey, d; for Searcy.

1950

Jan	Ralph Hutchinson, tb; for O'Brien briefly 1111 Club		(10feb50)
Mar	Ille; O'Brien; JL; Wasson; Humphrey. 1111 Club		(07apr50)
?	Floyd Bean, p; for Wasson at one point		
Jun	Ille & O'Brien left to join Hodes at Rupneck's Replacements were Don Slattery, tp; Georg Brunis, tb.		

1951

Jan	Benny Woodworth, tp; Brunis, tb; JL; Wasson; Humphrey. 1111 Club		(09feb51)

May   Danny Little, tp; for Woodworth
Jul   Jack Ivett, tp; for Little   1111 Club   (05oct51)
Sep   Woodworth, tp; Mike Riley, tb; JL; Wasson; Humphrey.
       1111 Club   (19oct51)
late Oct George Winn, tb, euphonium; for Riley. 1111 Club   (30nov51)
Dec   Dick Haas, tp; Winn; JL; Wasson; Humphrey. 1111 Club (25jan52)
1952
early Bill Tinkler, tp.   1111 Club   (22feb52)
Spring Georg Brunis, tb; rejoined.   1111 Club   (04jun52)
Jul   Brunis took over 1111 Club band. Lane moved to Preview
       Lounge, with Floyd O'Brien, tb; and Don Ewell, p.   (27aug52)
Nov   Russ Phillips, tb; Bill Pfeiffer, d; joined Preview Lounge
late   Lark Merriman, tp; Phillips, tb; JL; Lloyd (or Floyd) McCann, p;
       Pfeiffer, d., Preview Lounge
Dec   moved to Famous Tap, with O'Brien, tb.   (14jan53)
1953
Spring O'Brien, tb; JL; Doc Cenardo, d; others?   Famous Tap?
Jun   moved to the Normandy, with O'Brien & Cenardo   (01jul53)
Aug   Jasper Taylor, d; joined Hollywood Show Lounge   (09sep53)
?   Nap Trottier, tp; JL; Don Ewell, p; others?
Dec   moved to the Moulin Rouge   (30dec53)
1954
       Lane worked with Georg Brunis band at The Red Arrow, Stickney
1955
early Lane took over band. Bill Tinkler, tp.   Red Arrow (23mar55)
Mar   Jack Ivett, tp; Sid Dawson, tb; JL; Jack Condon, p;
       Hap Gormley, d.   Red Arrow
early Benny Woodworth, tp; Dawson; JL; Art Hodes, p; Gormley, d.
       Red Arrow
Spring Jim Cunningha, tp; for Woodworth.   Red Arrow
late summer Mel Grant, p; for Hodes; rest as before   Red Arrow
fall   Bob Cousins, d; for Gormley   Red Arrow (19oct55)
late   Cunningham; Dawson; JL; Grant; Cousins. Red Arrow (14dec55)
1956
Jan   Dave Remington, p; for Grant   Red Arrow (30may56)
Apr   Lane left Red Arrow for a "long vacation"(Red Arrow) (30may56)
Summer Del Lincoln, tp; Marty Nichols, tb; JL; Grant, p; Dale Parman, d.
                                        Harlem Lodge   (25july56)
late   Lane moved to Los Angeles
1958/1959/1960
       Playing weekends at the Officers' Club, Terminal Island naval base.
1961
Spring Don Kinch, tp; Al Jenkins, tb; JL; Marvin Ash, p; Doc Cenardo,
   d.   The Roarin' 20s, Downey   (06jul61)

Jun   Wild Bill Davison, co; Pete Bielmann, tb; JL; Ash; Cenardo.
   same   (20jul61)
(Davison's stay was brief. Lane at The Roarin' 20s for most of the year.)
1962
early   Garner Clark, tp; Warren Smith, tb; JL; Freddie Lent, p; Nick
   Pelico, d. Mardi Gras (01jan62)
(Lane played at The Mardi Gras Steak House in Orange County at
   weekends January to July.)
Summer Irvan 'Irv' Stumph, tp; Warren Smith, tb; JL: Tom McKenzie,
   p; Doc Cenardo, d.   The Roarin' 20s
Summer Bill Campbell, p; for Mckenzie (Thu/Fri/Sat)   (16aug62)
fall   Bob Higgins, tp; for Stumph.   The Roarin' 20s   (13sep62)
1963
early   Irving Goodman, tp; for Higgins   The Roarin' 20s (31jan63)
Spring Irvan Stumph, tp; for Goodman. Nappy Lamare, bj; Harry
   Babasin, b; occasionally sat-in.   The Roarin' 20s   (20jun63)
Fall   Jerry Burns, tp; Al Jenkins, tb; JL; James Worley, p; Nick
   Pelico, d. (5 days a week)   The Roarin' 20s   (07nov63)
1964   Lane remained at The Roarin' 20s.
1965
late Summer Irvan Stumph, tp; Al Jenkins, tb; JL; Bill Campbell, p; Bill
   French, d.   (07oct65)
   Sunday's at Jack's for Steaks, Catalina Island, and at Officers' Club
   Long Beach.
1967
Fall   Wes Grant, tp; Al Jenkins, tb; JL; Don Owens, p; John Perret,
   d.   (still The Roarin' 20s?)
                              Wonderbowl

1972
late   Irvan Stumph, tp; Warren Smith, tb; JL; Tom McKenzie, p;
   Doc Cenardo, d.   (various engagements)   (IM jan73)
1973
Spring Dick Cary, tp, p; JL; Nick Fatool, d; others.
Sky Room   (IM jun73)
 (at Breakers Hotel, Long Beach)
1980
Jun   Bill Stumph, tp; Al Jenkins, tb; JL; Kenny Sands, p; Bob
   Raggis, wb; Bill French, d. the Reef, Long Beach   (IM jul80)

References:

The Chicago Reader, January 23, 1981 "Leona and Johnny Were Sweethearts" (Chuck Sweningsen)

Autonetics Skywriter, 1960s, "John Italiane of Purchasing Known as 'Banker with a _____"The Saga of Johnny Lane's Clarinet: as told by Johnny himself)"

Chicago Sun-Times, October 4,1977, "Clarinetist Lane Returns For A Set" (Jerry De Muth)

The Mississippi Rag, February 1990, "Floyd Town: His Story" (Derek Coller)

The Mississippi Rag, May 1992, "Reminders of a Forgotten Era" (Warren Vache, Snr)

The Mississippi Rag, August 1992, "Coming of Age in the 1950s: Chicago Traditional Jazz Clubs" (Thomas B. Gilmore)

Johnny Lane (excerpt from interview) with unidentified interviewer, Downey, CA, early 1960s

Buzz Knudsen   interview with Jim Gordon

Down Beat   numerous issues

Acknowledgements

Grateful thanks are expressed to all those musicians and collectors named in the text, and to the following: American Federation of Musicians (Local 407), Nick and Jean Carter, Dick Cary, Gilbert M. Erskine, Marty Grosz, Pete Goulding, Merrill M. Hammond, Wayne Jones, Bob Koester, Gene Kramer, Floyd Levin, Paige van Vorst.

George Zack: The Unforgettable

Until the recent arrival of the German Commodore record of piano solos, many collectors will probably have been limited to the first 1939 Muggsy Spanier Bluebird session for examples of George Zack's piano playing. The reasons for this will become clearer later in this piece, but first let's set the scene with some details of Zack's life and career.

He was born July 20, 1910, the first child of George and Barbara Zacek of 1165-19th Street, Chicago, Ill. George Zacek was a professional musician, playing clarinet, saxophone and other wind instruments at dances and in beer halls. He was also director of the marching band of the Great Lakes Naval Academy. One Sunday, as the family was enjoying dinner, Father suddenly got up from the table and, announcing that he was tired of family life, walked out of their lives for ever. Oro "Tut" Soper, another fine Chicago pianist, remembers George junior telling this story and that "he'd never seen his dad after that incident".

George took piano lessons as a child but after a while the tutor realised that she could not teach him any more. He then attended the Chicago Conservatory of Music for four years. Just how Zack became infected by the jazz bug depends on who tells the story. His sister Muriel says that he left home when he was about 16 to join a theater group as an actor and pianist and probably heard jazz during a tour of the South. His wife Helen, who died in May 1985, said that he heard a band in the street when he was about 14 and, shortly afterwards, ran away to New Orleans where he played in a brothel. This matches Zack's own version, told to Bob Coates, of how, already tired of all the "paper work and theory" at the Conservatory, he was shaken by jazz one day when standing on a corner on Wabash Avenue. A wagon came by carrying a band that King Oliver had at the Sunset Cafe. Zack was fascinated, not having heard jazz before, and followed the band all the way to 31st St. A little later, he met Louis Armstrong and Muggsy Spanier and found that he never wanted to go back to the conservatory. On the other hand, Zack also told George Hoefer that he wanted to be a

George Zack, c. 1944.

1976

𝕷𝖎𝖋𝖊 𝕸𝖊𝖒𝖇𝖊𝖗

TUCSON MUSICIANS' ASSOCIATION
LOCAL 771, TUCSON, ARIZONA

𝕿𝖍𝖎𝖘 𝕳𝖔𝖓𝖔𝖗 𝕻𝖗𝖊𝖘𝖊𝖓𝖙𝖊𝖉 𝖙𝖔
GEORGE ZACK

IN RECOGNITION OF FAITHFUL SERVICES
AS A MEMBER OF THE TUCSON MUSICIANS'
ASSOCIATION, TUCSON, ARIZONA.
(This card is valid only for the year indicated.)

concert pianist until one day Director Rudolph Ganz hammered his knuckles with a copper-edged ruler. He quit on the spot and went off to Memphis where he met Georg Brunis and others of the New Orleans bunch who were playing on the steamer *Capitol* anchored on the river. The year was 1924.

However the break came about, Zack decided that his piano playing from then on would be of the barrelhouse persuasion and he got a job with a band led by trombonist Mush Oliver. Bob Sawyer was on trumpet and Jimmy Lytell on clarinet. The band eventually went to Indianapolis and played the Circle Ballroom. During this time the band went to Richmond, Indiana, to record for Gennett. No records are known under this particular Oliver's name but, in any case, Zack thought that the records had been issued as being by the Original Indiana Five. Apparently some of the Oliver men were associated with that band but just how this ties in with what was basically a neighborhood group is not known. In any case, all known Indiana Five Gennetts were recorded in New York City. Zack told Hoefer that he had copies of the records until one day when in a fit of frustration he'd smashed his collection of about a thousand 78s. Thus, it may be that we'll never know which records were the ones on which Zack made his debut.

The pianist went from Oliver to play with the Jimmie Joy band at the Brown Hotel in Louisville, Kentucky, and at Castle Farms in Cincinnati, Ohio. This year was 1927. They had to play light music for dinner sets but were able to let fly with jazz during the evening dancing. Zack used to be featured, he said, playing and singing *You Rascal You* and claimed he was on the band's records during this period. If he was they have yet to surface and band members of the time do not recall him.

Then he went back to Chicago and various bands including Eddie Neibauer's for about four years as well as spells in bars playing solo piano and, no doubt, singing. He also worked with Henry Halstead's band in Chicago and Kansas City - the Muelbach Hotel in the latter - and claimed to have recorded with them. Among other jobs in this period, he was fan-dancer Sally Rand's accompanist during the 1933 World's Fair in Chicago.

Early in 1939 and still working the bars in Chicago, Zack was contacted by Muggsy Spanier who was putting together a small band. The pianist fell in with the idea as did clarinetist Rod Cless:

Muggsy came along with his proposition .... he had a nice line-up: Brunies on trombone, Pat Pattison, Bob Casey, George Zack and Marty Greenberg. Ray McKinstry came in a little later. We didn't rehearse very long. Everybody in the band worked out arrangements to use as a guide on certain tunes... Muggsy got a contract from Ernie Byfield of the Sherman Hotel... we opened in April.

It was this personnel which went into Victor's Chicago studio on Friday the 7th of July of that year to cut the first four titles by the historic band: Big Butter and Egg Man, Someday Sweetheart, Eccentric and That Da Da Strain. Zack got space to solo on all four and provided more barrelhouse piano to form the introduction to Someday Sweetheart on which he can also be heard comping nicely behind the soloists. On That Da Da Strain the Hines influence is rather stronger than elsewhere. Official issues of these records in recent times are curiously lacking in availability. Young collectors will probably have to try for secondhand copies but it's hard to imagine an established collection without them.

Some sources have it that Zack was replaced by Joe Bushkin during the August of '39 but others place Zack still with the band when they opened at Nick's in New York's Greenwich Village during November. Certainly Bushkin played the second Victor date on the 10th (as well as the third and fourth sessions that month and the next). Ralph Gleason told of when

> ... George blew into town with the Spanier band and opened at Nick's as high as a kite... no one was disappointed. I'll never forget that night... we called for Black and Blue and Snowball. Art Hodes had told us that Zack could sing them like Louie. And he could. Roaring away with his big tawny head rocking back and forth and his enormous hands played on the keyboard, he sang and sang and played and played. I had never heard anything like it.

Either way in regard to Zack and Bushkin, after the former left the Spanier band he was in New York and played various places, including often Ross's Tavern, for something like five years. He played a lot of Milt Gabler's jam sessions and at the lectures that Ralph Berton gave (including one where he shook the polite society ladies in the audience by finishing a fast number, downing the last of his drink and turning to his audience bellowing, 'Let's all go to a cheap hotel'.) Berton was running a small jazz appreciation society and the first evening featured three pianists, Zack, Art Hodes and Sam Price. In *Eyewitness Jazz*, Marvin Goodman reported that

> Zack was the first performer... and really electrified us that night. He played some absolutely terrific piano, reminiscent of early Hines, with amazing power and drive .... he was inspired and the results were wonderfully thrilling.

During 1944 in New York, Zack was recorded by Bob Thiele for his Signature label. In any event, Thiele didn't issue the sides but dealt them off to Sam Meltzer who put out three of the four on his Century label. Dan Qualey tried to get the pianist to record for his Solo Art label but never got anything down that was any good, no doubt because of Zack's drinking habits. It was also reported that he recorded for Blue Note but, again, the sides have never appeared. Milt Gabler obtained good results but often the sessions were troubled. He wrote in a 1980 letter,

> I do not believe that I ever found him sober after high noon. His wife adored him and watched over him. Commodore kept him going as well. I had him straightened out enough to make the record dates, for I paid him with cash any time he could appear straight enough to play. I booked the studio and sometimes I got lucky and other times we struck out. I tried to use him for band dates, but he never made any of them. Still, I loved the sides I made with him and believe the better titles will enhance his memory beyond the Muggsy Ragtime sides. They will all be issued in good time.

Milt Gabler, who kindly supplied details of his Commodore sessions, said

> Note that they are piano and drum duets and not solos with drum accompaniment. The traps are balanced differently. I had been to some strip joints on Skid Row in Chicago during WW2 and for a two-bit beer you could watch an unending series of has-been strippers perform to piano and drums accompaniment. One place had a trio with Boyce Brown on alto sax so I remember it clearly. The drums and piano worked as a duo with the drummer playing a rhythmic tune like the melody. I tried to get this effect on the Zack-Wettling and Zack-Alvin sides. I used Danny when George was not available. Zack liked Danny as they had worked together. Wettling was super and just what I wanted, but then again he was always my man."

George Zack (piano and vocal: 4002)
Max Kaminsky and George Zack (trumpet; piano and vocal; 4003)

March 23, 1944

T1930-3	Black and Blue	Century 4003
T1931- v?	Snowball	not issued
T1932- v	Oh Baby, Look Out (GZ)	Century 4002
T1933- v	Havin' A Ball (GZ-MK)	Century 4003

Reverse side of 4002 is a Dick Wellstood recording.

George Zack and George Wettling (piano; drums)

April 14, 1944

A4758-1	A Monday Date No 2 Commodore	6.25895
-2	A Monday Date	
	Commodore 651, FL20,001, CEP4, 6.25895	
A4759-1	Lizzie's Dream (GZ)	Commodore 6.25895
-2	Lizzie's Dream No 2 (GZ)	Commodore 6.25895
A4760-1	Kansas City Stomps No 2	Commodore 6.25895
-2	Kansas City Stomps	Commodore 597, 6.25895
A4761-1	In the Barrel -Part 1 (GZ)	Commodore 6.25895
-2	In the Barrel -Part 2 (GZ)	Commodore 6.25895

June 20, 1944

A4783-1	Bugaboo	Commodore 598, 6.25895
-2	Bugaboo 2 No 2	Commodore 6.25895
A4784-1	Shoe Shiner's Drag	Commodore 6.25895
-2	Shoe Shiner's Drag No 2	Commodore 6.25895
A4785-1	Sizzlin' 'Stakes (sic) (GZ)	Commodore 6.25895
-2	Pickin' up 'Stakes (sic) (GZ)	Commodore 6.25895

July 19, 1944

A4794-1	Sunset Cafe Stomp	(see note)
-2	Sunset Cafe Stomp No 2	Commodore 6.25895
		(see note)
-3	Sunset Cafe Stomp	Commodore 6.25895
A4795-	If I Could Be With You	
	Commodore 650, FL20,001, CEP4	
A4796-	Sweethearts on Parade	Commodore

A4794-2 appears on 6.25895 with a small section of A4794-1 spliced in to replace a goof. The take used of A4795 is not known; neither do we know how many takes of this were made nor of A4796 but all this will presumably be clarified when the second Zack Commodore LP is issued.

A4822-1	Ace in the Hole	Commodore 648, FL20,001, CEP3
A4823-1 v?	Snowball	Commodore
A4824-1	Lazy River	Commodore
-2	Lazy River	Commodore 566
A4825-1	I Never Dreamt	Commodore 649, FL20,001, CEP3

George Zack and Danny Alvin (piano and vocal; drums)

March 16, 1945

A4851-1	Hood Stomp (GZ)	Commodore 598
-2	Hood Stomp (GZ)	Commodore
A4852-1	Blue and Brokenhearted	
		Commodore 648, FL20,001, CEP3
A4853-	Everybody Loves My Baby	
		Commodore 649, FL20,001, CEP3
A4854-1 v?	Black and Blue	Commodore

April 19, 1945

A4855-1	My Melancholy Baby	Commodore
-2	My Melancholy Baby	
		Commodore 650, FL20,001, CEP4
A4856-1	Shim-Me-Sha-Wabble	Commodore 599
A4857-1 v	Snowball	Commodore 566
A4858-	Angry	Commodore 651, FL20,001, CEP4
A4859-1	Farewell Blues	Commodore 599

July 19, 1945

A4860-	My Daddy Rocks Me	Commodore
A4861-	Chimes Blues	Commodore

As noted earlier, the future Commodore LP will do no doubt clarify takes used above where these are at present unknown. The Commodore records with three-digit numbers are 10" 78rpm and 597/598/599 were issued in album CR9 **Barrelhouse Stomps**. FL20,001 is 10" LP entitled Party **Piano of the Roaring Twenties** and CEP3 and CEP4 are 7" extended-play versions of this. 6.25895 is a German 12" LP entitled **Barrelhouse Piano 1944** and there is no U.S. equivalent of this, although it should be available from specialist dealers at least. All compositions known to be originals by Zack are marked '(GZ)' above.

All the foregoing sessions were made in New York City, most if not all of the Commodores at WOR, 1440 Broadway, but by the turn of the years 1945/46 George Zack was back in Chicago. He seems mainly to have played piano bars and occasional Hot Club of Chicago affairs. One of these sessions was held March 17 at the Moose Hall, 1016 North Dearborn, with two bands: Zack's Windy City Five with Johnny Mendell, trumpet; Bud Phillips, clarinet; Pat Pattison, bass; Hey Hey Humphrey drums. Pianist Floyd Bean led his Toddlin' Town Quintet; Bill Stapleton, trumpet; Boyce Brown, alto; Jack Fonda, bass; Lou Finnerty, drums.

Yet another never-issued record session took place in 1947 when Zack cut some sides with cornet man Doc Evans and reedman Bud Jacobson. But the last-named apparently played piano, so just how Zack fitted in here is a mystery which will likely remain for ever unsolved.

The Bee Hive, a Chicago joint, had a band around the end of 1948 and into the following year which was led by trombonist Miff Mole with Zack and Art Gronwall taking turns at the piano. Others present included Fred Greenleaf, trumpet; Darnell Howard, clarinet, and Baby Dodds, drums. John Schenck set up a session at the same venue on March 20, '49 in which Zack was accompanied in some solos and songs by Danny Alvin's drums. That same evening a band with Zack and Alvin had Bill Price, trumpet; Jimmy James, trombone, and Bob (The Sheriff) McCracken, clarinet. The band was billed as George Zack's Bar Room Boys which, as far as the pianist was concerned at least, was fairly appropriate.

Towards the end of 1949, Zack was playing solo at a piano bar, Sandra's on West Division, Chicago, and Schenck's Bee Hive blow the day before New Year's Eve again had two bands, one of which had Zack with Lee Collins, trumpet; Jimmy James, trombone; Jug Berger, clarinet; Boyce Brown, alto, and Danny Alvin, drums.

Schenck also organized a recording session one Saturday in probably the August of 1950. This took place in the upstairs room of Seymour's record shop on South Wabash. This was by Jimmy James Jas (sic) Band with Jimmy Ille, trumpet; James, trombone; Jug Berger, clarinet; Zack, piano and vocal, and Freddie Flynn, drums. Four sides were cut, Sit Right Down And Write Myself A Letter, Black and Blue (with Zack singing) and a two-part Royal Garden Blues, issued on Seymour 78s. Only the first two titles have been heard. This session is so obscure as to be omitted from the discographies but, thanks to Jim Gordon, the chance to listen to his rare 78 confirms reports that it was a drunken shindig but the music was ferociously hot.

John Steiner remembers another session in Seymour's upper room with Zack playing and rocking and 50 people crammed in and all stomping in time, the ceiling below moving. He also vaguely recalled an occasion when some wire recordings were made with Zack, a forgotten trumpet man, Jim Beebe on trombone, and one (Eddie)? Chamblee on clarinet. This took place on Broadway on the North Side somewhere around the 3200s.

Zack moved to Tucson, Arizona, during 1952 and played at many piano bars and clubs in the area: the Stallion Room of the Westerner Hotel, the Play House, Gus and Andy's Crystal Palace (where Frank and Peggie Snyder heard him "playing the piano and (he) was the only entertainment; he was a little bombed but we had a small visit"), the Brass Rail, the Circus Lounge, the Dunes and the Casino Ball Room amongst many others. Al Saunders recalls, "In over 20 years in Tucson he played with everyone from Dean Armstrong's Arizona Dance Hands to my Old Pueblo Jazz Band but mostly he performed solo or with only a guitar". Saunders also remembers that his first job with Zack was a street fair on Broadway in January 1954 and the last at the Aztec Inn during September 1974.

But some touring was done, and Helen Zack spoke of doing the driving while they moved from one gig to another, often for periods up to six months. During the late '50s, Zack had a spell with a band co-led by Ray Bauduc and Nappy Lamare. There was also touring with Bob Scobey's San Francisco Band during 1958. Bob Coates reported the band playing

> ... at the Villa, a bar on the outskirts of Madison, Wisconsin. George Zack had replaced fellow-Chicagoan Floyd Bean about a month previously, having just recovered from a bout of alcoholism about which he was remarkably frank.

Inevitably, Zack was involved when star musicians came to Tucson. Towards the end of November 1960, the Tucson Press Club sponsored a concert at the Santa Rita Hotel. Wild Bill Davison was the headliner and the five-piecer which accompanied the cornetist was organized by George. Another fine cornet man, Pete Daily, was at Gus and Andy's during July 1965 with a band including Zack, as well as AFM local official Al Saunders on banjo amongst other local talent.

Ill health finally forced Zack to give up full-time work during the mid-'60s although he continued to play at private parties. As will have been gathered already, drinking hindered his musical career and there were many spells of lay-offs for drying out. Dan Mahony saw him once and said "he could hardly stand but he played fine piano". Oro "Tut" Soper noted "He was too generous and drinking ruined his career before it really got off the ground." Ralph Gleason wrote of "Zack's enormous capacity for enjoyment... and his capacity for eating and drinking and all other things." Wayne Jones reported that "George Zack, the slightly legendary pianist, came back to town for a gig, but fell off the wagon and went back (from Chicago) to Arizona."

> George was a huge man — about 6'2" and solidly built. Auburn hair, blue eyes, sort of space between upper front teeth and a golden smile. His piano hands were the largest ever; I think he could stretch a twelfth, maybe not cleanly but that's quite a stretch,

said Tut Soper, describing Zack. Pete Daily called him a 'great keyboard man with one hand as big as my two." Ralph Gleason wrote graphically "his great hands make a piano rock as he roars away singing - he *enjoys* it." Jim Gordon remembers him at the Bee Hive when "he would come up behind you and slap your back so hard you'd almost fall to the floor." John "Jax" Lucas recalled going to a bash in which Zack was involved. He said,

> Going into the affair, George met me at the door and it was clearly implicit that a five dollar bill would be appreciated ... he played up a storm ... I don't know how far my five dollars had gone towards encouraging George to play the way he did. I don't know how many others he'd waylaid on the way in, but I was absolutely flabbergasted when I was leaving the party when George was again at the door and a couple of people handed over a little something and he said to me. 'Oh, I'm sorry, I got some bad news for you.'

Of his playing, John Steiner says, "He was a rhythm section in himself, like Joe Sullivan and Ralph Sutton." John Lucas observed that the difference between Zack's piano on the first Spanier Bluebird session and that of Bushkin on the others "is absolutely astonishing." Lucas doesn't decry Bushkin's work but states that "Zack was manifestly an individual piano player." Milt Gabler again: "When I first heard him play solo, what with those large hands of his, he floored me. I always had the feeling that he was the link from Hines to Stacy. There was something old-timey and barrelhouse in his playing. Barrelhouse was it because he was that kind of man." Ralph Gleason put it like this:

> Give him a ballad like Someday Sweetheart or an old standard like Dixieland One-Step, Grandpa's Spells, Bluin The Blues or That Da Da Strain and similar raggy numbers and he really plays, with big smashing chords and terrific rhythm.

Anyone with some appreciation for solid two-handed jazz piano should make up for any lost time by listening to the Commodore 12"er listed above. From the first fleet take of A Monday Date (and the no less wonderful second choice) through to the happy and bouncing Sunset Cafe Stomp, there's a solid 40-or-so minutes of superior and rare music. And should there be anyone out there who doesn't know about George Wettling... In between, there are plenty of Jelly Roll tunes given the Zack treatment - individual and firm but respectful of the master. Plus there are originals, all on blues lines, you'll enjoy regardless of first and second take choices.

By 1977, all the high and low living, all the booze and all the smoky, airless saloon atmosphere had had their effect and George Zack was coming to the end of his devil-may-care life. Pneumonia set in, and death came to the big man on the 7th of November of that year. A few days after the cremation, a memorial service was attended by friends, musicians and others. They had a jam session and played all the tunes Zack had loved. Helen Zack expressed it this way: "George said that after he died he wanted everyone to come to the house and get loaded and high and have a ball. So I'm going to see that they do."

George Zack recorded one title with Wild Bill Davison and his Commodores for Commodore records on January 19, 1945. This was:

A4843   A Ghost Of A Chance   Commodore 635

He was too drunk to continue beyond this first title and was replaced by Dick Cary, who was in the studio as a spectator.

Jack Gardner: a Truly Lusty Pianist

In the early days of jazz Chicago was awash with fine white jazz pianists. Among those who went on to achieve their own special fame were Joe Sullivan, Jess Stacy, and Art Hodes, and among those who never quite made it were Tut Soper, Pete Viera, Floyd Bean, Mel Grant, George Zack, Frank Melrose, Mel Henke and Chet Roble. Another was Francis Henry Gardner, better known as Jack Gardner or even, on account of his weight, Jumbo Jack Gardner. (One report gave his weight as 400 pounds, though another stating 260 pounds seems the more likely.) Care must also be taken to avoid confusion with a *different* Jack Gardner, whose Dallas orchestra recorded for OKeh in 1924 and 1925.

Born in Joliet, Illinois, August 14, 1903, our Jack Gardner began piano lessons at the age of eight. In his Hot Box obituary for *Down Beat* George Hoefer wrote: "His unmusical parents were amazed when his talent on the piano began to emerge .... when he started lessons with George Stahl, an old German music master." When the family moved to Denver, Colorado, the youngster worked in a music store and, this was 1921, played in a band led by Benny Goodman - a violinist. Next came a job with Doc Becker's Blue Devils at the Coronada Club, followed by a stay with a Boyd Senter group which included Glenn Miller.

Returning to Chicago he was in George 'Spike' Hamilton's band (with Glenn Miller, Pat Pattison and Bob Conselman) for a no doubt short-lived engagement at the Opera Club. There was a spell with Fred Hamm's orchestra and Brian Rust lists him on a Victor session recorded in Chicago on December 17, 1925. Three titles were made, one of which was a rejected Hangin' Around. Later, in the summer of 1926, he worked with violinist Art Cope's band at the Vanity Fair cafe on the northside. Eddie Condon was also in the band for a spell and historian George Hoefer has referred to "the then infamous Condon-Cope-Gardner singing trio". Condon, in We Called It Music, recalled the floor show, with dancers, singers, comedians and chorus girls, that the job lasted ten months and that he dated the bass player, Thelma (Coombs) Terry "all that winter".

Jack Gardner

Gardner told *Down Beat* writer Sharon Pease: "I benefited mostly by working and listening to the Chicago boys, but I believe I was most influenced by Jimmy Noone, Earl Hines and good old Zutty Singleton." In the same paper, four years later, he told John Lucas that his two top pianists were Earl Hines and James P. Johnson.

According to John Steiner, Gardner was working for a music publisher in Chicago in 1924 and 1925 and about this time began writing songs. His first tune, Hangin' Around, was recorded by Merrit Brunies for OKeh in 1926, but his big hit, in partnership with Spike Hamilton, was Bye, Bye, Pretty Baby. Among those who recorded the song in the 1920s were Abe Lyman, Jan Garber, Nathan Glantz, Joe Herlihy and Jack Hylton, while Benny Goodman did so in 1947. Vic Dickenson sang it on one album. Other songs were You're Wonderful, recorded by Nat Shilkret, and My Baby Came Home, recorded by Red McKenzie.

Early in 1927 Gardner became a leader at Chicago's Commercial Theater. This has been reported as a nine month engagement, with Floyd O'Brien, Bud Freeman, Eddie Condon and Dave Tough included in the personnel during that time. Hoefer told how this booking ended:

> They played between shows and during the newsreel. The gig came to an abrupt end during a jam session on Clarinet Marmalade while on the screen Marshal Foch was laying a wreath on the Tomb of the Unknown Soldier. It was Dave Tough's drums that did the trick.

There was a short stay with Jean Goldkette in Detroit and a theatre tour with vocalist Gene Austin, an association which was to be revived twenty years later. (That the Goldkette stay was very brief is confirmed by John Steiner's comment: "If there was a Goldkette connection he did not mention it to me during the several years we lived together".)

Gardner's first jazz recording date, though he is hardly heard, was with Wingy Manone's Club Royale Orchestra - a quintet - in Chicago on April 9, 1928; Downright Disgusted and Fare Thee Well (Vocalion 15728) were made, with Wade Foster, clarinet, Bud Freeman, tenor, Ray Biondi, guitar and Gene Krupa, drums.

Interestingly, clarinetist Bill Reinhardt, of Jazz, Ltd. fame, also recalled a recording with Manone and Gardner:

It would have been between 1928 and 1930 that I recorded with Wingy Manone, in an old Brunswick studio on South Wabash Avenue, with Jack Gardner, piano, and a fellow named Floyd Hinkley, alto saxophonist. I don't remember anybody else. I was playing North Side Chicago, some chop suey house, with this Floyd Hinkley and Art Hodes playing piano.

In the early 1930s Gardner was with Phil Spitalny at the Century of Progress and in 1933 at the Cafe De Alex with violinist Maurice Sherman. This was a Dixieland group which included Carl Harris on trumpet and Rosy McHargue on clarinet. *Down Beat* for September 1934 shows Maurice Sherman leading his octet at the College Inn, in the Sherman Hotel, still with Gardner and McHargue, plus Joe Rushton.

The August 1935 issue continues to show Sherman at the College Inn and still with Gardner and Rushton. Hoefer also lists a Joe Hooven as a member of the band, which "used 36 arrangements originally made for a group Jimmy McPartland had at the Beachview Gardens".

When, in April 1936, corporation lawyer, capable amateur pianist and jazz enthusiast Squirrel Ashcraft organised a Decca recording session the band was Jimmy McPartland's Squirrels. The personnel was McPartland, cornet, Joe Harris, trombone, McHargue, clarinet, Dick Clark, tenor, Gardner, piano, Dick McPartland, guitar, Country Washburn, tuba, George Wettling, drums. The titles were Eccentric, Panama, Original Dixieland One Step and I'm All Bound 'Round with the Mason-Dixon Line. Gardner is Sullivan-esque on Dixieland One Step and has a couple of other acceptable solos.

Hoefer says that Gardner went to New York in 1937 and early that year he was working at the Carlton Hotel in Washington, D.C., in a band led by violinist Sande Williams. (The tenor player in the band was one Jack Tarr!) The accuracy of these dates is uncertain; a *Down Beat* report stated that Gardner left the Williams group to join Harry James, and that would have meant he was with the violinist for nearly two years.

In January 1939 Harry James left Benny Goodman to form his own orchestra and Gardner was a founder member, remaining with the trumpet star for eighteen months, until he was fired for drunkenness. He told John Steiner that he complained when James sacked him, "but I didn't throw up".

Peter Levinson, in his biography of Harry James, Trumpet Blues, writes:

> Al Lerner joined the James band on June 30, 1940. He was hired to replace Jack Gardner on piano, but... Harry had neglected to give Gardner his two-week's notice. On Lerner's arrival for his first gig the bandstand was set up with a piano at either end with Gardner seated at one of them.

Gardner passed out during a show at the Paramount just as guest Bea Wain was starting her signature tune and Lerner had to fake the piano part.

The James band recorded many titles between February 1939 and July 1940, the best known featuring Gardner being the two-part Feet Dragging Blues. Because of this association with James he was voted into 15th position in the pianist section of the 1940 *Down Beat* readers' poll.

Other titles from the Brunswick and Columbia recordings by the James orchestra are also worth hearing for, among others, his raggy solos on Sweet Georgia Brown and Comes Love, a short but neat solo on I Found A New Baby, a Basie-ish introduction to two versions of Flash. He is into eight-to-the-bar for Back Bay Boogie and Two O'Clock Jump, and is similarly effective in his long introduction to St. Louis Blues, from a 1939 Hotel Sherman broadcast. Cross Country Jump on the same airshot also has a good solo. Note too his accompaniment on the Harry James quartet version of Sleepytime Gal.

At times one wonders if Gardner's playing really fits the swing style which Harry James was presenting, but it does introduce a touch of earthiness into the polish and brassiness of the band. And the many James' recordings do offer a rare opportunity to appreciate Gardner's ability.

There is a "More Informal Sessions" album, MIS-3, which includes titles recorded at Squirrel Ashcraft's over a number of years. One number from 1939 is What Is This Thing Called Love, on which Gardner plays a satisfactory solo, alongside Bill Priestley, cornet, Wade Foster, clarinet, Joe Rushton, bass-sax, and Hank Isaacs, drums. One assumes that the Harry James orchestra had an engagement in Chicago at the time.

One Gardner story is told in the notes to the 1980 Princeton Bix Festival album. The tune Jelly Roll is dedicated to the memory of

Jack Gardner. "It was his favorite tune and always reminds us of his reply to a request he wasn't anxious to fill. When asked if he could play the Barcarolle, Jack's answer was, "No, but I can play Jelly Roll and it's every bit as good."

Returning to Chicago. Gardner, as George Hoefer put it, worked "solo jobs and occasional stints with Dixie combos, as well as in groups playing behind strippers, where he could improvise freely and experiment". For the rest of his life Chicago continued to be his base, with occasional forays to other locations where there was work, as the next few paragraphs show. Some of these jobs are known from brief and occasional mentions in *Down Beat*.

About July 1941 Gardner took a band into Nick's in New York, with Gordon "Rip" Thornton, trumpet; Milton Fields, tenor; Marty Blitz, bass, and Billy Exiner, drums. This was not a typical Nick's personnel. Could it have been a short engagement or as a Monday night band?

In December 1941 he played with a big band led by Bud Freeman and organised for a four-night booking at the College Inn, plugging a gap between engagements by the bands of Woody Herman and Alvino Rey.

According to a John Lucas story in *Down Beat* (September 15, 1944), Gardner, after leaving James, worked with Joe Marsala at the Hickory House, with Ray Conniff at Nick's, and Marty Marsala at the Band Box. The article also reports that "Jack's best kick came when he played a *March of Time* broadcast in place of Count Basie." One can surmise that these engagements were during the 1942/43 period, before he signed with C.R.A. as a single act about mid-1943.

Towards the end of 1943, following the demise of his big band, Muggsy Spanier played a number of gigs in the Chicago area with a sextet. It is likely that Gardner played some of these dates as he was pianist for three titles which Spanier recorded for World Transcriptions on November 15, 1943 - Three-Twenty-One Blues, I've Found A New Baby and Baby, Won't You Please Come Home. Fellow Chicagoans in the personnel were Bud Jacobson, clarinet, and Pat Pattison, bass, plus Warren Smith, trombone and Frank Rullo, drums. Gardner has solos on the first two tracks, with that on the blues particularly worthy.

In April 1944 Jack Gardner was at the Dayton Hotel in Kenosha, Wisconsin, and around October of that year he was leading a trio, sax and drums, at the Silver Palm on Wilson Avenue, on the North side of Chicago. George Hoefer reported: "The trio plays on a raised platform back of a zig-zag bar where a string of stripteasers perform". And on June 30, 1944 John Steiner recorded three titles by Red Nichols, backed by Gardner and Vic Engles, drums - Cheerful Little Earful and I've Got A Woman (She's Funny That Way), issued on Steiner-Davis 507, and Smoke Gets In Your Eyes (unissued). The piano solo on I've Got A Woman (on CD on Vintage Jazz Classic VCJ-1009-2) is flowery yet in context.

Also for Steiner in 1944 were three piano solos. Doll Rag, with Baby Dodds on drums, recorded January 31, and Bye, Bye, Pretty Baby, and Rolling Around The Roses made June 30. The first two titles were on Steiner-Davis 508, but Rolling Around remains unissued. Doll Rag, Gardner's interpretation of Paper Doll, generates a vigorous swing when he moves into up-tempo, with Bye, Bye, Pretty Baby not far behind.

Two takes of Jelly Roll, no doubt from the Steiner collection, were made in October 1944 by Bobby Hackett and Jack Gardner, with good piano solos on both. He also recorded two tracks with Rosy McHargue, playing well on Indiana and stomping away on the medley of My Baby Just Cares for Me / I Got Rhythm.

In April 1945 Gardner made at least two appearances at Boston Jazz Society meetings, on the 9th with George Hartman, Johnny Windhurst and Danny Alvin, and on the 23rd as soloist with Charlie Vinal's Rhythm Kings. John Steiner reported that Gardner had recorded with the Milt Herth Trio, with whom he played months, but had been unable to find these as issued records. Perhaps working with Herth explains the "long absence" mentioned in *Down Beat* for November 15, 1945, "Jack Gardner returns in the Loop after a long absence, at Elmer's."

He appeared with Jack Teagarden in February of 1946 at a Hot Club of Chicago concert, when the impressive trumpet section was Sterling Bose, Charlie Teagarden and Muggsy Spanier. He recorded with Bud Freeman in September 1946, issued on Steiner-Davis and Classics 975, playing a long, basic but effective blues-y opening solo on Ontario Barrel House (SD-506). With altoist Bill Dohler added, Gardner also makes satisfactory contributions, both solo and accompanying, to Taking A Chance On Love/You Took Advantage Of Me (SD-504) and Ribald Rhythm (SD-506).

In *Tell Your Story* Eric Townley says that Gardner was sharing an apartment with Steiner on Ontario Street at this time, but Bob Koester recalled Steiner telling him that Gardner lived in a basement apartment that Koester once had at 102, E. Bellevue. Steiner was in 104. However, John Steiner also told Tor Magnusson that he had lived for a long time in a studio-laboratory at 1637 N. Ashland Avenue and that this "had many rooms, as you can correctly suppose". Gardner was one of those resident at 1637.

1947 began with a four-week engagement at the Grandview Inn in Columbus, Ohio, and in July he briefly replaced Don Ewell at Jazz, Ltd., before spending August and September, presumably as a soloist, at Polly's, "new jazz spot on North Michigan Boulevard". During October and November he was the pianist at the Blue Heaven in Las Vegas, a casino owned by Gene Austin.

He played the final three weeks at Tin Pan Alley before it closed, in October 1948, then "filled in with Doc Evans' Bee Hive unit temporarily," as *Down Beat* put it. In November 1948 he was in clarinetist Johnny Lane's band at Rupneck's, leaving in January 1949 to work as a single at the Cipango Club in Dallas. Presumably this was a month's gig as in February he was back in Chicago, at the Hi-Note, working opposite Max Miller's trio, followed in April by the Tower on N. Wabash. At the end of 1949 he was reported to be playing as a single at the Clayton Hotel.

On March 21, 1949 Gardner recorded three titles (St Louis Blues, Cherry, Embraceable You) for John Steiner, with Johnny Lane, clarinet, and Jack Goss, guitar, but these are undistinguished. He recorded again for Steiner on June 20, 1950. Pee Wee Russell, passing through Chicago, had called on Bud Jacobson and the pair visited Steiner in search of a drink. The titles were Blues (a piano solo), You Took Advantage Of Me (a trio with Jimmy James, trombone, Bud Jacobson, clarinet), and Louise (quartet, the trio plus Pee Wee Russell on clarinet).

Starting in 1950 Bill and Crickie Priestley helped Ashcraft revive the 'Sessions at Squirrel's', with four or five annual weekend sessions being organised. Two titles (You Took Advantage of Me, Poor Butterfly) with Gardner in the personnel, come from July 1950 and were issued by John Steiner on his 10" Private Issue 2. The album labels state 'Informal Session at Squirrel's: The Sons of Bix's'. Poor Butterfly is a feature for bass saxophonist Spencer Clark, but

Gardner plays a long introduction to You Took Advantage of Me which is worth hearing, although he is heavy on the bass. Spencer Clark told collector Paul Burgess that he thought Gardner played drums on some of the other 1950 titles,

From July 4, 1952 Pennies from Heaven is a piano solo, nearly five minutes of sustained improvisation, included on Paramount CJS-108. It is a recommended sample of his playing. Gardner is listed as 'Jarvis Farnsworth" on this issue and, to quote John Steiner, "the pseudonym was used to avoid conflict with Musicians Union policy about unauthorized recordings with non-Union men. He chose the name".

Writing about the Priestley sessions, Herb Sanford in his book, "Tommy and Jimmy: The Dorsey Years," says that Ashcraft called Gardner

> one of the very greatest of the *full* pianists. Arthur Schutt was one of his heroes, and Teddy Wilson told me that his first real conception of tenths bass came to him from listening on radio when Jack was playing with Maurie Sherman at the College Inn in Chicago.

Gardner played with George Brunis at the 11-11 Club in August 1952, though his stay with bands rarely lasted long, as if he preferred to find work as a soloist. Chicago collector Jim Gordon recalled: "I used to hear Jumbo Jack Gardner at a place near Rush Street called New York Bar. Jack was solo there and I heard him play some wonderful stuff. He was a great pianist". (One of Jim's visits was on New Year's Eve of 1953.)

Collector Merrill Hammond said:

> I knew Jack Gardner very well ... I would rate him as an outstanding orchestral jazz pianist, although I cannot rate his solo work as high. He was a very personable fellow and extremely devoted to jazz.

In his tribute to Jack Gardner in *Record Research* (No. 17, March-April 1958) John Steiner recalled that "Jack had lived with me for five of the past fifteen years" and described him as "one of the truly lusty pianists of our era". He concluded the tribute:

> The stories of Jack's sweetness and whimsy are unending. A new one from the hospital where they were draining fluid from his distended tummy a few days before his death goes like this: An

intern who had become intimate (and everybody quickly did with Jack), held up a beaker of the yellow stuff and asked, 'Have a nip, Jack?' To which Jack replied, 'No, I guess I'll pass this one - as long as I am to be on tap for awhile.'

Pianist and organist Les Strand was active in Chicago in the 1950s and met Jack Gardner when "he was playing solo piano in some lounge here in Chicago". Writing in 1991, Strand recalled Gardner's style:

His piano style was very interesting to me in that he would *deliberately* phrase tune in a way that suggested an incorrect number of beats within the segments of melody, but he *always* readjusted so that the beat count came out right in the overall presentation. This made for some very interesting listening. Not once did he ever fail to rescue the overall melodic and rhythmic shape of the piece but he kept one in suspense, anticipating disaster than never occurred.

Jack had an excellent harmonic sense: he was not a bopper but didn't sound old-fashioned at all. He was *fun* to hear! He was a very unique pianist; not a technical marvel, but with all the ability to do what he wanted to really express himself, which is what counts, in my opinion.

Gardner was undoubtedly a forceful and swinging pianist. He could be heavy-handed at times and flowery, perhaps over-busy, at others, but as his recordings with Harry James and for John Steiner show, at his best he deserved his place in the gallery of Chicago jazz pianists.

Jack Gardner moved to Dallas, Texas, towards the end of his life, the city where he died on November 26, 1957.

Chet Roble: A Chicago pianist

Names of obscure musicians litter the histories of jazz. They are recalled for their brief stay with a famous band or for being members of an influential group. Some participated in a classic record session; many were fortunate to record at all. John Steiner's chapter on "Chicago" in *Jazz*, edited by Nat Hentoff and Albert McCarthy, is full of such names. At one point Steiner writes:

> For example, pianist Chet Roble, in the early 1940s, reincarnated the Noone Apex Club sound remarkably, using clarinetist Bud Phillips, altoist Boyce Brown and a full rhythm section.

"Remarkably" is perhaps poetic licence, but who was this pianist who recreated the Noone Apex Club sound?

Chet Roble was born Chester Wroblewski in Chicago on 13 April 1908. His introduction to the piano began with lessons taken as a form of exercise after suffering a broken arm. At Chicago's Schurz High school he and drummer Wally Gordon were together in a band. Presumably this was Gordon and Roble's Chicagoans, who, were patterned, as Roble told Jack Tracy, "after Condon and McKenzie's Chicagoans, some band in those days."

On leaving the University of Illinois he endured, among other jobs, a spell in insurance, before becoming, in 1932, a professional musician, touring for eighteen months with Ace Brigode's band. John Steiner reports:

> Chet had met and worked with Boyce Brown for weeks or months at Liberty Inn with drummer Earl Wiley's trio backing comedians, strippers and for dancing, before joining Gray Gordon who offered more money.

There were engagements with the orchestras of Henry Gendron and Carl Schreiber followed by work as a soloist and as a leader. Referring to influences, John Steiner says:

> Chet told me that he had heard Louis Armstrong, Earl Hines and Bebe Hall at the Sunset. He had been influenced at first by Hines, or perhaps inspired was the word. But then, it was Zurke who set him on the path to a style.

Chet Roble, Chicago, 1951

Cairo Lounge, Chicago, June, 1947.Left to right: Boyce Brown, Chet
Roble, Sammy Aron. (Courtesy Sammy Aron)

boyce · chet · sam

To add to his jazz credentials, Roble was married to Ginny Reinhardt, the sister of Chicago clarinetist and 'Jazz, Ltd.' club owner, Bill Reinhardt.

A Don Gold sleeve-note says that Roble "began a two-week booking at Helsing's Vodvil lounge on Chicago's north side. He remained as chief custodian of the piano for four years." This extended booking covered the period from sometime in 1940 until the summer of 1944, when he was able to recruit a small band. This is probably the band to which John Steiner referred in *Jazz*.

Chet Roble's Sextet
Eli 'Bud' Phillips, cl; Boyce Brown, as; Chet Roble, p; unknown g; sbs; d.
Private recordings, Chicago, c. 1944

Copenhagen
Riverboat Shuffle
I Surrender Dear

It has been assumed that John Steiner made these recordings, but he says:

Certainly, I would have wanted to record the Roble Sextet. But I must confess that I cannot recall having done so. In the mid-1940's, thousands of my records, including hundreds of acetates, were destroyed in a fire ... If I did have something to do with recording the Roble Sextet, it may have been having them record during the day (when I couldn't be present) at Myron Bachman's studio. Myron was a trombonist who could make fellows feel at ease.

I Surrender Dear is in part a pseudo-classical exercise, but the first two titles are straightforward jazz performances, indicating that Roble was able to perform satisfactorily in a jazz context. Boyce Brown's is the individual voice, with Roble displaying a touch of Bob Zurke in his solos. (Drummer Bill Pfeiffer was reported to have been with Chet Roble in 1942, but it is perhaps more likely that he was in this 1944 band?)

The sextet played twenty-four weeks at Helsing's before dispersing, but Roble was back there around August 1945, this time in a trio setting with Boyce Brown and bassist Sammy Aron. From this point the trio remained unchanged for the next four years, generally playing long engagements in Chicago clubs with names such as The Vanity, The Delta, The Cairo and The Argyle.

(A provisional listing of the trio's engagements is given at the end of this article.)

Marty Grosz recalls:

> At one time he (Roble) had a trio. The altoist was Boyce Brown, making a living. When the group played 'Hawaiian War Chant' Boyce had to roll up his pants legs and don a grass skirt. He had the legs of a singed pullet. You get the idea.

At a Dave Garroway concert presentation at the Civic Opera House in Chicago on 4 May 1947, *Down Beat* praised the trio's performance:

> With Illinois Jacquet, Georgie Auld, Chet Roble and their groups, Sarah Vaughan and cornetist Jimmy McPartland there, it was Chet's group ... that not only saved the concert from an inglorious ending but almost stole it away from the bigger names. ... Chet's trio, with Boyce and Sammy, went back on for an unscheduled half hour, killing time until Jacquet's group arrived. With some good jazz — Boyce's alto outstanding — and clever routines, they walked off to about the best hand of the evening.

In 1948 *Down Beat* reported that the trio had "apparently ... adopted the bastard mixture of swing and dixie and bop that seems to be what lots of musicians are playing nowadays. But Boyce alone would be worth a trip northward to Argyle street."

In May 1949 Charlie Spero, clarinet and tenor, joined as replacement for Boyce Brown, and the trio seems to have survived until early the following year. By April 1950 Roble was working solo as a pianist/singer, back at 'Helsing's' where he stayed into 1951. He also started to make an impact on local television. There were occasional jazz concerts with trumpeters Bill Tinkler or Jack Ivett, trombonist Floyd O'Brien, and clarinettists Bud Jacobson or Johnny Lane, but primarily he worked in cocktail lounges, notorious for their debilitating effect upon pianists with jazz leanings. 'The Rocket' and 'The Key' were other locations he played, but in December 1951 he started a residency at the piano bar of the Sherman Hotel. This was to last, with few interruptions, for the rest of his life.

Television became increasingly important, starting with Treasury Department shows with a trio, followed by other regular solo spots, culminating in a Friday (later Sunday) night A.B.C.

(later N.B.C.) network show, "Stud's Place", featuring Chicago historian, personality, and author, Studs Terkel.

In a 1951 *Down Beat*, Jack Tracy could write:

> TV may be criticised for doing little for jazz and jazzmen so far. But it has given Chet a chance to act naturally and not like a puppet. And to prove that musicians are really people.

Following the success of "Stud's Place", Terkel began, in 1952, a regular Monday night session at the 'Blue Note'. Entitled "I Come For To Sing", it featured Roble, Big Bill Broonzy, folksinger, guitarist Win Stracke (who was also in "Stud's Place"), and Elizabethan tenor Larry Lane. After about a year, late in 1953, the show switched to the 'Blue Angel' for a short stay.

It was in 1952 that Roble signed his first recording contract, with the small Chicago firm "Topper". This was reported in *Down Beat* for 18 June 1952, and the release of one record, with Ace In The Hole on one side, has been confirmed, but no other details have been traced so far.

In 1953 Roble was recorded by Argo, the jazz label of the Chess organisation. The resulting LP is listed in Michel Ruppli's discography of the Chess label by its catalogue number and Roble's name only. Fuller details of the album on Argo LP-16, titled **Chets Chats** are:

Chet Roble, p/v; Joe Hazdra, g; Sid Thal, sbs; Wally Gordon, d.

Chicago 1953

Sugar; I Can't Believe That You're In Love With Me; I'm In The Market For You; The First Baseball Game; Easy Living; Have Another One, Not Me; Lil' Augie Is A Natural Man; Memphis In June; Do You Know What It Means To Miss New Orleans; Judy; Lazy River.

(Thal and Gordon also worked in tandem on the 'Jazz, Ltd.' recordings by Sidney Bechet, Muggsy Spanier, Doc Evans and Don Ewell.)

Argo may have been a jazz label, but this is not a jazz album. As Jack Tracy says: "I produced his Argo LP and it was done for love, not to enrich a jazz lover's library." Certainly it is a better-than-average collection of songs and surely a token of Roble's work at the Sherman Hotel. John Steiner draws attention to the good and typical piano chorus on Sugar.

Questions about Roble's jazz abilities have produced varying responses. Trumpeter Bill Tinkler said, "Chet Roble was a good player - not too much on the jazz side," while collector Merrill Hammond commented: "He was very busy in the Chicago area. I would rate him as a first rate jazz pianist but certainly not outstanding." Marty Grosz remembered him as, "an enthusiastic, entertaining pianist whose relationship to jazz was tenuous. He masked his lack of talent and sensitivity through manic showmanship." A view from a different angle was given by Jack Tracy, a *Down Beat* editor in this era,

> Chet Roble was a dear friend of mine who really wasn't too great a piano player or much of a singer, but he was perhaps the ideal piano bar personality, and he was loved in Chicago and never (I mean NEVER) out of work. For years he was at the piano bar of the 'Well of the Sea' in the Sherman Hotel and everybody knew him, and he knew everybody. Seemingly he never forgot a face or a name, was always laughing and happy, always knew the latest ribald stories and music gossip. He was just fun to be around.

In a 1982 letter to Bert Whyatt, a Chicago pianist with a higher jazz reputation, the late Tut Soper, wrote of his forty years friendship with Roble:

> He too loved jazz and baseball, was a fine swimmer, and about 6 feet two inches tall. Taller and heavier than I. A truly fine looking man and one who by dint of hard work succeeded in the music business far and above anything he'd ever dreamed. He was frustrated as far as his jazz career was concerned but he made it big as an entertainer. We played much golf together and we attended many ball games as Cubs' bleachers fans in conjunction with many jazz musicians including Bud Freeman.

Also recalling the Sherman Hotel days, John Steiner says,

> Chet played dozens of private parties every year. Often he would play for an early evening affair until 9 or 10 pm. Then to the grand piano in the 'Scuttlebutt Lounge' where there was also the bar for the eastern half of the Sherman Hotel basement. The lounge was in a room between a restaurant called 'Well of the Sea' and the biggest room, the 'College Inn'. Overflow crowds waited in 'Scuttlebutt'. Continuous piano activity was considered necessary, so Hots (his only and legal name) Michaels was

brought in as a second pianist, and lounge music started at about 7 pm and continued until after 2 am.

Tut Soper recalled the tragedy when Chet Roble's daughter died and how, subsequently, the Robles parted, with Ginnie Roble moving to Florida.

Chet Roble died of a heart ailment on October 31, 1962.

It cannot be disputed that he was an extremely popular figure on the Chicago music scene. Tut Soper was unable to attend Chet Roble's funeral, but recalled that over 3,000 people were there. The *Chicago Tribune* obituary referred to him as "Mr. Chicago" and as "one of the many mayors of Randolph Street in its heyday," but as a jazz player the adjectives already used, 'enthusiastic, entertaining', are perhaps the ones most applicable. And all those years in partnership with Boyce Brown must redound to Chet Roble's credit.

The Chet Roble Trio Provisional listing of engagements. All locations are in Chicago, unless otherwise shown. Months are estimates, based upon *Down Beat* news items, except for specific dates.

Chet Roble, piano; Boyce Brown, alto; Sammy Aron, bass

1945	August to December (or beyond)	Helsing's

1946	uncertain dates	Isbell's (Washington & Dearborn)
	uncertain dates	Isbell's (Brym Mawr)
	July	The Vanity
	September to December	The Delta

1947	February 11 (opening date)	The Cairo
	March to May	The Skyride (12 week engagement)
	May/June	The Clover, Peoria
	June 19 (opening date)	The Cairo (for "18 weeks or more")
	December	The Lido, South Bend, Indiana

1948	January/February	The Rocket
	February	Forest Park Hotel, St. Louis, Missouri
	April 5 (opening date)	The Cairo

June 29 (opening date)	Castle Inn, Ventura, California, (for eight weeks)
August 31 to October	The Argyle (closed by I.R.S.)
October	Mickey's (Milwaukee & Cicero)
1949 May	The Cairo (Charlie Spero replaced Brown)
July	The Brass Rail
July/August	The Capitol
September to October 23	The Zebra, Green Bay, Wisconsin.
October to December	The Cairo
1950 January	The Brass Rail

Down Beat for 6 October 1948 reported

A steady stream of substitutes invaded the Argyle recently, when altoist Boyce Brown of the Chet Roble trio, went into hospital for a check up. Among them were clarinetists Bob McCracken and Charlie Spero, and cornetist Paul (Doc) Evans.

Evans was there September 17-20, before joining Jazz, Ltd. However, despite these reports, Sammy Aron says that Brown did not go into hospital and there were no substitutes!

Floyd Bean: The Forgotten Ones

The Jimmy McPartland session for Decca's Chicago Jazz album, produced by George Avakian and issued in 1940, would have been for most jazz buffs in those days their first hearing of pianist Floyd Bean. By then he had been on the scene for two decades but opportunities to record had rarely come his way. As it was, another decade and more had to pass before he made it to a studio again.

Some references have it that he was born in the small town of Grinnell, Iowa, on August 30, 1904. In a 1963 interview, however, Bean said that his birthplace was an even smaller town, Ladora, in the same state. His father, a plumber, was not musical and his mother 'tinkered' on the family reed organ so it was not until he was at high school in Grinnell, and became involved, on bass drum, with the school band, that music came to him. More importantly, he enjoyed 'fooling around' on the school piano and then took lessons on that instrument from George Leins (aka Lyons), leader of a band called The Mississippi Six.

By 1918, Bean had become a professional musician, working with the Hawk-eye Melody Boys, a band which played at a roadhouse, the Linwood Inn, on the Mississippi about seven miles out of Davenport. During this period, Bean recalled,

> ... a trumpet player by the name of Bix Beiderbecke used to come out from town (Davenport) and sit in with us. He hardly ever played trumpet, however, but liked to noodle around on the piano. We knew he was a wonderful musician but he had only a local reputation then. When our trumpet player left we thought of hiring him but we needed someone who could carry the lead on new sheet music and Bix couldn't read. Bix showed me a lot of new things about piano, (such as) playing tenths. I'd never heard of that before; always played octaves in the bass.

Thereafter, Bean moved to Muscatine, a larger town with a toll bridge to Illinois. From that base he worked with many local bands in both states. By 1924 he had wandered as far as Fond du Lac, a resort town in the southern tip of Lake Winnebago in Wisconsin.

Brian Shanley, Dave Black, Bob Scobey, Floyd Bean. Bob Scobey's band in Toronto 1958.

He was with bandleader Cy Mahlberg who, the following year, employed trumpeter Bunny Berigan. Over the next few years, Bean jobbed with many bands including that of Fred Dexter, then very popular with dancers in the midwest. In the August of 1930 Dexter recorded in Richmond, Indiana, for Gennett. Brian Rust's personnel in *Jazz Records 1897-1942* for this session names another but Bean was in no doubt that he was on piano.

By 1931/32, Bean was employed as staff pianist at radio station WOC in Davenport and also worked in trumpeter Jimmy Hicks's band for which he wrote some arrangements. (This may well have been somewhat earlier. Bean recalled Beiderbecke sitting-in with the Hicks band while in Davenport with Paul Whiteman. According to *Bix: Man & Legend*, the cornetist was in that city for the last time in January, 1931, though not then with the band. He died the following August.) Bean's early models had been Rube Bloom and Lee Sims but "... then I heard Earl Hines and I knew this was the real thing."

WOC merged with WHO of Des Moines and Bean lost the staff job. He formed a five-piece Dixieland band which played at a place called Claus' Dine-and-Dance. "Then," said Bean, "the Depression came along and things really got bad. There was only one piano job in town and another man had it. My band was working seven nights a week for $15 a man. I pulled out and went to Chicago."

He studied arranging and also, as was the tradition, worked with local bands before settling in for a long spell with Eddie Neibauer's Seattle Harmony Kings.

> It was a good band for those days, 10-piece. We worked four seasons in Chicago, alternating between the Casino Moderne on the south side and going in the summer to an open-air place on the north side, the Wilshore. I was doing all the band arranging.

Around 1937, Bean became a member of Jimmy McPartland's busy band at such places as the Three Deuces (named for its number on North State Street: 222) and the Hotel Sherman on the corner of Clark and Randolph Streets.

The hugely successful Bob Crosby orchestra was in crisis during its spring 1939 season in Chicago. Pianist Bob Zurke wanted to leave to form his own band and had to be replaced at short notice. Pete Viera was fixed but could not join immediately because of contracted work elsewhere and then had health problems. Joe

Sullivan was set but not yet available so Bean, then working as solo pianist at the Deuces, was chosen. The third of four Decca sessions in April produced Rose Of Washington Square and Penthouse Serenade. The latter has some fine Eddie Miller tenor, then, after the vocal duet by leader Crosby and Marion Mann, Bean has two four-bar spots leading to Irving Fazola's clarinet solo.

The fourth batch was that by the Bob Cats which gave the world Shakespeare sonnets set to music by Englishman Arthur Young and played in a generally Dixieland manner. Perhaps astonishingly, these come off very well indeed. Marion Mann had an excellent singing voice but it pays to listen to the instrumental goings-on behind her. Bean can be heard happily comping during It Was A Lover And His Lass and Sigh No More Ladies and has a good solo on the latter.

Discographers should note that Bean also played the second Chicago session, despite what the books say. He noted the titles and the dates in his diary. However, what little piano there is to be heard is quite anonymous. He remained with the Crosby band for its next engagement, in Milwaukee, but returned to Chicago when it went on to New York and Sullivan came in.

Bean was in Jimmy McPartland's band at the Off-Beat Club (no trace of its location seems to remain) when, six months later, came the Chicago Jazz batch mentioned in the opening paragraph of this article. With the cornetist were Bud Jacobson on clarinet, Boyce Brown on alto, Dick McPartland on guitar, Jim Lanigan on bass, drummer Hank Isaacs and, of course, Bean on piano. The opener, Jazz Me Blues, inevitably brings Beiderbecke to mind and is nicely relaxed with well-taken breaks including one by Bean who also has the first solo. Another recollection is China Boy for the 1927 McKenzie-Condon OKeh record which also included McPartland. This later version has a run of solos including a chorus by Bean shared with Lanigan on the bridge. Sugar does not feature the pianist but he takes a very good solo on The World Is Waiting For The Sunrise, the arrangement of which seems odd until you realise that the out-of-tempo intro with its gloomy arco bass is intended to illustrate the moments before dawn. That aside, an excellent session very adequately preserving Chicago style as it was at the end of the decade.

The next year, Bean worked with Boyce Brown at the Club Silhouette on Howard Street and was in Wingy Manone's band later. He had his own trio at the Barrel O'Fun and then leaving the jazz scene, at least in terms of gainful employment, worked as arranger for singer Eddie Howard who was backed by an orchestra led by Lou Adrian. Records were made for Columbia but the output was purely popular. In complete contrast, Bean then spent most of a year in the Boyd Raeburn band but, because of a union ban, no records were made. By 1944, he was in the dance band of Eddie Stone, as pianist and arranger. With Stone as lyricist, they wrote a song entitled I Never Thought I'd Sing The Blues which was recorded by Stan Kenton with the vocal by June Christy.

Chicago in the mid-1940s must have been exciting for jazz piano enthusiasts. Joe Sullivan had a spell at the Hotel Sherman and both George Zack and Floyd Bean could be found at one or another of the many bars and clubs. On at least one occasion, in March 1946, the latter two, leading their own bands, were together on a bill for a Hot Club of Chicago concert.

Jess Stacy, struggling to keep together a big band, suffered a broken finger and had to use substitutes for gigs. For an engagement at Chicago's Band Box in the fall of 1945, Bean was recruited as first pianist (that is, he undertook the basic work of pianist in the band). John Chilton noted that his time with Stacy was as 'second piano' and that he made some arrangements.

Another recording session, and very obscure at that, was in 1946 by a band led by Carl Bean, a cousin of Floyd. Reportedly, the pianist had a good solo on Blue Skies. This was for the Tower label which had virtually no distribution.

Bill and Ruth Reinhardt had opened their club. Jazz, Ltd., at 11 East Grand Avenue in Chicago, in June, 1947. The band had the usual never-ending stream of personnel changes down the years but by the turn of 1947/48 Bean was part of the group led by Sidney Bechet. There was no trumpeter (hardly needed, and, in any case, the stand was too small for more than a five-piecer), the trombonist was Munn Ware, the drummer Danny Alvin and the co-proprietor was, as always, on clarinet. Bean returned several times to Jazz, Ltd., including a fairly long run during the winter of 1949/50, at first with Muggsy Spanier, George Brunies and Sid Catlett. By the spring, Miff Mole and Zutty Singleton had replaced Brunies and Catlett and then in June, Fred Greenleaf took over from Spanier.

Between spells at Jazz, Ltd., Bean was pianist in a band led by singer-banjoist Clancy Hayes. Also present were Jim Beebe on trombone and Brian Shanley on clarinet. When Richard Nixon was running for president in 1949, the Republican party had the band record a ditty entitled Vote For Richard Nixon! In the event, they didn't use it very much because, according to Beebe, they thought it a little too raucous.

In the March of 1950, Spanier made the first of his several recording sessions for Mercury. He used what was almost the Jazz, Ltd. band: Brunies, Bean, Catlett plus Darnell Howard on clarinet and Truck Parham on bass. The performances were typical Spanier with the fast numbers played hell-for-leather and the slows with much depth of feeling, especially in blues. Of the latter, Feather Brain is an excellent example with muted Spanier cornet and Howard's mellow clarinet and the entire side enhanced by Bean's sympathetic playing. Bean's feature was his own composition, Lazy Piano Man. He had put this on paper 10 years earlier and named it Back Room Blues. It was published in a 1940 issue of *Down Beat* to accompany an article on Bean by Sharon Pease. The Spanier version has the band playing the five bars of introduction, Bean soloing for 12, the band taking the first four of the next and then Bean again. Spanier has a low, throaty, muted chorus and the band takes the closer with the piano well to the fore.

Spanier had decided to form a band for touring and it was eventually engaged to play at the Railroad Fair in Chicago at the beginning of June. It played at a venue called Dixieland Village where pianist Tut Soper, who had been unhappy for some time, was replaced by Bean. Bean was very happy, despite all the travelling, and said that

> ... his association with Muggsy was a great pleasure. I was with him the years of 1950, 1951 and 1952. I took one leave of absence for seven weeks from January 31, 1952, and rejoined on March 27 in Akron, Ohio. I finally left permanently on December 21, 1952.

These are extracts from his careful diary which produced details of transcription recordings cut at the Merchandise Mart and at Universal Studio in Chicago. Details of these are included in the discography which is in this writer's book on Spanier.

That work also provides some details of the band's itinerary from which the following list of cities played in 1950/51 gives some idea of what was involved: Salt Lake City, San Francisco, Los Angeles, Boston, Philadelphia, Toronto, Chicago, Denver and back to San Francisco by early June.

George Brunies (by now Georg Brunis) had been leading at the Eleven-Eleven Club (at that number on Bryn Mawr Avenue) from 1951 and Bean came into the band after he had left Spanier. Apart from a brief period in 1958 when he was with the Bob Scobey band, he stayed with Brunis until round the turn of 1959/60. The Scobey band was more or less that of Clancy Hayes of several years earlier: the leader on trumpet, with Jim Beebe on trombone, Shanley, Bean, Hayes, Rich Madison on helicon (he also played bass trumpet), and Dave Black at the drums.

Bean went back to Davenport in 1961 and worked locally and then finally settled down in Cedar Rapids. In 1970 he said:

> I'm semi-retired and still play in a local quartet two or three nights a week. Also do some occasional work as a single and a little teaching and some arranging.

But his health was declining and he died on March 9, 1974.

He had no distinctive style at the piano, having listened hard to and been influenced, he said, by Earl Hines initially, followed later by Teddy Wilson and Art Tatum. In his perceptive notes to a Jazzology LP of Spanier recordings made for World Transcriptions, Hal Smith commented that Bean was "an excellent, though curiously underrated jazzman, whose style is a unique melange of Joe Sullivan, Earl Hines, Jess Stacy and Art Hodes". So, a fine and reliable pianist who worked with many of the greats of jazz and is deserving of some attention.

Most of the recordings he made are unavailable other than through specialist collectors shops and dealers. Apparently still not on compact disc, and worth seeking out is Chicago Jazz (includes the McPartland 1939 session), Decca DL-8029, Brunswick LST8042 or Coral CP38; then the Muggsy Spanier long-play records on Mercury and subsidiary labels and Rare Custom 45s on IAJRC 42 as well as the above-cited Jazzology which is J115. The Bob Crosby April 1939 sessions are on DHDL128 in Halcyon's compact disc series on that band.

Bill Reinhardt: Jazz, Ltd. - and more

I was born in Chicago in 1908, my birthday is September 21st. While in high school I worked in the A&P stores to earn enough money to follow Jimmy Noone and Johnny Dodds around the South Side on weekend nights. I would see Dodds at Kelly's Stables and Jimmy Noone at the Eldorado Club, which I for years called The Rado club until I learned that the "do" lights on their sign were burned out. I saw the sign and my friend and I joked about it each time we went there - I'm wondering if they contrived the blacked-out letters purposely (other sources say the two letters had been shot out. Certainly the word "Rado" does not appear in any available Spanish dictionary —DC/BW). It was in the basement of an old building and a thin door separated the club from the rest of the basement - and two bowling alleys. If the band was playing not too loudly, the chatter from a 'strike' did much to shatter the musical mood.

My entry into the dance band business was when I was attending the University of Illinois. I only attended university for one year, but prior to going there I had been fooling around with a saxophone. French horn was my main instrument at that time, which I played in Lake View High School. When I went to the University of Illinois I got into the concert band, under the direction of Austin Harding, of which I was very proud.

I lived in a place in downtown Champaign, Illinois, called College Hall. Across the hall from me lived a fellow named Miles Rinker, who was the brother of Al Rinker, one of the original Paul Whiteman Rhythm Boys. He heard me fooling around with this French horn. I didn't know jazz from a bale of hay, but I did make sounds on the horn which sounded like jazz to him. He played alto saxophone with a band called Louis Schwab and his Illini Orioles on the campus, and immediately started contriving to get me into the band. We went downtown to the music store and traded my alto sax for a tenor, which is what I needed for this Schwab band. So we played quite a few dates and the French horn was a big success.

Summer vacation was at hand and Schwab made contact with a fellow, King Richards, to take us on the road. As I recall, the first

Bill Reinhardt
at Jazz, Ltd.,
Chicago,
c. November,
1950.
(Courtesy
John Miner)

Ruth Sato
Reinhardt,
Miss Japan 1933

stop was to be Beloit, Wisconsin. Everybody was enthusiastic; we were asking Richards, "What about this? What about that?" In Beloit we found out that this job had been booked about three hours prior to our appearance. Because of the short notice there was hardly anyone in the audience. It was the same in Madison, Wisconsin. He didn't have a single date booked. Schwab had a little money but the sidemen had none. The leader doling out dollar bills one at a time made it rough.

Schwab got in touch with Richards's people and found out he had escaped from some sanatorium. We had this wild ride to Eau Claire, Wisconsin, to deliver Richards, and here, sure enough, were the men in white coats! We went on our merry way and tried to get a date here and there. The leader booked several days in a dance hall in Milwaukee. We were all gathered in a hotel room, when there's a knock on the door. Who's there, but King Richards. He said 'Well boys, they weren't good enough to hold me. Where can we go from here?'!

We went from Milwaukee to Michigan City, Indiana, where there was another ballroom, right on the lake. We were there about two weeks. After a week or ten days a man in the audience asked to see me. Fred Dexter was the man's name. He had played for a number of years at the Wisconsin Roof in Milwaukee. Why in the world he ever hired me I do not know, because I couldn't blow my nose. I still had the French horn, but this to any knowledgeable person must have sounded awful. He needed a man badly as some guy had left at the last minute. He was playing a resort pavilion at a place called Hudson Lake, Indiana, not far from Michigan City.

At any rate, this was a fast band. The men all went on to good things. The clarinet player, Slats Long, went with Raymond Scott in later years. Walt (Fats) Fellmen was the other saxophone; worked with name bands. Trumpeter Itch Shulkin went to the Hollywood studios. Dale (Mick) McMickle, the other trumpet player, was first trumpet with Glenn Miller. Alex Palocsay, the trombone, was with Fred Waring. Bob White, the drummer, was with a lot of bands, with Freddy Martin for about twelve years. The bass player was Mylan Olds, the pianist was Paul Konestrick and Fred Dexter played violin.

We went on the road to Wisconsin, Illinois, and wound up in Buffalo, New York, to play a Christmas season in this ballroom. The band was ahead of its time. It tried to pattern itself after

Benny Pollack. Consequently, if a band plays above the head of the general audience, nothing happens. There was a band from Canada playing opposite, five or six pieces, and each man had a sock cymbal, played with this heavy sock thing. The audience loved them; ignored us. We wound up in a place at 48th and Broadway in New York City called The Everglades. This was a place with a floor show, a line of girls, and several acts, and I was flabbergasted. I had never even seen the inside of a nightclub at that time. This was maybe early 1928.

That was a fairly successful engagement. Name people, Walter Winchell, lots of celebrities, used to frequent this club.

Musicians used to hear us. Benny Goodman was there. We were living in an apartment building at 130 West 47th Street. I was with some of the livelier members of the band, although I didn't belong there, because I preferred sleeping. But they had sessions there, in the apartment, near every night of the week, and the big star was Jack Teagarden - his first time really out of Texas. He hit New York like a tornado. We had a man with a guitar, never heard too many horns. Men came from all over New York - Red Nichols - Miff Mole got his first hearing of Teagarden. I remember him sitting there, very interested. That was really my first introduction to jazz. Then too, they had records. This was where I heard my first McKenzie-Condons, and all those Bix records were coming out like mad. So my love kept increasing with hearing these things.

We were scheduled to finish at The Everglades, but in the last days of our engagement Cass Hagan came in. He liked our little band, so he purchased it from Fred Dexter and took us on the road doing college dates and, for the summer, took us to the Pelham Heath Inn, which was a summer out-on-the-road nightspot, owned by the mob. We stayed with that band until the fall of 1928, at which time Cass Hagan had no jobs, so the band broke up.

At one point I started a New England vaudeville tour with Freddy Rich, but an abcessed tooth caused me to cancel. I went to work for a Paul Specht unit at a place on Broadway and stayed there for a few months until I decided I'd had enough of New York and came back to Chicago. Almost immediately I fell into club dates until the spring of 1929, when Sol Wagner hired me. I did a place called The Frolics, which was a very well-known nightclub. Stayed there through the summer of 1929, and the crash came and business went haywire.

It would have been back around between 1928 and 1930 that I recorded something with Wingy Manone, in an old Brunswick studio on South Wabash Avenue in Chicago, with Jack Gardner, piano, and a fellow named Floyd Hinkley, alto saxophonist. I don't remember anybody else. I was playing North Side Chicago, I guess, near Evanston, some chop suey house, with this Floyd Hinkley, and Art Hodes playing piano.

Wingy Manone? A wonderful character, and he had that good old New Orleans sound; feeling. He would speak to the audience and tell them, "I'm glad you came to hear the truth."

Following Sol Wagner I did a few dates in and around Chicago. Finally left and went to Florida to play Albert Boucher's Villa Venice nightclub. Following that I went to New York and did various jobs there. I was approached by some people who had a place called The Ship Ahoy in New Rochelle and I put together what I thought sounded like a little jazz band, which it was, and people enjoyed it. In the band Johnny Strouse played drums, and a fellow named Tabby Haverfield played very good piano. From time to time I would go into New York and bring back men to play for a day or two, such as Joe Mooney playing piano.

One night I went to the Hickory House in New York. I made regular visits from then on, I so admired Joe Marsala and that whole band. Joe Marsala inspired me to try solo work on the clarinet. I made a record with Marty Marsala, and in the course of something I was playing on the playback, he said, "Boy, you play so much like Joe." Yes, I enjoyed him so much.

After leaving The Ship Ahoy I did some work in a place called The Nut Club, and latched on to doing the Monday night sessions at Nick's for about two months. The men at Nick's were George Stacey, trumpet (brother of altoist Jack Stacey, with Jimmy Dorsey), Frank Orchard, trombone; Gene Schroeder, piano; Danny Alvin, drums. I can't recall the bassist. This was when I enlisted in the navy.

(John Miner's *Down Beat* researches show Bill Reinhardt working in 1935 at the Westchester-Biltmore Country Club; and in 1941 at the Crystal Cafe, Brooklyn. A sleevenote also gives him at Club 18, where he enjoyed watching comedians like Joe Frisco and Jackie Gleason.)

The French horn went out with Cass Hagan's band. I never got it out again until I joined the navy. I knew they always wanted

French horns, so I got it out and started woodshedding. Joined the navy playing the French horn, although I wound up doing everything with the band. I met my wife in a club in New York. I was playing there on an off-night. We got married in Norfolk in June, 1942, following my enlistment. Ruth had a great show business career. She was in the chorus, but she invented some things. Ruth was the first U.S. born Japanese to appear in a Broadway show. She performed with people like Fred Astaire, and she was with Milton Berle quite a while. She worked for Vinton Freedley, the Broadway producer, then with Billy Rose for a long time. (Walter Winchell said of Ruth Sato, who was Japanese-Irish, "Ruth Sato — a Japanese doll with brains!")

I joined the navy in Norfolk, Virginia, and I went through boot training with the Ninth Sea Bee battalion. When I finished training I immediately joined the band at Camp Allen. That was the summertime, and then they moved us to Camp Perry in Williamsburg, Virginia. The big thing was that I didn't have to live on the base. I got out of the navy in 1945. I did very little work at that time, because I was too busy putting Jazz, Ltd. together. Nick's served as an example for the club and we opened it in 1947. [June 11th 1947 at 11 East Grand Avenue, Chicago.] It should have been larger. We were looking all over for a location and couldn't find one. We came upon this place and it was a very likely spot, except for the size. It only seated about 85 people. It was unfortunate, because we opened to a line waiting to get in, and that's the way it stayed, practically all the time we were there, from 1947 to 1960, until we moved to a larger location.

This room was designed by Hugo Weber and Emerson Waeffler, who were artists at The Institute of Design in Chicago. I got talking about this 30" ledge inside the room, and Weber said, "I make you a nice statue." He made Ziblid, a statue ridiculing women in general, I think. The right arm was extended, with a great big hand on the end of it, the grasping aspect. The neck on top of the body was long, the rubber-necker curiosity. We brought her with us when we moved. Only drawback, it took up so much room with that long arm. So we donated it to one of those causes they have on television.

I think the best record we at Jazz, Ltd. made was one that was picked up by Atlantic. Starts off with Panama, the flip side starts with Sensation Rag, I think.

I always enjoyed Sid Catlett. I enjoyed Bechet. He gave the drummer hell; didn't approve of his taste. Joe Sullivan'? Good piano player. Don Ewell I always enjoyed; I was responsible for bringing him out of Baltimore. Nap Trottier, he played real nice. Norm Murphy was a great supporter of mine. Joe Wiedman, another supporter, played trumpet with Will Bradley, his chief claim to fame. One of the tastiest trumpet players was Fred Greenleaf. And oh yes, I enjoyed Marty Marsala.

On May 2, 1960 Jazz, Ltd. moved to larger premises at 164, East Grand Avenue, Chicago. A brochure for the club produced after this date says: "Jazz, Ltd. is a night club dedicated to the Jazz of the '20s and World War I era. It is a club where people who are not necessarily Jazz buffs can spend some time and enjoy themselves. It is a club for the discriminating, the fun-loving and well-mannered person who likes to frequent a well run and safe night spot." The club was closed on Sundays, and the Thursday night band was Franz Jackson's Original Jass Stars. There was a $2.50 minimum but no cover charge.

In the second Jazz, Ltd. location we had a space where customers could dance if they wanted to. It was always my contention that jazz music was originally intended to play for dancing, and to play, for the most part, tempos that people could dance to, for which I received a lot of criticism from men in the band. They got hung up on the Chicago style routines; there's some men who can do it right, but for the most part these guys just can't keep time. But I never expect the boss to be regarded kindly. [Jazz, Ltd. closed its doors for the last time on February 26, 1972.] After Jazz, Ltd. closed I continued to book dates with my own band. I had a good reputation, and we had an awful lot of publicity while we had the club. Eventually I was approached to take a band into the Blackstone hotel, with the same instrumentation that I had used in the club, and some of the men that had played with me on Jazz, Ltd. I was there about three months. About a year later they asked me to come back.

(Flaming Sally's was the name of the room in the Blackstone, so-called because the waitresses wore flaming red wigs. The first engagement lasted from January 7 to April 6, 1974, and the band's opening personnel was reported in the press as: Bobby Ballard, trumpet; Harry Graves, trombone; Bill Reinhardt, clarinet; Claude Johnson, piano; Ed Wilkinson, bass, tuba; Marshall Thompson, drums. Bill Reinhardt also recalls Spanky Davis, trumpet; and

Steve Bahr playing with the band at some time. Harry Graves's attitude had not pleased Reinhardt and his replacement for the second engagement was Jim Beebe.)

Jim Beebe plays trombone very well. I was responsible for his being a leader. When I left the Blackstone I just figured he was the logical one to have the band. He had a good jazz knowledge, and he stayed there on the job for a couple of years, I guess. He's been a leader ever since. This time I left because I wasn't feeling too well. When I turned in my notice I was too tired. I started booking club dates again until we decided to come to San Diego in 1978, the first of May I did a few dates out here and I played that Solana Beach Friday cocktail session, one day a week. I learned that the promoter was hiring some union men and some non-union, and scale didn't mean much, so I left. About that time I began having some trouble with my ticker. Arrhythmia (irregular heart beat) set in, and following that I discovered one of the arteries had an obstruction. (The obstruction was cleared and a pacemaker inserted to govern the heart beat.)
Naturally, since that time I'm on a permanent diet. Exercise is important. I found that walking these hills gave me greater benefit than just swimming.

This interview took place in May 1992 in San Diego. Bill Reinhardt, looking lean and fit, carried his 84 years like a man many years younger. Sadly, Ruth Reinhardt died on 9 December 1992 after a long illness.
Bill Reinhardt died in San Diego on January 23, 2001.

Notes:

1 Pianist Chet Roble married Bill Reinhardt's sister.
2 Bill Reinhardt recalls that Bill Challis did some arrangements for the Cas Hagan Band.
3 Further information about Bill Reinhardt and Jazz, Ltd. may be found in the following publications:
   a)   *Hot Man* by Art Hodes and Chadwick Hansen (Bayou Press)
   b)   *Sidney Bechet, Wizard of Jazz* by John Chilton (MacMillan)
   c)   *The Jazz Legacy of Don Ewell* by John Collinson and Eugene Kramer (*Storyville* Publications)
   d)   *The Mississippi Rag,* November 1977 (Article by Don Ingle); August 1992 (article by Thomas B. Gilmore)

Bill Reinhardt — A Discography

Original issues only, with thanks to Jim Gordon, whose records provided the basis for this listing

Wingy Mannone, t; Bill Reinhardt, cl; Floyd Hinkley, as; Jack Gardner, p; others
Chicago, Illinois 1928-1930
unknown titles   Brunswick   unissued

Above details from Bill Reinhardt. Studio was on South Wabash Avenue. Session date was probably in 1929 as Reinhardt spent little time in Chicago in 1928 and 1930.

No Band Title
Lloyd Ballard, c; Bill Reinhardt, cl; Don Ewell, p; Beale (Bill) Riddle, d.
Annapolis, Maryland 1941
Everybody Loves My Baby   Unissued acetate
Above details from *The Jazz Legacy* of Don Ewell.

The following group of sides, all prefixed UB, were made on the same day despite the varying band personnel and wide variation in numbering. They appeared originally in a Jazz, Ltd. 78 album in a limited pressing of 1,000 copies retailing at $7.50. These issues bear no band titles and the record titles appeared in inverted commas. Subsequently, all sides have been copiously reissued in microgroove formats with the artist credits shown below:

SIDNEY BECHET Jazz, Ltd. ORCHESTRA
Munn Ware, tb; Sidney Bechet, ss; Bill Reinhardt, cl; Don Ewell, p; Sid Thall, sb; Wally Gordon, d.
Chicago, Illinois c. February 1949
UB9101 Maryland, My Maryland   Jazz Ltd 201A
UB9102 Careless Love   Jazz Ltd 201E
UB9103 Egyptian Fantasy   Jazz Ltd 101A
The reverse of Jazz Ltd 101 is Maple Leaf Rag, a piano solo by Don Ewell (matrix UB9104).

DOC EVANS DIXIELAND BAND
As above, but Doc Evans, c; replaces Bechet.
UB9181 Wolverine Blues   Jazz Ltd 301A
UB9182 It's A Long Way To Tipperary   Jazz Ltd 301B

MUGGSY SPANIER JAZZ LTD ORCHESTRA

As above but Muggsy Spanier, c; replaces Evans.

| UB9183A | A Good Man Is Hard To Find | Jazz Ltd 401A |
| UB9184 | Washington And Lee Swing | Jazz Ltd 401B |

All the 1949 and 1951 titles issued on CD, Delmark DE-226

DIXIELAND AT JAZZ, LTD.

Doc Evans, t; Miff Mole, tb; Bill Reinhardt, cl; Ralph Blank, p; Sy Nelson, sb; Doc Cenardo, d.

Chicago, Illinois mid-1951

Tin Roof Blues	Jazz Ltd (un-numbered LP)
High Society	Jazz Ltd (un-numbered LP)
Jazz Me Blues	Jazz Ltd (un-numbered LP)
The Charleston	Jazz Ltd (un-numbered LP)

This was Jazz, Ltd. Volume One. This is dated by Jepsen as 1949, probably because of the previous Doc Evans session in that year. The estimate of mid-1951 seems more likely, based upon a similar personnel working in the club at that time.

JAZZ AT JAZZ, LTD.

Norm Murphy, t; Dave Remington, tb; Bill Reinhardt, cl; Max Hook, p; Hal Carnes, sb; Freddie Kohlman, d.

Chicago, Illinois 1956

Sensation	Atlantic 1338 (LP)
I've Found A New Baby	Atlantic 1338 (LP)
Just A Closer Walk With Thee	Atlantic 1338 (LP)
Farewell Blues	Atlantic 1338 (LP)
Panama	Atlantic 1338 (LP)

All titles issued on CD, Collectables CON-CD-6250. There is some confusion over the year for this session. Jepsen gives February 1960. However, the sleeve to Volume 5 (which is dated 1964) refers to "eight years ago". Thus 1956 if the 1964 date is accurate! However, a similar personnel worked at the club early in 1957 and again in 1958, so perhaps 1957 is a more likely date.

Marty Marsala, t; Harry Graves, tb; Bill Reinhardt, cl; Max Hook, p; Kenny White, sb; Doc Cenardo, d.

Chicago, Illinois 1956

Savoy Blues	Jazz Ltd JL-1003 (LP)
Bluein' The Blues (sic)	Jazz Ltd JL-1003 (LP)
The Battle Hymn of The Republic	Jazz Ltd JL-1003 (LP)
The Saints	Jazz Ltd JL-1003 (LP)

Milenberg Joys   Jazz Ltd JL-1003 (LP)
   Jazz Ltd JL-1003 is a 10" LP. These sides were also included in Atlantic
1338 (see above) a 12" issue. All titles, except The Saints, issued on CD,
Collectables COL-CD-6250 The third title was arranged by Ralph Blank.
Jepsen again lists this session as February 1960, however the sleeve
says the club has been in operation for nine years. The club opened in
1947, thus 1956 seems appropriate. Additional circumstantial evidence
against the 1960 date is that Doc Cenardo moved to California in 1957.

ART HODES ORCHESTRA
   Fred Greenleaf, t; Dave Remington, tb; Bill Reinhardt, cl; Art Hodes, p; Truck
Parham, sb; Fred Moore, d.

Chicago, Illinois 12 June 1957

DE-100 St. Louis Blues	Dotted Eighth DELP 1000 (LP)
DE-101 Riverside Blues	Dotted Eighth DELP 1000 (LP)
DE-102 Livery Stable Blues	Dotted Eighth DELP 1000 (LP)
Washington And Lee Swing	Dotted Eighth unissued
South Rampart Street Parade	Dotted Eighth unissued
Bourbon Street Parade	Dotted Eighth unissued

   DELP 1000 titles also on (CD) Jazzology JCD-46. Other titles without
Bill Reinhardt were recorded at this session.

BILL REINHARDT'S JAZZ LTD BAND
   Joe Wiedman, t; Dave Rasbury, tb; Dave Remington, tb/p; Bill Reinhardt,
cl/v-1; Earl Washington, p; Mike McKendrick, bj/g; Quinn Wilson, sb/bb; Freddie
Kohlman, d.

Chicago, Illinois 1964

Clarinet Marmalade	Jazz, Ltd. (Volume 5)
Canal Street Blues	Jazz, Ltd. (Volume 5)
Bill Bailey	Jazz, Ltd. (Volume 5)
Just A Little While To Stay Here	Jazz, Ltd. (Volume 5)
Georgia On My Mind -1	Jazz, Ltd. (Volume 5)
The World Is Waiting For The Sunrise	Jazz, Ltd. (Volume 5)
Lassus Trombone	Jazz, Ltd. (Volume 5)
Georgia Camp Meeting	Jazz, Ltd. (Volume 5)
Tiger Rag	Jazz, Ltd. (Volume 5)
Shake That Thing	Jazz, Ltd. (Volume 5)
That's A Plenty	Jazz, Ltd. (Volume 5)

   The sleeve says: 'The 11 tunes recorded give you an idea of what has
been going on at Jazz, Ltd. for 17 years." This would suggest the year
of recording as 1964.

BILL REINHARDT'S BAND

Don Ingle, t/arr-1; Ray Sassetti, Nap Trottier, t; Jim Beebe, Bill Corti, tb; Bill Reinhardt, cl/arr-2/v~1; Joe Masek, cl/as; Eddie Higgins, p; Doc Schliesmann, bj; Quinn Wilson, bb; Barrett Deems, d; band vocal -2

Chicago, Illinois 1968

W4KB-2939-1 Illinois (By The River Gently Flowing) -1

Jazz Ltd 821J-2939

W4KB-2940-1 Just A Closer Walk With Thee -2

Jazz Ltd 821J-2940

The above is a 45 rpm T issue.

Bill Reinhardt Bands

Compiled by John Miner, with additions by Derek Coller. With the exception of the first entry, all personnels are for bands appearing at Jazz, Ltd. They are taken from news items in *Down Beat*. Issue dates, where noted, are shown in brackets. Appearance dates are estimated from these issues. Additional information has been quoted from John Chilton's *Sidney Bechet: The Wizard of Jazz*, Art Hodes's *Hot Man*, Manfred Selchow's *Profoundly Blue* and John Collinson and Eugene Kramer's *The Jazz Legacy of Don Ewell*.

Bill Reinhardt (on clarinet) is shown by his initials.

1941 c. May George Stacey, c; BR; Gene Schroeder, p; Danny Alvin, d
Playing at the Crystal Cafe, Brooklyn, NY (01jul41)

1947 11 June Paul 'Doc' Evans, c; Munn Ware, tb; BR; Don Ewell, p;
Danny Alvin, d. (02jul47)

August Jack Gardner, p; replaced Ewell (10sep47)

November Sidney Bechet, ss; BR; Munn Ware, tb; Mel Grant, p;
Danny Alvin, d. Floyd Bean, p; replaced Grant.

1948 6 February Lionel Prowting, p; temporarily replaced Bean.

February Dick Wellstood, p; replaced Prowting.

March Bechet, ss; BR; Ware, tb; Wellstood, p; Bob Saltmarsh, d.

6 June Bechet's residency ended.

? Doc Evans, c; Munn Ware, tb; BR; Carroll Lee, p; Bob Saltmarsh, d.

late July Enos 'Doc' Cenardo, d; replaced Saltmarsh. (11aug48)

? Don Thompson, tb; subbed for Ware; Joyce Lacy McDonald, p;
replaced Lee. (25aug48)

25 August Sidney Bechet, ss; BR; Munn Ware, tb; Don Ewell, p; Wally
Gordon, d. Bechet had five-week. contract. (08sep48)

Oct./Nov. Doc Evans, c; then Johnny Windhurst, t.

(20oct48/04Nov48)

23 November Sidney Bechet, ss; BR; Ware, tb; Ewell, p; Johnny Vine, d. (15dec48)

? Wally Gordon, d; replaced Vine.

1949 12 January Muggsy Spanier opened, with Munn Ware, tb; BR; Don Ewell, p; Wally Gordon, d.

April Muggsy Spanier, c; Munn Ware, tb; BR; Joe Sullivan, p; Wally Gordon d.

summer Muggsy Spanier, c; Don Thompson, tb; BR; Joe Sullivan, p; Sid Catlett, d. 20May49)

Sidney Bechet, ss; Big Chief Russell Moore, tb; BR; Lloyd Phillips, p; Sid Catlett, d.

20 September Sidney Bechet left, with two weeks of contract remaining.

Doc Evans, c; and Jack Ivett, t; filled in until Muggsy Spanier arrived as featured guest.

c. November Muggsy Spanier, c; Georg Brunis, tb; BR; Floyd Bean, p; Sid Catlett, d.

1950 c. May Muggsy Spanier, c; Miff Mole, tb; BR; Floyd Bean, p; Zutty Singleton, d.

June Fred Greenleaf, t; replaced Spanier. (28aug50)

c. July Fred Greenleaf, t; Miff Mole, tb; BR; Mel Grant, p; Zutty Singleton, d.

c. August BR on vacation. Doc Evans, c; Al Jenkins, tb; Art Lyons, cl; Mel Grant, p; Doc Cenardo, d. (08 Sep 50)

c. November Marty Marsala, t; Eddie Schaefer, tb; BR; Ralph Blank, p; Sammy Dean, d. (15 Dec 50)

1951 c. January Sid Catlett, d; replaced Dean.

c. February Bill Tinkler, t; Miff Mole, tb; BR; Ralph Blank, p; Sid Catlett, d. (09 Mar 51)

March Doc Cenardo, d; replaced Catlett, who died March 25.

by summer Doc Evans, c; replaced Tinkler.

1953 ? Jack Ivett, c.

? Art Hodes was house pianist for a time.

fall Les Beigel, t, replaced Nappy Trottier.

1954 c. May Jack Alexander, t; Miff Mole, tb; BR; Mel Grant, p; Doc Cenardo, d

? Harry Graves, tb; replaced Mole.

1956 early Nappy Trottier, t; Jack Reid, tb; BR; Tut Soper, p; Walt Gifford, d

early Norman Murphy,t; Dave Remington, tb; BR; Ray Dixon, p; Walt Gifford, d.

late Art Hodes, p.

1957 early Norman Murphy, t; Dave Remington, tb; BR; Eddie Higgins, p; Freddie Moore, d.

summer Alvin Alcorn, t; BR; Freddie Kohlman,d; et al.

1958 ? Norman Murphy, t; Dave Remington, tb; BR; Max Hook, p; Freddie Kohlman, d.

Oct./Nov. Del Noel, t; Dave Rasbury, tb; Ed Hall, cl; Max Hook, p; Freddie Kohlman, d. (Ed Hall's engagement was for six weeks, while Bill Reinhardt was on holiday.)

1959 early Thomas Jefferson, t.

1960 c. January Switch to seven nights a week policy: Dave Remington band on Sunday and Franz Jackson band on Thursday.

2 May Joe Wiedman, t; Dave Rasbury, tb; BR; Max Hook, p; Quinn Wilson, tu; Freddie Kohlman, d; Blanche Thomas, vo. Tut Soper, intermission pianist.   (04Aug60,Chicago *Daily News* 30Apr60) Red Saunders, d; subbed for Kohlman, who had a broken wrist.

fall Floyd Bean, p; replaced Hook.

? Rozelle Claxton, p; replaced Bean.

late JoAnn Henderson, vo.

1961 Jan.-June Tut Soper, intermission pianist. Franz Jackson led Thursday night band.

July-Nov. Clancy Hayes, bj/vo; Jackson led Thursday night band.

1962 c. February Lil Armstrong, p: Bobby Lewis, t; Jim Beebe, tb; BR.   (12apr62)

c. March Bobby Lewis, t; Jim Beebe, tb; BR; Eddie Higgins, p; Quinn Wilson, tu; Freddie Kohlman, d.

summer Dick Oakley, t; Jim Beebe, tb; BR; Eddie Higgins, p; Mike McKendrick, bj/g/vo; Quinn Wilson, tu/b; Freddie Kohlman, d.

? Dave Rasbury, tb; replaced Beebe.

? Earl Washington, p; replaced Higgins.

1963 c.spring Don Ingle, t.

summer Mike Parker, t.

1965 early Emanuel Sayles, bj; replaced McKendrick, who had foot surgery.

1967 early Rollo Laylan, d; replaced Kohlman.

late Don Ingle, t; Bill Johnson, tb; BR; Rozelle Claxton, p; Emanuel Sayles, bj; Dave DeVore, b; Barrett Deems, d.

1968 summer Don Ingle, t; Jim Beebe, tb; BR; Rozelle Claxton, p; Art Sandly, bj; Quinn Wilson, tu/sb; Barrett Deems, d.   (05Sep68)

late Tommy Gekler, tb; replaced Beebe.

1969 early Max Hook, p; replaced Claxton.

early Duke Kane, t; replaced Bill Bachmann.

summer Dave Phelps, p.

1972 February Bobby Ballard, t; and Marshall Thompson, d; were in the last band to play at Jazz, Ltd.

Clarinetists who subbed during Bill Reinhardt's vacations, etc, included: Art Lyons (1950), Dick Pendleton (1951), Frank Chace (1952), Darnell Howard (1954), Chuck Hedges (1957), Ed Hall (1958), Albert Nicholas (1959), Jimmy Granato (1965), Pete Fountain, and Bobby Gordon. Other musicians known to have worked at Jazz, Ltd. include Sidney De Paris, tp; Ralph Hutchinson, tb; and Zinky Cohn, p.

Left to right: Bill Reinhardt, Wally Gordon, Muggsy Spanier, Joe Sullivan, Munn Ware. Jazz Ltd, c. April, 1949. (Courtesy Bill Reinhardt)

Bill Reinhardt: Jazz Ltd - and a little more

Our piece in *Storyville* 154, 1 June 1993, aroused quite a lot of interest including letters from musicians and others variously involved.

Bassist Harlow Atwood, a little younger than Bill Reinhardt, wrote:

I met Bill in 1930 or 1931 when he and I both lived in White Plains, N.Y. An eager young drummer then, I met Reinhardt when I sat in at The Farm, a roadhouse on the Bronx River Parkway north of White Plains, for Buddy Wagner, the drummer/leader of a mid-sized, stocks-reading band. The guitarist was Theo Kuriss (spelling?), the pianist Ernie Harris, Sol Pace was on clarinet and alto, Bobby Kuzemano (spelling?) [no doubt the Bob Cusumano who was with Dorsey, Clinton and Whiteman in the late 1930s. DC/BW] was on first trumpet, Rusty Jones was on trombone, and Bill was the first player I ever saw blowing clarinet on a clear plastic mouthpiece.

Next, in 1932 I sat in at Armonk's (N.Y.) Log Cabin, a huge roadhouse (old term for speakeasy out in the boonies), with Bill Whelpley's band which included Whelpley on violin, George Blum on trumpet, Ernie Harris on piano, Bill King on tuba and bass, and Reinhardt, Chubby Landis and Stewie Anderson on sax/clary. This date is firmly fixed as late Summer or early Fall of '32 by the fact that King and Anderson segued into the rehearsals for Charlie Barnet's first big band (yeah, he beat them all for mounting the first white swinging big band; Charlie then was a 17 years-old pothead fugitive from Moses Brown Prep in Providence, R.I.) which boasted the legendary Jack Purvis on trumpet and Scoops Thompson (he sold drugs by the scoopful!) on guitar. The two wildest dudes I ever met in the business. That band, by the way, opened the brand-new Paramount Hotel, owned by Charlie's family, on New Year's Eve of '32-'33 and lasted exactly one set. Barnet's mother, shocked to her socks by Purvis's romping charts, fired Charlie herself. I was sitting at Charlie's table and heard the conversation.

[Barnet, born October 1913, would have been 19 at that time; no matter - that doesn't spoil the story! - DC/BW.]

As for the Village Nut Club stint, I hung out over there, not only because George Stacy [no 'e'; the Monday night trumpet man at Nick's] and I roomed together then in the Village, but because I also knew Frank Orchard who played valve trombone, guitar and piano and also sang and M.C.'d. Frank's first move on that job was to seduce the hatcheck girl, Miriam, who was the owner's popsie. Then he plowed her into persuading The Op [the club operator, presumably - DC/BW] to fire Reinhardt and to hire Orchard as the leader. He installed a 2 1/2 times life-size photo blow up of himself at the club's street entrance and then topped himself by hiring Reinhardt as a sideman.

The sets were pure Mack Sennett. Frank would tinkle a piano intro, then switch to rhythm guitar for the opening chorus, grab his guitar and up to the mike to sing/play a chorus, then do the sock chorus on trombone lead and finally sprint back to the piano for the ending. Plus, of course, introductory blather.

Next, something of a conversation we had with Chuck Sweningsen at the 1994 IAJRC Convention:

I was assistant editor of *Down Beat* from '48 to '49, approximately a year, and I used to go to Jazz, Ltd. a lot because it was near where I lived at the YMCA and I could walk over there from the office. Muggsy was playing there during the time I was with *Down Beat*. If they didn't have enough paying customers to fill all the tables they'd let me sit at a table instead of standing at the little bar they had there. The musicians were expected to go and mingle with the audience. There wasn't any place else to go. There was a men's room and that was about it. But there was a little slip of a room behind the bandstand where you could get in sideways to put in instrument cases and coats and hats in wintertime. Incidentally, the men's room was the best place to hear the band. You could hear the piano real well. You couldn't hear it too well out in the audience.

When you worked at Jazz, Ltd. you really worked. They started at nine o'clock. They had a four o'clock licence and the last set would end about 3.30 except on Saturday nights when it would end a little after four o'clock as they had an extra hour's time on the licence.

Trumpeter Don Ingle, who worked at the second location (164 East Grand), underlined Chuck's closing remarks:

It was a hard band to stay on as Bill was a stern taskmaster and wanted everything played the same way every time. And the job was a marathon - six hours a night, five nights a week.
[...] The house policy: never, never, a woman at the bar, and no women un-escorted. Ties and jackets or no entry. No food served, just honest drinks. The club's small 'deuce' tables sometimes had six or seven people crammed around them. No monkey business. Ruth was known to toss out big burly guys who got disorderly. Short as she was, she simply cowed tough guys with her glare and her New York accent. One tough cookie she.
The tent cards on the tables said, 'We just played it' and 'The Saints is a $20 tune'. On the wall back of the band was a sign saying 'Peace,' with Yankee and Confederate emblems. Up front was Ziblid, the avant garde sculpture of a stylised broad with an outstretched arm. She was the only 'lady' allowed to stay up at the bar!
In the back was a small storage area where the band took breaks and played tonk, a card game. The bare walls were too much for my doodling nature to avoid using so, by the time I left, they were covered with cartoons and other sketches I made to pass the time between sets.
One night, Dick Gehman, writer for *New Yorker* and other magazines, came in and stayed all night and then every night for a week, telling us endless Eddie Condon stories. He was a regular whenever in town, as were Carl Sandberg, Tallulah Bankhead, Dan Dailey, Maurie Wills and many other American sports figures.
Pianist Dave Phelps was on the band earlier than listed [Summer 1969] then came back a second time. When I joined the band in March of 1963, Earl Washington was playing piano. Earl left and the band split the week with Art Hodes two nights and Dave Remington three nights.
Mike Parker replaced me late in August of 1963 when I went back to California to work with Matty Matlock and Rosy McHargue, so late Summer of '63 is correct. There were at least four other trumpeters in the interim before I returned but I only know of Norm Murphy for sure as one of them. Believe Freddy Greenleaf may also have been one of them - a fine Detroit player.
I returned to Jazz, Ltd. in early March of 1965 after the stint in LA with Rosy. Stayed on the band through Labor Day (first

Monday in September) of 1968. According to Ruth, I had the most accrued total time on the band of any trumpet man, just over four years.

The trumpet chair tended to be a revolving door. I stayed so long because my skin in thick and a steady gig is nice to have (until it's burn-out time). When I left I didn't touch a horn for nearly a year after, switching to my journalist hat after moving to Michigan.

Not listed was the Thursday off-night band. Art Hodes led it at one time, with Bobby Lewis, trumpet; Dan Williams, trombone; Jimmy Granato, clarinet; Earl Murphy, bass; Jerry Coleman, drums. Another Thursday band was led by Lil Armstrong with the same sidemen except Whitey Myrick on trumpet.

On the 45rpm recorded 1968, Joe Masek is listed as alto sax - should be tenor. Bill is listed for arranger for side 2, but I arranged the enlarged rubato beginning and ending for the added horns. No big deal, but it is one small correction. In my time with the band I added a few dozen charts and had written several for Bill as early as 1954.

Very appreciative of the article as is Jean, my wife. She worked for Ruth as a waitress when I played there and she and Ruth were good buddies.

Max Hook told us:

I put in something like five years altogether at Jazz, Ltd., adding up three or four stretches as resident pianist (to give it a high tone). I was on two albums. I remember quite distinctly the anxiety and fuss connected with the recording we did on which Norm Murphy was the trumpet. Not the session itself, but keeping him sober in the days leading up to it - and through the session. An eloquent jazz player but prone to succumb to the classic refuge of the 'Wicked Jazzman' - the ingestion of vast quantities of alcohol.

In the same vein, there was Dave Rasbury, who put in a long stretch at Jazz, Ltd. Trombone, of course, and dyed-in-the-wool trad player. Breakfast for Dave began with a shot and a beer and the day continued with the methodical consumption of beer, booze, pills, pot (as I remember) and tobacco.

Bill and Ruth ran a tight ship. Ruth was tireless in her role as co-owner and Maitre-D'. She was such a vital and dynamic person. The Reinhardts permitted no nonsense in their club. You came to hear the music, not to be rowdy and obnoxious. Customers were kept in their place. If they got out of line they were courteously but firmly shown the way out.

Among the many musicians I worked with at Jazz, Ltd., I particularly value Quinn Wilson, Doc Cenardo (who was responsible for getting me my first job there), Marty Marsala, and Freddy Kohlman. Quinn was such an accomplished bass man, brass and string, having worked a good part of his career with Earl Hines. I also had the opportunity to work briefly with Edmond Hall, during one of Bill's vacations, which was a great kick for me.

Jazz, Ltd. was, of course, a mecca or haven for traditional and mainstream jazz. I came into contact with musicians I might not otherwise have known — Art Hodes, Tut Soper, Red Nichols, Doc Evans are some names which come to mind.

A few oddments: George A Borgman's article on pianist Eddie Higgins in *The Mississippi Rag* of March 1996 mentions that Higgins was in the Monday off-night band in 1952. By November 1956 he was with Bill Reinhardt in the band five nights a week alongside Norm Murphy, Dave Remington and Freddie Moore. On March 24 the following year the band played a Sunday concert at the Civic Auditorium, La Porte, Indiana, with guest star Art Hodes. Higgins left Jazz, Ltd. shortly thereafter.

Brian Williams wrote that during a visit to the U.S. in 1965 he was in Chicago around 8-9 August and spent a very pleasant evening at Jazz, Ltd. The personnel on that occasion was: Don Ingle,t; Dave Rasbury, tb; Bill Reinhardt, cl; Earl Washington, p; Emmanuel Sayles, bj; Quinn Wilson, sb/bb; Freddie Kohlman, d.

Concerning the Solana Beach gig, Art Pilkington reminds us of an article about bassist Bob Finch in *The Mississippi Rag* for January 1994. In 1981 Finch was invited to bring a band into the Belly Up Tavern. He had Reinhardt front the band and Ruth suggested the band should be named the Chicago Six. The last Friday, at least, the band included Dick Cary and Johnny Varro and Reinhardt stayed for about six months. Bill Reinhardt remembers the Chicago Six (but doesn't recall Cary and Varro — 'two of my favorite people') and played with the band until 'found out by illness.'

Readers of *The Noel Coward Diaries*, edited by Graham Payn and Sheridan Morley, will relish the entry for 31 August 1947. He and Tallulah Bankhead watched Carmen Miranda's show at the Chez Paree and then went to two jazz clubs. He loathed them both. He concluded his entry for the day:

> We were driven back into Chicago and returned to a beastly little club and given a table right under the trumpet, whereupon I walked out and came home. I am forty-seven and sane.

Both George Snurpus and Al Jenkins believe this could well have been Jazz, Ltd. The chances are that the two clubs were the Blue Note and the Reinhardt venue.

In 1994, thirteen titles by Jazz, Ltd. bands were reissued on a Delmark CD, DE-226. These were the twelve from the sessions plus Bluin' The Blues, claimed to be previously unissued. In fact, it is the version of that tune made at the second session. There is a fourteenth track containing an interview with Bill and Ruth Reinhardt in which Ruth admits 'we were old-fashioned' and tells of how her ban on women wearing slacks came to be abandoned.

The CD notes contain fascinating memories by Jim Beebe and Wayne Jones of the club and of those who played there. Those recollections are a bonus adding to the fine music which we heartily commend.

Art Hodes' biography, *Hot Man*, has some interesting reminiscences about Jazz, Ltd. and Ruth Reinhardt. On the latter, Hodes underlines Don Ingle's description of the lady's toughness. Tough she certainly could be, but some correspondence and a telephone conversation in the 1970s revealed a helpful and charming person.

Word from Bill Reinhardt at the end of March '96 said, "I just sold my clarinet - after a long lay-off, too many notes in the clarinet part to try returning so I might have a go at valve-trombone (as you know, Brass is not new to me and I think I could manage the slower moving part)."

Seems there's no stopping Bill - he recently went to Milligan's in La Jolla and sang *Sister Kate* with the Bobby Gordon band! Nor must we forget that Harlow Atwood introduced Bill to his good friend Patricia and the pair of them happily married on 23 September 1994.

We sent a copy of the above to Bill Reinhardt. He enjoyed it and approved generally. However, he says that,

> ...the Nut Club experience (was done) briefly to help a friend. At that time, I had already enlisted in the navy and I was waiting for a call from them. Frank Orchard did ask me to come in and front the band and there lies a humorous tale. I arrived at the club opening night to find my name on the front of the marquee in lights. Not 'Bill Reinhardt' but 'Bill Rein' and the reason given me was that what with the war against Germany, Reinhardt sounded too German. They did subsequently change this. Meantime, I went to Nick's for Monday nights as relief band until the navy called me shortly thereafter. I never would appear as a sideman in the Nut Club.

Bill Reinhardt was playing in New Rochelle in the late 1930s when he was painted by an artist for the front page of *The Saturday Evening Post*. Bill was used as the model for the four musicians playing different instruments shown on the front page of the April 15, 1939 issue.

The Dotted Eighth label was a cooperative venture between the Reinhardts and H. Daniel Birchard of Indianapolis.

Bill Reinhardt was mugged (fractured pelvis and knife cut) in February 1998 while taking his daily constitutional. (*Rhythm & Blues*, Spring 2001)

Ruth Reinhardt was interviewed by Studs Terkel on his radio show on March 16, 1964. The interview is available on-line.

Dan Lipscomb: Talk about Two-Handed Piano

In the course of researching the career of Jess Stacy[1], I tried to contact other musicians who had been active in Chicago in the 1920s and 1930s. Early in 1982 I asked Chicago drummer and writer, Wayne Jones, about Dan Lipscomb, a Chicago pianist of long-standing, though known only for his participation in the 1928 Paramount recordings of Charles Pierce and his Orchestra. Wayne responded to my query by telephoning the Musicians Union (AFM Local 10) for Lipscomb's address. I wrote to Lipscomb – and I received a reply.

Here then is the text of the letter, sent from 10606 Mercury Drive, Apache Junction, AZ 85220, and dated May 4, 1982. It was written in reply to mine of April 3, 1982, in which I asked for any recollections he had of Jess Stacy and of the various clubs in Chicago in the 1930s.

> Dear Mr. Coller
> I had hoped to send you a typewritten copy of my discourse. My wife took my dictation in shorthand. Then we discovered that our typewriter is inoperative. She then had to transcribe her notes. We had them xeroxed but the copies did not turn out too well, so I am sending you the handwritten pages. This was quite a hassle and accounts for the delay in replying.
> I hope my remarks will be of some value to you.
> You would not know, of course, that I lost my eyesight about twenty years ago and gave up playing[2].
> I enjoyed hearing from you.
> Sincerely,
> Dan Lipscomb.

Attached were six lined pages, handwritten, with the following text:

> Jess Stacy has been my idol for many, many years. During the twenties and the early thirties, Jess was working in a band directed by Floyd Towne at The Midway Gardens[3], which was

only a few blocks from where I was working at the Pershing Ballroom. Our paths crossed quite often, but I never have known in detail about his playing engagements. These were things that musicians in those days seldom talked about. During this period, I cannot say exactly what date, there was a salute on radio to Bix Beiderbecke, who was the idol of all musicians. I turned on the show, not knowing that Jess was on the programme, and was surprised to hear him playing Bix's composition, "In A Mist", which he did beautifully.[4]

I made a record with Bix in the early thirties which was more or less a dud.

I recall meeting Jess one time at Wabash Avenue and Van Buren Street in Chicago's Loop, and he had his portable piano keyboard, which he carried with him always. He demonstrated it to me. At that time he was playing in a downtown Chinese restaurant. I lost track of him and haven't seen him since that time.[5]

I am sorry I can't tell you any more personal things about Jess. As you know, Jess is a very private person.

I will relate some of my personal experiences that I think will convey a more intimate impression of the times. During the early twenties I worked in a club owned by Al Capone. It was on Wabash Avenue and he visited the place practically every night in the week. I had an opportunity to meet real gangsters close up. The manager of the club was one of Capone's top lieutenants. I recall one night accompanying Sophie Tucker who was billed as "The Last of the Red Hot Mamas". She asked me to play "Some of These Days" in F sharp. The boys in the band all looked at each other as much as to say he can't play in that key, but she asked for F sharp and she got F sharp. I was a hero about the place for a few days.

I don't mean to insert myself in this rendition; I am only telling you these things because they are my own experiences.

I also played in a nightclub in Burnham, Illinois, a suburb just south of Chicago. Everything there was gangster controlled. I have often repeated this story about the time I worked in one of these joints. It involved another pianist named "Horsey" because he always sounded hoarse. A customer kept goading Horsey to play some more. It was after five o'clock in the morning. Horsey had played all night and was ready to leave. The customer kept insisting. The episode ended when Horsey pulled out a gun and shot the guy. He never served a day in jail because he worked for Al Capone.

I went to work one time in a small private home that they were using as a substitute for a saloon. They were serving near-beer or some kind of beer and whooping it up until all hours. I never did know who lived there or anything else about the circumstances, but I thought it was a strange place to be doing business. That was what prohibition was all about, illegal booze anywhere you could get it.

In another location in Burnham I worked for a married couple who had a small nightclub and the operation of the club was something else. They had one customer who was a meat packer. He went out there every six months. He would call to tell them he was coming and they would practically close the place to the public. There wasn't anyone there but the one customer, the hosts and the help.

The owner and the customer would shoot craps on a blanket. I heard one thousand, two thousand, three thousand. It was something. Then someone would say, "That's enough of this. Everybody back to the tables." Drinks were ordered, the band would play, the girls would resume singing and the festivities would go on until no one could sit up or stand up any longer. Then the hosts would put the meat packer to bed. His visits usually lasted three or four days, perhaps a week. When he had had his fill he would call a cab and go back home. Then the club would reopen to the public.

I would like to tell you that in those days musicians did not quit their jobs. They sold them. The job would be worth as much as the "take" in the kitty. You could sell a job to anyone who was looking for a change.

You have probably seen "The Untouchables", the old television series starring Robert Stack as Elliott Ness, the government agent who led his forces against the mobsters and the speakeasies they operated throughout Chicago and the outlying areas. It was a very lively time and this series tells it like it was. It is still being shown here on late TV.

Getting back to the episode which involved "Horsey", I knew about it because I was subbing for him at the time.

D.N.L

The following month I wrote to Lipscomb, thanking him for his helpful letter and also requesting some biographical details and perhaps a photograph. Unfortunately, there was no reply.

Howard Rye's delving into the archives (draft registrations, census returns, local newspapers) has provided a wealth of material about Daniel Norwood Lipscomb and his family, with surprising results. There is also some information about musical activity.

Dan Lipscomb was the youngest of three sons born to Daniel and Mary Lipscomb, who were married January 25, 1882 and resided at 210 Covington Street, Crawfordsville City, Indiana. The children were Roy Francis (born April 6, 1887), Clarence Pearl (born January 20, 1894) and Daniel Norwood (born December 8, 1896). Their race was stated to be black. Roy's 1917 draft registration lists him as a barber, married, Caucasian.[6] [Crawfordsville City is 152 miles south of Chicago.]

June 1, 1913 – Jackson orchestra to play for 66th anniversary of Crawfordsville church. Personnel James Wooden, J.W. Hall, coronet (sic), Norwood Lipscomb, trombone, Eugene Jackson, violin; Mrs. Eugene Jackson, Italian harp.[7]

1916: Daniel Norwood Lipscomb listed as a Junior at Wabash College, Crawsfordville. And a joint winner of the Sophomore Declamation Contest.[8]

On February 23, 1917, D. Norwood Lipscomb of Wabash College was scheduled to speak on the subject of "War and Peace" at the annual Indiana State oratorical contest in Indianapolis. [9]

June 5, 1917 – Draft Registrations for Daniel Norwood, 21, student, and Clarence Pearl, 23, musician "employed in public", list both as single. Daniel is "African," Clarence is "Negro".

June 13, 1917: Daniel Norwood Lipscomb received diploma from Wabash College, and honoured among Day Triangular Intercollegiate Debaters and as a representative in the Intercollegiate Oratorical Contest. [10]

November 12, 1918 – Privates First Class Clarence P. Lipscomb and Daniel N. Lipscomb, of Base Hospital 10, was due to sail on the Empress of Asia from Hoboken, New Jersey.[11]

June 7, 1919 – was the date of sailing for the MSS Matsonia, from France (St. Nazaire) to New York. Pfcs Daniel Lipscomb and Clarence Lipscomb were among the passengers.[12]

January 22, 1920: the family was still residing at 210 Covington Street, Crawfordsville City, IN. Dan (barber, shop) and Mary, Clarence P. & Daniel N., (both listed as "musician. Orchestra"). The census shows the family as "White".[13]

By 1923 the family had moved to 592 Ingraham Avenue, Hammond, Indiana. Daniel Sr was shown as "watchman"; his sons were employed at American Steel Foundries, Daniel Jr. as a clerk.[14]

This was Dan Lipscomb's home until at least 1941. Hammond, in addition to being a major steel manufacturing town in that period, was only 21 miles south of a major jazz centre, Chicago.

One could speculate that Lipscomb worked as a professional pianist between about 1920 and 1928 – at least some of the time.

Ingraham Avenue would have been in West Hammond, and in 1924 that community voted to become Calumet City, Illinois.

1926: Daniel Sr listed as "foundry worker"; Clarence as Salesman, Ritter Music Co.; and Daniel Jr. as musician. At the same address.[15]

1928: At same address. Daniel Sr. labourer, Clarence, driver, Prosperity Cleaners and Dryers, Daniel N. clerk, American Steel Foundries.[16]

February-April, 1928: recordings with Charles Pierce and his Orchestra.

February 23, 1929 – Dan Lipscomb played and sang at birthday party arranged by Mr. & Mrs. Phil Novak of 17th Street, Hammond.[17]

1930 Census (April 12, 1930) gives the family living at 592 Ingraham Avenue: Daniel (barber, retired) and Mary Lipscomb, Roy (barber, private firm), Clarence (salesman, jewels) and Daniel (secretary, brokage).

September 5, 1931 – Dan Lipscomb and his brother Clarence, Hammond musicians, were slightly injured Saturday night in an auto accident when they were returning from Cedar Lake where they had been playing. A passing motorist sideswiped their car and forced them into a ditch.[18]

1935: same address; Daniel (barber) and Mary Lipscomb; Roy (barber), Clarence (beer tavern), Daniel (clerk).[19]

1937: same address: Clarence now shown as a cook. Neither Mary nor Daniel Norwood are listed.[20]

[It seems reasonable to assume that Mary Lipscomb died in about 1936; Daniel Sr. about 1938, and that Daniel Jr. married the same year.]

1939: 592 Ingraham Avenue is now shown as home of Daniel N. Lipscomb Jr (clerk), his wife Thelma, and (no doubt) son Daniel Lipscomb.[21]

February 17, 1939 – Dan Lipscomb "played several selections on the piano" at a fathers and sons banquet sponsored by the

Methodist Brotherhood of the East Chicago Methodist Church, Hammond, Indiana.[22]

1941: 592 Ingraham Avenue is home to Daniel (steel worker) & Thelma, and Daniel.[23]

April 27, 1942: Draft registration confirms address and name of wife, giving employer as Youngstown Sheet & Tube Co., East Chicago Lake, Indiana. The report gives Daniel Norwood Lipscomb as white, 5'8" and 165-lbs.

February 9, 1943 "piano selections were given by Dan Lipscomb" during a Lions Party dinner party at the First Methodist Church in Hammond, Indiana.[24]

c. 1978 moved to Apache Junction, Arizona.

January 1986: Daniel Lipscomb of Apache Junction, Arizona, died. [25]

The Chicago AFM reported that Lipscomb had been in Apache Junction since 1978. It was about 1970 that Wayne Jones last saw Lipscomb. "It has been about 12 or 13 years since I saw him. He was surely in his late 60s then, although quite vigorous and vital."

It is intriguing that Roy Lipscomb was passing as white as early as 1917, but the other members of the family did not do so until 1920.

The only known Lipscomb recordings are the seven Paramount titles by Charles Pierce and his Orchestra, recorded in Chicago at three sessions in early 1928. These were a source of confusion for some years. Paramount 12640 contained *Jazz Me Blues* and *Sister Kate*, one pressing using these titles from a session with Muggsy Spanier and Frank Teschemacher, another a session with Charles Altiere, cornet, and Maurie Bercov, clarinet. It is said that there are only two known copies of take -7. Fortunately there have been LP and CD releases of all the takes listed below.

The details are:

CHARLES PIERCE AND HIS ORCHESTRA

(Muggsy Spanier, Dick Fiege, co; Frank Teschemacher, cl; as-1; Charles Pierce, as; Ralph Rudder, ts; Dan Lipscomb, p; Stuart Branch, bj; Johnny Mueller, sbs; Paul Kettler, d).

Chicago – February 1928

20399-1	Bull Frog Blues	Paramount 12619
20400-3	China Boy -1	Paramount 12619

(Charlie Altiere, co; Maurie Bercov, cl, as; Pierce, as; Rudder, ts; Lipscomb, p; Branch, bj; Mueller, bbs; Kettler, d).

Chicago - March 1928

20469-3	Jazz Me Blues	Paramount 12640
20470-4	Sister Kate	Paramount 12640

(Spanier, co; Jack Reid, tb; Teschemacher, cl, as-1; Pierce, as; Rudder, ts; Lipscomb, p; Branch, bj; Mueller, sbs, bbs-2; Kettler, d.)

Chicago - April 1928

20469-5	Jazz Me Blues -1	Paramount 12640
20470-7	Sister Kate	Paramount 12640
20534-2	Nobody's Sweetheart -1,-2	Paramount 20616

In addition to the oddity of the same titles being recorded in March and April and being released with the same catalogue number, it is strange that there were changes to the routines. The March titles run for three or more minutes, whereas those from April are down to 2:20. *Jazz Me Blues* follows the same lines, though with each section and solo shortened and with variations in the final choruses. The changes to *Sister Kate,* which is taken at a nice steady tempo, are more evident, with the added trombonist taking the opening solo. There are differences in the opening and closing ensembles and in the placing of the various breaks.

The difference between Spanier and Altiere is quite marked, of course, but Bercov does well in the Teschemacher role. All versions make effective use of stop-time choruses.

Lipscomb's only heard contribution, on *Sister Kate,* is interesting. His solo on take -7, though brief, does differ in approach to the better and longer solo on take -4. Although it may be unfair to judge a musician on the basis of a chorus or two, it does suggest that he would have been worth hearing at greater length. Certainly Wayne Jones thought so. He said, "Jesus, he was *really good.* Talk about *Twohanded piano!*"

The John Steiner Archives at the University of Chicago no doubt contain more information. Any member in the Chicago area who wished to pursue this would be looking for Box 125, Folder 5, and Box 179, Folder 8.

Bert Whyatt, in his notes to "The Recordings: Muggsy Spanier 1924-1928," (Retrieval FJ-108) refers to Dan Lipscomb confirming that Charlie Altiere played cornet with Charles Pierce for Paramount. It seems likely that this quote came via John Steiner.

Sources:

1 Jess Stacy: *The Quiet Man of Jazz* (Jazzology Press, 1997)
2 Wayne Jones last saw Lipscomb c. 1970, presumably before Lipscomb's sight failed. Perhaps "almost twenty years ago" was an approximation.
3 Stacy was at the Midway Gardens with Town(e) from c. January 1927 to mid-1928,
4 Stacy is known to have played *In A Mist* on Benny Goodman Camel caravan broadcast of September 6, 1938.
5 Stacy is known to have played two Chinese restaurants in 1929.
6 1910 Census
7 *Indianapolis Recorder*, May 31, 1913
8 *The Annual Catalogue*, 1916
9 *Indianapolis Star*, February 22, 1917
10 *Indianapolis Star*, June 14, 1917
11The National Archives at College Park, MD.
12 Ibid
13 1920 Census
14 *Hammond City Directory*, 1923
15 *Hammond City Directory*, 1926
16 *Hammond City Directory*, 1928
17 *Lake County Times*, February 25, 1929
18 *The Munster Times*, September 8, 1931
19 *Hammond City Directory*, 1935
20 *Hammond City Directory*, 1937
21 *Hammond City Directory* 1939
22 *Hammond Times*, February 28, 1939
23 *Hammond City Directory*, 1941
24 *Hammond Times*, February 11, 1943
25 U.S. Social Security Death Index

Frank Chace: Chicago Clarinet

The name may not be too familiar, if at all. We had been aware of Frank Chace's jazz clarinet on records for several years but only comparatively recently did it dawn that his playing was rather special. Touches of Frank Teschemacher and a lot of Pee Wee Russell and a great deal of attention to the melody line. All of which is important. Then there's his ease in ensemble and his flowing solos and clean, comfortable sound. Pianist Butch Thompson, also a clarinettist, put it very well,

> Chace is the kind of player for whom the phrase 'musician's musician' seems to have been coined. His obvious reverence for Russell is tempered by great intelligence, and like Pee Wee he has technique, lyricism and sheer nerve to spare. His is serious playing that rewards serious listening. On top of that, Chace swings.

Chace didn't gain an entry in Chilton because he was born after 1920 and Grove missed him completely so it became necessary, as always, to discover something about him. Not just recorded work but about his life in music and perhaps even about his life. Scattered in time came morsels and bigger bites but not getting very far until news of Frank's death stirred belated progress. He once asked 'Have I become something of a cult figure? Marty Grosz suggested long ago that our "tawdry efforts" [on records] might become known to a few people - as few as collectors of 18th century pewter.'

Frank Chace was born in Chicago on July 22, 1924, and 'picked up clarinet in 1947 after army service to see whether I could find out what that incredible pied piper was up to.' That 'pied piper' was Pee Wee Russell, of course. Chace had a year at Yale and then was drafted. In 1943 the army sent him to Los Angeles, where he did a nine month course at UCLA, and first heard Russell in a record shop.

> In those days you could listen in a booth. They had some Commodores and I got the impression that these were the real

Frank Chace, 1964. (Courtesy Wayne Jones)

jazz guys and even if you didn't know what the hell was going on you should listen until you did. And I remember the first one; I saw "Pee Wee, clarinet" and didn't know which, who, where it was. I think it was either Tappin' The Commodore Till or Life Spears A Jitterbug. He plays some kind of introduction or something and I didn't know what it was. He did it in his most extreme manner, of course. After a while the Commodores got through to me.

He had copies sent home to Chicago and

... listened to them on furlough and found that I'd memorized all his playing.
There were other delights. In '43 during my magical stay in LA I heard Joe Sullivan and Big Joe Turner at the Sewannee [sic] Inn on the north side. The buddy I was with told me to ask Joe Sullivan to play Peg O' My Heart; he actually played it for me! I learned later how he was with requests, I remember, at the Hangover in 'Frisco and other places, he was pretty brusque with requests. But that's all right, he's a great guy! Eddie Miller and Nappy Lamare came in to visit him when we were there. LA was like a little village to me, somehow. A little entertainment village, like everybody knew each other and had a fine time. Bob Zurke at the Hangover Club, just a few steps away from NBC, where all those wonderful radio programmes took place with the orchestras featuring jazz musicians.
Then, luckily, I got stationed at Fort Monmouth, New Jersey, in '45, so a half hour by Pennsylvania Railroad into Penn Station and the subway down to Nick's every night. At Nick's it was the Muggsy Spanier band: Joe Grauso, Bob Casey, Gene Schroeder, Miff Mole, Spanier and Pee Wee. I thought Pee Wee understood the universe and accepted it all. I thought he was the great mentor. I saw Pee Wee with his button eyes, his amused and amusing stare over the audience and what came out of his horn was unbelievable. Still is. I've no idea how he did it. None. The army sent me to New York in '45 and I heard, for example, at Town Hall a recreation of four tunes from the Strut Miss Lizzie date. The only substitution was Schroeder for Bushkin. I'd virtually memorized those Eddie Condon 1938 records while on furlough and then hearing them, another version, live like that! A tremendous thrill for me.

Chace started to play clarinet when he got home after the war.

One became available to me from an old high school buddy and I only picked it up because of curiosity to see what Russell was doing.' He played 'a little flute' in what they now call middle school and he later regretted quitting because 'I lost all the high school years of music education that I might have learned for free. No, I only picked up clarinet after Pee Wee inoculated me, he kind of poisoned me or whatever you call it.'

By 1951 he was on his way to that target and took part in a recording session at Princeton with a band including multi-instrumentalist John Dengler and guitarist Marty Grosz. A somewhat rare 10" vinyl eventually resulted. Around this time, Grosz recalled,

> A bunch of us played at a bar called the Rathskellar off Fordham Road in the Bronx, NY. I was not the leader. In fact there was no set leader. I persuaded Dante Bolletino who had the Jolly Roger label to record us.

Chace, Grosz, Dengler with pianist Dick Wellstood and others recorded, at Dengler's insistence, at New York's Steinway Hall. 'They came out on Jolly Roger as Marty Grosz and his Cellar Boys', said Grosz, 'first because we did them in a cellar and we were thinking of Wingy Manone and his Cellar Boys too. But Pops Foster had the biggest name among us so, when Danny Bolletino got chastened there, he reissued them as Pops Foster and his Big Eight on his newly-named label Pax, which was LP. The originals were 78s so I bridged that gap.' Chace, years later, declared it represented "the nadir of recorded music'.

Chace meeting Marty Grosz was of benefit to both men. Grosz told Martin Richards,

> I met a clarinet player named Frank Chace in Evanston and we got together. He took me to his house and gave me an education in jazz. Up until then I'd had certain likes but he really gave me an education. He played Pee Wee Russell and Frank Teschemacher for me, which stayed with me for the rest of my life because they are probably my two favourite clarinet players, and some of my favourite jazz. He played me the Pee Wee solo on One Hour; he was crazy about it. Over and over, I mean, twenty times in a row! And then we'd go out and clear our heads and take a walk and come back and he'd play it some more. He'd discovered

that quirky, sawtooth kind of thing and I was under the spell. We would sit for hours and hours in his apartment and then afterwards we'd sometimes go down and play with Lee Collins. We'd sit in and dream.

Early in November that year Chace was working in a band led by Wild Bill Davison at George Wein's *Storyville* Club at the Buckminster in Boston's Copley Square.

I wasn't supposed to be in a band with Davison at *Storyville*. I went up there with the Johnny Windhurst gang, but once getting there learned that Windhurst and Bill simply traded places at Condon's and *Storyville* for a couple of weeks. So the third week Windhurst came up and played with what presumably was his band.

In 1956 Savoy Records issued eight titles taken from airchecks with three more added on another compilation some years later. Another thirty years on Chace played in New York with Davison at George Wein's Carnegie Hall concert. He was introduced as Frank 'Chance'. Chace thought that Davison 'just strung together phrases without much relevance to the song'.

The years of delay from recording to producing a disc was repeated in the spring of 1952. Chace was in the band with trumpeter Jack Ivett and pianist Don Ewell at the Barrel Club in St Louis. Lee Collins replaced Ivett and then Dewey Jackson came in. College student Bob Koester - later the proprietor of the Jazz Record Mart - was there and 'He and his pals barged in one Saturday night, took over the front table and recorded us. Neither we nor the boss wanted any part of it. Koester said he couldn't issue the recordings because Dewey Jackson's wife wouldn't allow it for some reason.' Over fifty years later, Koester issued eight tracks when technology enabled a labour of love to sufficiently improve quality for a Delmark compact disc.

Soon after that St Louis gig he was in Europe

As a ringer in the Amherst College Dixieland Five to entertain US Army troops around the continent. I remember the views from the boat-train, Harwich-London from The Hook Of Holland. I visited England only briefly but yearn, like Bud Freeman, for the English countryside.

Chace returned from Europe.

It must have been around September 1952. Luckily Pee Wee was there at Terassi's. Dicky Wells, he could break your heart, Joe Sullivan, Walter Page and George Wettling. The trumpet was a fat Jimmy McPartland. Jimmy would stand there, holding his horn over his belly, and Pee Wee and Dicky would be playing things that he had no idea what the hell they were doing. It was great fun.

Inevitably, Chicago remained Chace's base and he worked and recorded in 1954 with trumpeter Natty Dominque and trombonist Floyd O'Brien. Four tunes appeared on one side of a long-play and the performances match the band's title: New Orleans Six. Chace is a generation younger than most of the others but that doesn't seem to have troubled him and his too-few solo spots meld well in being rather less than his usual Russell and leaning towards Dodds. Not surprising because, as Hal Smith recalled, "Chace once admonished me for what he considered to be an incomplete list of favourite clarinettists. 'What? No Johnny Dodds or Omer Simeon in your hegemony?'"

Marty Grosz recalled that

After I was discharged from the army in 1954 I visited Chicago and stayed for 21 years. Frank and I played with Sid Dawson's Riverboat Ramblers in Toronto and in Columbus and Dayton, Ohio.

Then there was the long-lived Salty Dogs. With a varying personnel down the years, the Dogs recorded often. In 1955 there was a session where Chace was the clarinettist and, despite his doubts, in very fine form. We had a forty years wait - yes, yet another - until Windin' Ball put much of the session on a compact disc. The repertoire more than hints at an admiration for the Watters/Murphy jazz revival of the time. Chace wasn't entirely happy.

It's a different style of music, it's really not mine. I was fighting for my life. Those guys were pretty relentless. It was hard work. For the recording I stood a little closer to the mike. Trumpeter and record producer Birch Smith was hooked on the one-microphone theory, derived from William Russell of New Orleans, and in self-defence I stood a little in front of the band so that's why I'm a little over-recorded.

Down the years, Chace worked at Salty Dogs engagements as a substitute for regular clarinet man Kim Cusack. Drummer Wayne Jones said

> We were all in awe of Frank and, at the same time, delighted with our good fortune to know him and to have him on our bandstand, wherever it was. You did not dare take your ears off him and I like to think he made us all play better. I believe we all thought of him as superman. Even if he didn't like a tune or what someone in the band was doing, he'd just jump in. Pee Wee could be ornery and show his disdain but Frank would save the day!

Looking back years later, Chace commented,

> They had a fiftieth reunion at Purdue university last fall, 1997, but I didn't go. I was a ringer; the band started at Purdue and a number of Purdue guys are still in. I kind of walked off the band in '69. They had some terrible players in it and I just gave up on it.

Much more in Chace's preferred way was a session with pianist Dave Remington's Chicago Jazz Band. Marty Grosz noted that 'Dave's tastes were somewhat more "modern" than ours' but it is evident from his solos on such as Royal Garden Blues how happy he was. The band swings hard with verve and evident enjoyment of the repertoire. The coda to How Come You Do Me Like You Do says that theirs is the Condon way. Despite Grosz's mild reservations, the following spring, much the same line-up but with various pianists was at the Red Arrow in Stickney. Another good gig saved on disc was Chace's appearance as a guest at the Walker Art Centre in Minneapolis during the summer of 1957. He played both clarinet and bass saxophone with leader Doc Evans, a cornet player dedicated to classic jazz who rarely left his home city. Four titles were included in a three-disc album on the Soma label. I Found A New Baby gave Chace room for two solo choruses and then on At The Jazz Band Ball and his sparkling form is highlighted in the last chorus.

Marty Grosz was working in Chicago and area in the late 1950s and Chace was brought in from time to time. Inevitably, much was taped and, inevitably, finally got on to disc. One such was the Honoris Causa (work it out for yourself) band which devoted much time and labour on a batch of tunes associated with Bix Beiderbecke. All in good time, these appeared on an Empirical LP, then on Riverside and recently on a Good Time Jazz CD and all entitled Hooray for Bix! That the band rehearsed carefully is apparent and the results are a beautiful tribute. Chace doubles on baritone sax and his clarinet is wonderful on **Sorry** and that is but an example. Some of the unused takes turned up in England, along with other Grosz/Chace oddments, on John R T Davies's Ristic label.

Singer Lee Wiley was in Chicago in the August of 1959. A great favourite with jazz musicians - she recorded with Condon-ites, for instance - she was persuaded to spend time over a couple of days recording with some of the enthusiasts at Bill Priestley's home. Frank Chace was there with his clarinet sounding blissful on such as Hot House Rose. One hopes that some of these will be issued eventually.

During the 1950s there was an attempt to revive the atmosphere of the Prohibition Era speakeasies. Crowded long-bar, drinks, cigarette smoke, music and maybe a little space for dancing was what promoter Burton Browne aimed at creating in his Gaslight Clubs. Marty Grosz recalled, 'I got a job at the Gaslight Club in Chicago. In 1957 Frank Chace got the job on clarinet and got me on it. The piano player was Jess Sutton... he wasn't so much a jazz player but he could read anything you put in front of him.' Grosz told Martin Richards:

This was a key club in those days. You couldn't buy liquor on credit so you called it a private club and charged two or five bucks for a key and that made you a member. The tips were very good and it was good for the chops because we had to play long hours and there were only the three of us. We had to play all the Dixieland tunes; all the strains and everything! I used to have to do the drum tags at the end on the banjo. After five years, I'd had it with that. It was a manic atmosphere and I was drinking heavily every night. What we'd do is take a benny, you know, Benzedrine, so we'd stay peppy and then you could drink. You were wired and you could throw down the booze. I think Frank stayed about a year. The piano player we had used to play the melody along with Frank and it drove him nuts. He stood it as long as he could.

Perhaps that year was extended because in 1959 Marty Grosz was engaged to form a band which would provide a version of the jazz everyone believed personified the era. John Dengler recalled

I received a telephone call from Marty Grosz who was then working with a trio at the Gaslight Club. The proprietor wanted to use Marty as a keystone for several LPs, to be issued as the sort of thing representative of the Gaslight. He wanted at least six men and insisted on Frank Chace and Don Ewell and asked my help in filling out the band.

He brought in Eddie Condon-related musicians: trumpeter Max Kaminsky, Cutty Cutshall for the trombone and Gene Schroeder at the piano. Schroeder played evening sessions while Don Ewell, then in New York with Jack Teagarden, did the afternoon batches. Frank Chace - 'Last of the "hot" Chicago-style clarinettists' according to some sleeve notes - completed the front line. Grosz, in another interview, spoke of his twenty years in that city when he and Chace worked in the Gaslight there. 'They had a little room called the Speakeasy Room where the piano player wore a Keystone Kops uniform and they have a telephone booth you go through and you have to say "Joe sent me" and they had girls dressed up as flappers.' Recently Grosz said that

The Gaslight recordings were a disappointment to all of us. I had written little charts and spent hours picking our repertoire. For example, for an LP to be entitled Roaring Twenties At The Gaslight, I had selected tunes by Gershwin, Armstrong, Morton, Ellington, etc. At the last minute, as we were warming up in the studio, a messenger came from the boss, Sid Fry, a man of unquenchable mercenary proclivities, bearing a list of public domain tunes published before 1923 for which he needn't pay composer royalties. And so the sessions went.

From all of which it appears that Chace and Grosz spent much of a week in New York taking part in the recordings and the Chicago club managing without them the while. There were nine sessions over a five-day spell when the band recorded two dozen tunes which fitted the usually-held thinking of the days many decades before: show songs, sentimental ballads, something saying 'the good ol' South', even the comic Yes, We Have No Bananas, and all played in a rousting jazzy way. Grosz playing his banjo and John

Dengler's bass saxophone or brass bass added 'authenticity' and the records still remain listenable today, if hardly deep jazz, fifty years on. Grosz remembered

> Throughout the sixties Frank played jobs with various leaders. I managed to get Frank onto a band called Frank Hubbell's Village Stompers; dreadful, but it was work. This must have been around 1963. We toured westward of Chicago, winding up in Aspen, Colorado. Often we were together. I have photos of us clowning. And we met frequently at Bill Priestley's house in Lake Forest to play, often with visiting jazz players.

From that period came a session for the Chicago Historical Society in April 1964, with a band including pianist Tut Soper. But the next to appear on disc was made in Mendota, Minnesota, at the Emporium of Jazz in 1967. This was a roadhouse previously used as the Rampart Street Club by cornetist Doc Evans. In its thirty years it welcomed many great jazz musicians and they included, that April, trombonist Jimmy Archey - his last known gig - and pianist Don Ewell. The underappreciated Bill Price played comet and Chace completed the front line. At least forty numbers were taped. In 2002 - yet another long delay - twenty-five were put onto a two-CD set by George Buck. The music is of the to-be-expected twenties/ thirties standards, mostly very well played with the occasional clinker and Chace sometimes a little off-mike but all highly enjoyable.

At an undefined period in 1967, Chace was working in Aspen again where he was an unheralded member of the Village Stompers at the Jerome Hotel. Bob Wilber, Lou McGarity and Pee Wee Erwin flew in for a concert and hung around for a day or two. "Sometimes Frank and I would repair to Sunny's Rendezvous after work to sit in with Ralph" is how Grosz remembers it. That November, Chace was at RCA's Chicago studio with Marty Grosz and trumpeter Norman Murphy and others of the current scene including drummer Barrett Deems. Apparently intended for the Victor label, the nine titles cut still haven't seen release. The same could probably have been the case for another session that year but Vanguard had no fear and issued a dozen songs by folk singer Jim Kweskin accompanied by a jazz band including Chace. His solo on Memphis Blues wouldn't have disgraced his idol. Fellow reed player Kim Cusack said, "Frank sounds absolutely marvellous on that recording and leaves everyone in his dust. His solo on You're Not The Only Oyster ... is as inventive and creative a piece of music that ever was and a joy to listen to."

Work became patchy and Chace took employment with a company producing audio-visual training materials. He remembered that

> Bill Riddle called me in nineteen-seventy-something to play at Blues Alley in Washington. I had just taken a day job and I couldn't do it, but it would have been with Ewell and I would have loved to have done it.

Drummer Hal Smith and pianist Butch Thompson travelled to Libertyville in Illinois in April 1985 for an afternoon concert for the Good Time Jazz Club that featured Frank Chace. Butch Thompson was the leader and left his clarinet at home so that Chace would be the featured clarinettist. Similarly, John Otto, also an excellent clarinettist, played only alto sax at the concert. Two tunes were solos by Chace with the rhythm section and, in Anything For You, with Sweet Lorraine, well and truly make the highlights of at least the issued tracks. Smith returned two years later leading his Chicago Loopers with Chace again present. 'Those sessions were two of the highlights of my musical career! Frank was one of my heroes on clarinet.'

In June of 1986 a New York concert included a Chicago Jazz Summit band. Some of the musicians - Yank Lawson, Eddie Miller - hardly fitted that jazz category but Chace and others certainly did. Only one title, At The Jazz Band Ball, from the batch made was included on the Atlantic label. Chace seems not to have been excited by this, saying a dozen years later, 'I never bothered to listen to it.'

By 1998, Chace had more or less given up playing, saying he hadn't opened his clarinet case since 1996, when he played at the Chicago Jazz Festival. He continued,

> My horn is in tune now. For about thirty years it wasn't. My problem with that was innocence. I only learned a few years ago that if you leave the horn in the case a lot, the little micro-critters get in the pads and kind of tend to make them porous. I got my horn re-padded and I'm in clover.

Chicago record producer and store owner Bob Koester mounted one of his Sunday affairs on September 2, 2001: 'JRM [Jazz Record Mart] helps celebrate the Chicago Jazz Festival'. The then current Salty Dogs were featured and another band, a quintet including Chace, played a set. Wayne Jones was present and noted, 'I replaced the drummer for the last tune of that set. It was an experiment/trial to see if that grouping would work as Frank's band for the purpose of recording. Not bad but would need arrangements, planning and prep' to produce a good CD. Frank sounded not the least dimmed by the passing years and, apart from the all-grey hair, looked pretty much the same too; still not knowing what to do when not playing and looking mildly uncomfortable'.

Chace listened to many other reed players.

On the radio today I heard Muggsy and Teschemacher on There'll Be Some Changes Made. It still resonates for me. Tesch has such clarity, too, his sound is so bright, I can't believe it. I always had trouble with those descending phrases of Teschemacher's with Red Nichols, One Step To Heaven.

On such as Mezz Mezzrow, he had problems. He had some of the King Jazz Bechet-Mezzrow records.

I even like Mezzrow. No, I don't. His solo on Royal Garden Blues is probably the worst solo ever perpetrated on record. He just runs triads or some damned thing.

He admired Lester Young and liked to tell of his encounter with him in 1957 in Pres's hotel room in Indianapolis where he was playing at a club and Pres was in town with a non-JATP package tour. The drummer, Buddy Smith, in the band Frank was part of, suggested they pay a visit after the gig and when they got there Frank hung back while the others gathered around Pres. Noticing this behaviour, he beckoned Frank to come closer, addressing him softly as 'long-distance man'.

Larry Kart, a friend, who recounts that anecdote, says

Frank loved 'sheets of sound' Coltrane as much as he loved Pee Wee. I have a tape I made, in the mid 1970s I think, of Frank rehearsing with pianist Bob Wright where, among other things, they play superbly Trane's Lazy Bird and Dameron's If You Could See Me Now.

Chuck Nessa, another friend, tells of

the first time I met Frank was 1966 in the Jazz Record Mart where I was working. I knew him by reputation only and was thrown when he asked to hear Coltrane's Out Of This World. In a way it seemed an alternate universe had opened up.

He enjoyed Bob Wilber's playing;

I remember one morning going downtown and picking up Bob Wilber and Ralph Sutton and hauling them up to Bill Priestley's for R and R. I think they were with the World's Greatest Jazz Band at the time. I played John Coltrane's Lush Life for them and they were both horrified and angry. It really perplexed me. I didn't play the other side of the LP with three piano-less tracks because of Sutton, but Wilber complained bitterly how the piano player didn't know it and Coltrane played it wrong and missed Strayhorn's intent. But then, after listening the whole way through he kind of grudgingly agreed that he could play his instrument, Coltrane could, pretty good. I guess he is kind of particular. I'm not an intimate of his but I've run across him a few times. He's certainly a talented fellow.

Like so many other musicians, Chace had a period when he drank too much alcohol. Recalled is a session including such as Tom Pletcher and Bill Priestley when 'Chace got so drunk he fell off his chair without playing a note'. In June 1998 Chace said

I haven't been able to drink since '82, and the only fun I had listening to my own playing was when I was stoned, so you know it's rather hard. But the older stuff, some of it I can listen to.

Asked how he viewed audiences who don't listen but applaud, he thought it awful.

I hate applause after solos, anyway. Most of the musicians seem to treat jazz as an athletic contest. You know, trying to see who can jump the farthest, the highest, get the most applause. It's just absurd.'

By now it appears that Chace was in a depressed period and noted that his friend Grosz was somewhat that way too.

Get a job maybe every five years and you don't know who to play with and what songs to play. I wrote Marty that I'd been invited up to Milwaukee to hear one of their Dixieland party things and I told him I didn't want to do it. I'd probably be envious of all those fast clarinet players, except when they grin their appreciation at each other as each was trying to see who could pee the farthest.

He was 'horrified at recent trends' and unsettled about the Government, the Senate and the Constitution. He was reading a great deal and, among others, had discovered Kingsley Amis and Philip Larkin. He agreed that the latter was 'not far wrong' in thinking that the Rhythmakers records were a pinnacle of achievement while 'I know Amis regretted never being able to meet Russell. I think his last visit was '59 or something and he visited Condon's. Pee Wee wasn't there and he regretted missing the chance.'

Chace's health became patchy. Michael Steinman spoke with him briefly in September 1998 and he wasn't feeling well. 'He sounded deathly ill.' The following February, he told of going to the hospital to which his physician was attached.

But I never saw him. I remember paying off the cabby somewhere near the emergency room, and that's the last I remember. I don't remember going in any door. They found me on the floor. I woke up at the rehab place thirteen blocks away. I got this on account of a horsefly bite at the beach.

Six months later, Chace was coughing and blamed a 'bronchial thing' he couldn't get rid of.

This is a hangover from the tracheotomy they gave me. They told me I had a scar tissue there and that prevents me from shaking this thing off. I had cellulitis and the doctor told me that was only a start. Then I had kidney failure too and two weeks of dialysis and liver failure.

He recovered from all that and Bob Koester reported,

Vital clarinettist Frank Chace is back in action and we're hoping to get him in the studio soon. His Tesch - Pee Wee style of bitchy clarinet is all too rarely heard. When he comes into the Jazz Mart he's as likely to buy a Coltrane album as a Lee Wiley and will cut his first session for Delmark in June.

Wayne Jones says that, in truth, it didn't take place. However, he was well featured in a 2001 Sunday session at the Mart to

'Celebrate the Chicago Jazz Festival' along with the long-running, but often changed line-up, Salty Dogs with whom he had often appeared down the years.

Larry Kart told of visiting Chace at Christmas time in 2007:

> I paid a visit to Frank on Wednesday. Though he was not in good shape physically, worse off than he had been the week before, I was surprised that he had gone downhill so rapidly from there. On the other hand, Frank definitely knew that there was no way back for him from where he was. He was still all there mentally, remembering incidents from the fairly distant past with photographic detail and abundant, wry (sometimes caustic) wit.

Frank Chace, described in his *Chicago SunTimes* obituary as 'a staple on the Chicago club and recording scene for more than four decades,' died at a nursing centre in Riverwoods, Evanston, Illinois, on Saturday, December 28, 2007.

[Editorial note: Chace's recall of hearing the Eddie Condon 1938 Commodore titles again at Town Hall in 1945 seems to be a mis-remembering of the year. Condon's Town Hall concerts were in 1944. In 1945 they were at the Ritz Theatre. To the best of my knowledge, details have yet to be found. The Frank Teschemacher solos to which Chace refers were, of course, by the Chicago Rhythm Kings, April 1928, and Miff Mole's Molers, July that same year. BW]

The following compact discs feature Chace and appear to be currently available:

Atlantic 7 818442 **Chicago Jazz Summit**
Delmark DE246 **Dewey Jackson Barrel Band** GHB BCD461/2
Jimmy Archey & Don Ewell **Good Time Jazz** GT-GTJCD 1 0065-2
Marty Grosz Jazzology JCD371 /2
Chicago Loopers Jazzology JCD373/4
Butch Thompson J&M Records J&MCD8004
Marty Grosz **Trad Jazz** TJP2130
(multi artists) **Salty Dogs** Universe 25343
Jim Kweskin **Windin' Ball** WB105 Salty Dogs

Jimmy Ille - Cornet player from Biwabik

Parade music would seem to be the link between jazz and the circus, and perhaps one day someone will look in more detail at this connection. Undoubtedly circus bands provided employment for many musicians. One famous name of the swing era, Harry James, always springs to mind. He gained valuable training and experience with his father's circus band. Clarinetist Joe Darensbourg has spoken of the thrill of working with Al G. Barnes Circus in 1925 and, later, with the Pollock Brothers Circus. Punch Miller and Bunk Johnson were just two other New Orleans players to gain experience with circus bands.

One musician who has spent most of his life with a foot in each camp is cornetist Jimmy Ille (pronounced 'aisle'). He recalls: "My folks were in show business. My father played trombone and baritone, and my mother played piano. They were in a travelling stock company. In other words, they'd go into a town, put on different performances every night. I was born October 25, 1920, in a town called Biwabik, Minnesota. The show was there just for that week."

His parents' career was probably typical for show business in the early years of the [20th] century. They spent time with the Cotton Blossom showboat, the C.B. Primrose Minstrels, the Hi Henry Minstrels, Mrs Tom Thumb, Alphonse and Gaston, and the Forpauch and Sells Circus.

Ille grew up in California. His family moved to the Los Angeles area in 1926, and it was about then that he started to learn the trumpet. By the time he was thirteen he had become interested in jazz. In later years he was to number Louis Armstrong, Bunny Berigan, Harry James, Charlie Teagarden, Wingy Manone, and Sharkey Bonano among his favourite trumpet players. In 1935, when he was fourteen, his sister took him along on a date for Benny Goodman's opening night at the Palomar. His memories of Nate Kazebier and Bunny Berigan are still fresh today.

In 1939 Ille decided to join the army. He felt this was the best way to become a fully-fledged musician, but after a year in the

Jimmy Ille, Las Vegas, c. 1969. (Courtesy Jimmy Ille)

Jimmy Ille Band, at the Brass Rail, Chicago, c. 1952. Left to right: Eddie Higgins, piano; Jug Berger, clarinet; Bill Pfeiffer, drums; Jimmy Ille, trumpet; Al Jenkins, trombone. (Courtesy Jimmy Ille)

service he wanted to buy himself out. The threat of impending war prevented this, and by 1943 he was both a sergeant and a soloist in the 33rd Armored Regiment band in the 3rd Armored Division, stationed in England at Warminster. He has happy memories of England, including hearing the bands of Ambrose and Jack Hylton, musicians like George Chisholm - and tasting Hovis bread. On D-Day + 7 (June 13, 1944) he landed in France, and the next month the 3rd was taking part in the breakout from the Normandy beachhead. One close shave occurred when he was outside a tank making coffee and an '88' landed close by. Duties at this stage included escorting prisoners-of-war to the rear. Later, in France on leave, he was to play with Django Reinhardt.

Returning to the States at the end of the war with Germany he was discharged on August 30, and almost immediately joined the Gus Arnheim band in San Diego for a nine-month stay.

Leaving Arnheim he joined the Merle Evans band in the Ringling Brothers circus.

> I was the youngest guy in the band when I arrived, and half of the band had played with John Philip Sousa. Dynamite players. I saw the band rehearse for two weeks. We got on the train to Madison Square Garden, rehearsed about three days, and the show opened, but we'd only rehearsed the production numbers. There were five production numbers, including opening, aerial act, specialty, elephant act, and closing - but you'd got twenty or thirty displays in the circus. So on opening night we hadn't seen any of the music for the acts!

Jimmy Ille was to be in circus bands at frequent intervals between 1946 and 1975. "I spent a great part of my life on the circus. Seems to me, as I look back on it, I was either on the circus or with Mike Riley." About 1952 he was in Merle Evans band when it recorded much of the soundtrack for the Cecil B. DeMille film, "The Greatest Show On Earth."

> Merle Evans was a great man in my life. He was a marvelous man, and a great cornet player. I brought him to hear George Brunis one time and George knocked him out.

Ille's love of the circus and its music is only too evident. There is his pleasure in having the music for "a thing called *Idaho*, written around the turn of the century, by C. L. Barnhouse, who had a music publishing company in Oskaloosa, Iowa"; his admiration for circus composers like Russell Alexander Kaufgang, Fred Jewel, and Charlie Dougal; and his delight in seeing, on television news, a U.S. Army band marching through Moscow to the old circus tune, *Bravura*.

Though he has occasionally played trumpet, Ille favours the cornet. As he says,

> For years l had an English Besson horn. It's a fine, fine instrument. It's small; you can play and you can conduct. It feels natural in my hand. I have three Conn Victor models and I'm playing one built in 1959. If you listen to Louis on the first Hot Five records, when he's playing cornet, and listen to the execution, he's all over it. When he switches to trumpet, that tightens up, the sound changes a little.
>
> At the end of the season in 1948 I came home to Los Angeles and I was at a place called Club 47, owned by Ray Bauduc, Nappy Lamare and Doc Rando. I ran into trombonist Mike Riley, and he says: 'I got a chance to go in the Brass Rail in Chicago. You want to come?' So we left the next day, drove non-stop to Chicago. We organised the band out of a union book, while on the road. We had Kenny Sweet on piano; Hey-Hey Humphrey, drums; and Bud Jacobson on clarinet. It was a good band. We were in the Brass Rail for about a week and then they put us in the Capitol Lounge, next to the Chicago Theatre. We went for two weeks and I stayed there. That spring I didn't go back with the circus, I went out with Henry Busse. Then I came back in August and stayed in Chicago.
>
> I played with Miff Mole a lot. I knew Miff through Mike Riley because they were old buddies. Lee Collins had been playing at the Sky Club with Miff, and while he was gone I had a chance to play there.

Ille recalls hearing one of the bands at the newly opened Jazz, Ltd:

> The best band I heard down there was Floyd Bean, piano; Big Sid Catlett on drums; Bill Reinhardt on clarinet; Muggsy Spanier on cornet and George Brunis on trombone. It was marvelous too. You don't read too much about him but what a great player he was. Sid was a 'rounder.' He'd go out after work at night, go out to the Club De Lisa, get in that crap game out there.

Jimmy Ille found work at Mooney's, and then at other lounges. He recalls bassist Sy Nelson as one member of the band at Mooney's. He was working for the mob most of the time, and says that gangsters treated musicians wonderfully. By the end of 1949 he was back in the band at the Sky Club, with George Brunis, trombone, Johnny Lane, clarinet; Art Gronwall, piano; and Anderson Saucier ("he was loud") on drums. When Lane became a leader at the 11-11 Club he took Ille and Saucier with him, adding Floyd O'Brien on trombone and Roy Wasson on piano.

George Brunis was, to Ille,

> one of the most professional musicians that I ever saw in my life on a bandstand. He was a natural swinger. I remember the 11-11 Club, place held ninety people. It would be snowing outside and the people lined up half a block to get in.

But as Ille says,

> those guys like George Brunis, Floyd O'Brien, Al Jenkins - eliminate Jack Teagarden, he's a different thing - and Mike Riley, I'll put him in there, they knew how to play a trombone part. Give Floyd O'Brien a chorus and he'd swing that melody. He knew how to do it.

About April 1950 Ille left Lane for weeks to play an engagement at the Brass Rail with George Brunis. Completing the band were Pee Wee Russell, clarinet; Art Gronwall, piano; Bill Moore bass; Ray Luby, drums.

> Pee Wee was living out at Bud Jacobson's place; he was pretty sick. We were there with George about a month and then went back with Johnny Lane and Nick Alex. Nick Alex, the Greek, owner of the 11-11 Club, was the nephew of Gus Alex, who had the gambling for the Capone Syndicate. This was the same family, but he was a marvelous guy.

At one point the trombonist with Lane was Britisher Ralph Hutchinson, who later played with Muggsy Spanier. Ille recalls that Hutchinson joined Lane almost straight from the boat. The band now had Claude Hey-Hey Humphrey on drums, who was in the original Boyd Raeburn band. His nickname came about because he had an impediment in his speech, though "when he was sober he'd very seldom stutter."

On June 13, 1950, Art Hodes, who had returned to Chicago early that year, took a band into Rupneck's. The personnel was Jimmy Ille, cornet; Floyd O'Brien, trombone; Jimmy Granato, clarinet; Hodes, piano; Bill Moore, bass; Bill Pfeiffer, drums. Hodes said in his autobiography, *Hot Man*: "The band clicked from the very beginning. It had spirit and it had musicianship." Hodes was at Rupneck's until July 1951, but Ille had left about January of that year.

During 1950 one of Ille's rare jazz recordings took place when he was part of trombonist Jimmy James' Jas *(sic)* Band. Edgar 'Jug' Berger was on clarinet, George Zack on piano, and Freddie Flynn at the drums. This John Schenck session, held in the upstairs room of Seymour's record shop, was recorded and four sides were issued on the Seymour label. The titles were Royal Garden Blues (two parts), Black and Blue, and I'm Gonna Sit Right Down And Write Myself A Letter. Remembering Schenck, Ille says he also

> sponsored jazz concerts up above the Gaffer's Club. Jimmy James, myself, Lee Collins, George Zack, Danny Alvin, Big Bill Broonzy (nobody knew who the hell he was) used to come up there.

Ille was a leader at The Red Arrow for a time, with Bill Johnson, trombone; Jug Berger, clarinet; Bud Jacobson, piano; and Don Chester, drums. On July 17, 1951 he replaced Hodes at Rupneck's, opening with Al Jenkins, trombone; Berger, clarinet; Jack Condon, piano; Jim Pendergass, bass; Bill Pfeiffer, drums. Later replacements included Eddie Smeeth, guitar; Frank Chace, bass sax; and then Sy Nelson, bass; and John Carlson, drums.

Further *Down Beat* researches by John Miner show Ille at the Brass Rail during 1952 and for perhaps the next three years. Of this band Ille comments:

> Doc Evans had one of the all-time great trombone players, Al Jenkins. Al and I were together for years at the Brass Rail in Chicago. Everybody came to hear him. Jack Teagarden, Miff Mole; Count Basie used to come from the Blue Note; and all we had was five pieces. Had a good drummer, (the late) Bill Pfeiffer, Jug Berger on clarinet (he died a few months ago [1991?]), Eddie Higgins on piano.

Scott McLean was the clarinetist in early 1953, but by mid-1954 Berger was back, with Bill Johnson on trombone. In the fall of

1956 Ille had a band at The Whip in Chicago, with Marty Nichols, trombone; Ray Daniel, clarinet; Sy Nelson, bass; Buddy Smith, drums; but early in 1959 he was down to a quartet with Hots O'Casey, clarinet; Floyd Bean, piano; and Hey-Hey Humphrey, drums. In his autobiography reedman Drew Page recalls working at the Brass Rail in 1958 for four weeks with Mike Riley and playing opposite them was "Jimmy Ille's four-pieces."

To resume Jim Ille's recollections: "I left Chicago in November of 1959. I went to California, went through a divorce, and lived in back of Doc Cenardo for a couple of years." (Drummer Cenardo had a little cottage in his yard which Ille rented.) It was perhaps at this time that he again worked with Mike Riley at Riley's own club, the Madhouse. The band was Ille, cornet; Riley, trombone; Andy Kelly, clarinet; Sol Lake, piano; Hank Wayland, bass; Lou Diamond, drums; Bobby Scott, vocal. Ille says he recorded with Riley, but cannot recall the details. Mike Riley, who with Ed Farley wrote the 1935 hit The Music Goes 'Round and Around, is remembered by Ille as a "funny, funny man." He has many vivid memories of Riley's madcap humour.

> Then I went to Las Vegas. Joe Sagretto (?), who had been Louis Prima's road manager, was running the bar at the California Club on Fremont Street. I come walking by and saw him, and he gave me four days a week in there. I worked around those joints until 'Circus, Circus' opened. ('Circus, Circus' was a combined circus and casino.) A man had called Charlie Teagarden and wanted him to put a band in. Charlie said, 'Get Jimmy Ille'. Nat Brandwynne had the band at Caesar's Palace. I played a Capitol record of a circus band for him, we shook hands and then a day after the lease was finalised I signed a contract. So I'm in the Lounge in Caesar's Palace for a year before 'Circus, Circus' opened.
> That 'Circus, Circus' was great when it first opened (on October 18, 1968). I never saw anything like it. The kids could play those carnival games. But they weren't allowed on the casino floor. It had top acts and great Mexican flying acts. Fay Alexander, Willie Carson, Eddie Ward - these three did the stunts for Burt Lancaster and Gina Lollobrigida in "Trapeze" (the 1956 Carol Reed film) - and the Cabarettas. I set the music for the twelve hours of the show. I had the night band, Garnett Floyd Henry had the afternoon band, and I set all the music for the acts. We played an act every twenty minutes. There were two or three flying acts,

trapeze acts, on each six hour shift, and each one of those was on, I think, three times during the six hours. We played traditional American circus music, which is a different thing than any other kind of music.

When Merle Evans retired after fifty years, I was in 'Circus, Circus' and he recommended me to take his place with Ringling Brothers. I had played their show when it went indoors after the 1966 season. I went back, but it wasn't the same. The show had changed hands and all the circus people that I knew were gone, just like Bourbon Street today.

Around 1970-71 Ille worked with circus bandleader Howard Suarez (?), and alongside "a great circus drummer, Tex Maynard." Touring included trips to Mexico City.

In 1975 Jimmy Ille moved to New Orleans and began working on Bourbon Street. One group at the Blue Angel had Tony Mitchell, clarinet; Lloyd Ellis, guitar; Lloyd Lambert, bass; and Bob Gardiner, drums. In 1976 he recorded his only jazz album, on Blue Angel BAP7033N1 by the Jimmy Ille New Orleans Ragtime Band. The personnel were Ille, cornet; Tom Ebbert, trombone; Pud Brown, clarinet and tenor; Les Muscutt, banjo; Bruce Voorhies, tuba; Bob Gardiner, drums. Unfortunately it is a typical Bourbon Street production, with vocals, banjo solos, and a tuba feature. Ille remembers:

> Gardiner was with me on the circus. When I went in the Blue Angel I brought him with me. He passed away in Corpus Christi a couple of years ago (1990?). Good Texas drummer.

Also in 1976 his wife, Kay, died, but their daughter, Nellie, continues in the circus tradition. Like her mother, she is a bareback rider.

After an operation Jimmy Ille gradually cut back on engagements until nowadays, at the age of 73, he is retired, but occasionally persuaded to play a session. One such in 1992 was with Pud Brown on the riverboat *Orange Blossom*, and another was sitting-in during the French Quarter Festival.

He was certainly in good health and good voice on May 14, 1992, in Harry's Bar, when he gave Bert Whyatt and myself a generous amount of time and many happy memories, for which we are very grateful.

Jimmy Ille passed away in New Orleans on April 28, 1999.

In 1997 Laserlight released on CD, 12 819, The Grand Old Circus Band, "Authentic Circus Music by the Legendary Jimmy Ille." The 18 tracks include Entry of the Gladiators, Spana, Bombasto, and The Cantonians March. Ille does not play with the band. It is not known if he conducted or just lent his name. The sleeve notes also say that his career included work with the Cole Bros. Circus and the Clyde Beatty Circus.

Just Jazz magazine for February 2010 reported that when trumpeter Charlie Fardella left college he became a member of the Clyde Beatty Circus Band, a twelve-piece group led by Jimmy Ille. It toured extensively and visited New Orleans in 1976.

Other comments on the 1950 Seymour session will be found in the George Zack chapter.

Jimmy Ille outside Harry's Bar, corner of Decatur and Chartres, New Orleans, May 14, 1992.

Al Jenkins: Knocking down walls

Jack Teagarden died in 1964, but his powerful influence is still to be heard in the work of numerous trombonists, young and old, active today. One such, now in the veteran stage, is Al Jenkins. That he is not better known may have been due to his place of birth or the fact that he came late to jazz, but he has nevertheless contributed to our music for more than 50 years.

Al Jenkins was born in Newcastle, Pennsylvania, on December 19, 1913.

> Both my father and mother were born in Swansea, Wales, and came to the States in the late 1890s. My father taught himself to play enough piano to accompany himself as he sang hymns. Dad bought me my first trombone - wanted me to do theater work.

Mr. Jenkins, Senior, worked in a steel mill, and was anxious that his son would not follow in his footsteps. So, Al Jenkins did work in theater pit bands, but such work gradually faded away, especially in the smaller towns, and he later worked in saloons. His father would not have approved!

In 1933 his then girlfriend persuaded him to see the Paul Whiteman Orchestra, which was appearing at a local theater. His lack of interest changed to enthusiasm when he heard Bunny Berigan for the first time.

> I played in local dance bands and in 1937 played with my first jazz group. Trumpet player Bob Lamm, who later played and sang with Francis Craig (of Near You fame), was blind, so we used no music - good experience.

About 1940 he moved to Detroit, where his work, as he puts it, "was confined to nightclubs and theaters." In 1941 the society band with which he was playing was flown to Bermuda to play a benefit dance for the R.A.F. Later that year there was a four-month stay with the big band led by clarinetist Tommy Reynolds. He recalls taking part in a recording session with Reynolds, though no titles with Jenkins are listed in Brian Rust's *American Dance Band*

Al Jenkins, c. 1980. (Courtesy Chet Jaeger)

Left to right: standing, Al Jenkins, Doc Evans, Charlie Spero; sitting, Doc Cenardo, Mel Grant. (Courtesy Al Jenkins)

The Levee Loungers, Detroit, c. 1947. Left to right: Ephraim Kelley, Andy Bartha, Al Jenkins, Mickey Steinke, Steve Brown, Frank Gillis. (Courtesy Frank Gillis)

Discography. After a series of college dates and theaters, the band played at the Famous Door in New York.

Jenkins also did some casual theater and nightclub work with a famous name from an earlier decade, clarinetist Boyd Senter. This was a small group, with Senter still playing drainpipe clarinet and other instruments. Jenkins says "Everybody loved it. He was a big showman." He recalls Senter saying he felt cheap because he paid musicians like Jimmy and Tommy Dorsey only a little above scale at a time (1928/29) when he was getting a thousand dollars a night.

One of the jobs with a society band in a Detroit club was memorable for a reason other than music. The gangster owners kept insisting on unnecessary rehearsals, and on one particular occasion Jenkins had had enough. He left the bandstand and began to walk out of the club, whereupon one of the hoodlums came behind him, knocking him unconscious with a rabbit punch.

Pianist Frank Gillis, whose story was told by Jax Lucas in *The Mississippi Rag,* November 1985, was an active force for classic jazz in Detroit in the 1940s. Although Jenkins played a date or two with him shortly after moving to the city, Gillis reports "He was not a regular member of the jazzmen with whom I played and hung around with."

Jenkins came more regularly into this coterie when Frank Gillis returned from war service in 1946. After occasional gigs in 1946 and 1947, as Gillis says,

> Al began working steady with a group I was forming which was called the Levee Loungers. We had jam sessions and started working Tuesday nights, in about mid-1948, at the Wyoming State Show Bar.

The personnel were Andy Bartha, trumpet; Al Jenkins, trombone; Eph Kelley, clarinet, tenor; Frank Gillis, piano; Mickey Steinke, drums. Whitey Myrick was the trumpeter both before and after Andy Bartha's stay.

It seems that Jenkins was with this particular Gillis band from sometime in August 1948 until early December 1948. In 1949 he left Detroit to make his home in Chicago, and to join the Doc Evans band. He was with Evans for about a year, making his first released recordings, three sessions for the Joco label, in Northfield, Minnesota. These were subsequently issued as two albums on Jazzology, J-86 and J-87. Details are:

Doc Evans, tp; Al Jenkins, tb; John McDonald, cl; Carroll Lee, p; Willy Sutton, b; Doc Cenardo, d.

October 30, 1949

Titles: Milenberg Joys/Memphis Blues/Walkin' The Dog/Blues Doctor/Ostrich Walk/Willie The Weeper/ Doctor Jazz/Play That Barbershop Chord.

Doc Evans, tp; Jenkins, tb; Art Lyons, cl; Mel Grant, p; Biddy Bastien, b; Mickey Steinke, d.

April 5/6, 1950

Titles: Tishomingo Blues/Sidewalk Blues/Panama/Bye Bye Blues/Royal Garden Blues/Sleepy time Down South/Jimtown Blues/Dallas Blues/Pack Up Your Troubles/Missouri Waltz/ Copenhagen/Beale Street Blues/Weary Blues/Singin' The Blues/ I'm Gonna Sit Right Down/Buddy Bolden Blues.

It is easy to see why the band made an impression when the Joco records were issued. Tunes that had not then become hackneyed, a good ensemble sound, a lightly swinging rhythm section, the Bixian flavour of the leader's playing, the competence of the other musicians - it was a far cry from the hell-for-leather approach of the titles Evans made for Disc with Tony Parenti and Ed Hubble. There is fine ensemble work by Al Jenkins on all titles, and he solos on most of them. The Teagarden influence is to the fore on Sleepytime Down South, while Tishomingo Blues, Dallas Blues and I'm Gonna Sit Right Down and Write Myself A Letter are good examples of his solo work.

In addition to working at Jazz, Ltd. and other Chicago locations, the band also went to California in 1951, playing in Los Angeles and at the Hangover in San Francisco.

During the last few months of 1951 Jenkins worked for Jimmy Ille at Rupneck's. As reported by John Miner from his *Down Beat* researches, the band opened on July 17, with the front line of Ille, cornet; Jenkins, trombone; Jug Berger, clarinet; remaining constant, but with various rhythm section changes. For a time Frank Chace played bass sax in the band. After a period of a few months (the exact duration is not known) the band moved to the Brass Rail. Jenkins left there sometime in 1953. There were casual dates with Wingy Manone, and Marty Grosz recalls playing with Jenkins at the Velvet Swing in Nap Trottier's band.

1956 saw the best known of his few recordings, a session by Art Hodes for Mercury records, issued on EmArcy MG20185:

Muggsy Dawson, co; Al Jenkins, Jimmy Granato, cl; Art Hodes, p; John Frigo b; Hap Gormley, d.

July 31, 1956

Titles: Royal Garden Blues/Organ Grinder Blues/Randolph and Dearborn/South.

The trombonist is heard to good effect on each title, his blues solo on Organ Grinder being especially noteworthy.

Early in 1957 he played briefly at Danny Alvin's Basin Street club, with Jack Ivett, cornet; Jug Berger, clarinet; Mel Grant, piano; and Alvin, drums. George Zack was the pianist for a short time and his consort brought her close friend to the club. That close friend, an avid jazz fan named Renee, was to become Mrs. Al Jenkins. It was a very sad loss when Renee passed away last June [1994].

In August 1957 Jenkins moved to Los Angeles. Shortly after his arrival, he and George Zack, who was visiting, sat in at the 400 Club run by Happy Koomer.

Teddy Buckner was very popular then, in that same spot," Jenkins says. "He left and (Koomer) wanted somebody comparable. He liked dixieland music."

A couple of nights later, Koomer invited Jenkins to work there regularly, but Al said he had no union card. Koomer said not to worry about it and the card came through in two weeks! But Happy Koomer was something of a martinet. Jenkins was trying stop drinking, but Koomer insisted he mix with the customers and as a result Jenkins fell off the wagon. He stayed only a few weeks. The band at the time included Chico Alvarez, trumpet; Phil Gomez, clarinet; and Ed Garland, bass.

The years in Los Angeles are a kaleidoscope of casual engagements, including some circus work, plus the occasional steady job, so what follows is a listing of the memorable ones. Between 1959 and 1961 he worked mainly at the Roaring '20s club in Hollywood. One of the features was a girl on a swing. Jenkins says, "The place was packed, and the people that came in love the music. But we didn't bring them in, the girls did!"

Lucille Ball was one of the celebrities who visited the club, usually bringing a party. Jenkins played with two bands at the

Roaring '20s, which had a write-up in *Life* magazine. One group was led by trumpeter Garner Clark, with Al Jenkins, trombone; Bus Bassey, clarinet; Mel Bryden, piano; Woodie Bushell, bass; and Doc Cenardo, drums. The other was led by Pud Brown, reeds and bass; Jenkins, trombone; Phil Gomez, clarinet; Don Owens, piano; and Ray Bauduc, drums.

Around 1960 there was a short stay at the White Way Inn with a Wild Bill Davison group, with Bob McCracken, clarinet; Nappy Lamare, fender bass; and Charley Lodice, drums. This was when Davison was unsuccessfully trying to fix regular dates for himself on the west coast.

The following year Jenkins worked with clarinetist Johnny Lane, who was always finding regular employment. Jenkins was with Lane on at least five separate occasions between early 1961 and Spring 1980, playing alongside players like Don Kinch, Bill Stumpp or Irving Goodman on trumpet, Marvin Ash or Bill Campbell on piano, and Bill French on drums.

Jenkins recalls playing with trumpeter Rex Stewart in a short-lived band.

Rex Stewart, in the early Sixties, was a disc jockey in L.A. and a good one, I thought. (He) started a band, but found little work for it. I can only remember Max Murray on clarinet.

I did some work with Muggsy Spanier in '62 and '63 - the Showboat hotel in Vegas in 1962, also the Hollywood Bowl Dixieland concerts in '62 and '63. The Showboat band consisted of L.A. musicians plus Charley Clark on clarinet, who played in Chicago - very good. In the Hollywood Bowl (were) Muggsy, cornet; Al Jenkins, trombone; Barney Bigard, clarinet; Ralph Sutton, piano; Frankie Carlson, drums.

No one recalls the name of the bassist.

In this period, Jenkins began playing gigs with trumpeter Johnny Lucas, and this was another association which was to continue through the years, up to the present day. One gig, held at the Cal. Poly, in Pomona, was taped, and two titles were included in a Best of Johnny Lucas 1953-1973 cassette which Lucas circulated in the 1970s.

Johnny Lucas, tp, vo; Al Jenkins, tb; Jim Pugh, cl; Floyd Stone, ts; Connie Fay, p; Dolph Morris, b; Gene Washington, d; Lucille Lane, vo.

October 15, 1965

Titles: Black Butterfly/Song Of The Wanderer ["Lucas cassette"]

unissued titles were: Indiana /... None Of My Jelly Roll!/I Left My Heart in San Francisco/Do You Know What It Means to Miss New Orleans/Old Man River/I Found A New Baby/ Muskrat Ramble/High Society/Basin Street Blues/Mack The Knife/St. James Infirmary/The Saints/theme.

Al Jenkins considers this his best work to have been made available in recorded form. His long solo on Song of the Wanderer is excellent.

The day before the Lucas gig he played a date with Pete Daily's band at The Cup in L.A. - Daily, cornet; Gene Bolen, clarinet; Bill Campbell, piano; Lou Diamond, drums. This was just one of his jobs with Daily.

In 1963, 1965, 1966 and 1967 he made further appearances with Johnny Lane, and between 1968 and 1971 he recalls working with Dick Cathcart and George Rock.

Cathcart did the soundtrack for the "Pete Kelly's Blues" movie and television show. Later Dick attempted to commercialize the show - organized a band, played the Flamingo Lounge in Las Vegas, and that was it. The personnel consisted of Dick on cornet; myself on trombone; Bill Wood on clarinet; Fran Polifrani, tenor; Dick Cary, piano; Jud de Naut, bass; Charley Lodice, drums. Pretty good band. (This was 1968).

I worked with the George Rock band in late '68 to early '71 at the Silver Slipper and Desert Inn hotel, both jobs in Vegas. George Rock was Spike Jones' trumpet player for years; a fine trumpet player basically and adapted well to dixieland, which we played. Charley Clarke also in this band, and Nappy Lamare on banjo.

Many casual dates with John Lucas, Nappy Lamare, and Pete Daily continued through the 1970s, and in 1976 and 1977 Jenkins was at the Sacramento Jubilee with Pete Daily. There was also another visit to Las Vegas for a gig with Wingy Manone.

At the end of 1978 Jenkins joined the Nightblooming Jazzmen, led by cornetist Chet Jaeger, who says,

In my opinion, Al is one of the most under-rated players in jazz history. Al worked with the Nightblooming Jazzmen for about 18 months in 1979 and 1980. Actually his first gig as a 'permanent' Nightbloomer was New Year's Eve, 1978. His last was in June 1980. It was a joy working with Al. His ideas and ability to produce them on solos were outstanding, and his ensemble back-up work was flawless. He had to resign from the band for 'health reasons'. Part of the problem was the sheer physical strain of doing three or four day jazz festivals. Al is still the first one I call if I need a sub for local jobs. He still plays very tasty stuff and can knock walls down briefly when required to do so.

A job I remember several years ago was at a wholesale lumber yard grand opening. (We get some strange ones.) It had come up suddenly and I had four subs out of seven players, I am 6' 2" and I had Al and Phil Gomez on either side of me. Phil is much shorter than Al. I remember standing there and looking around and wondering where everybody went.

Al Jenkins was on two albums by the Nightblooming Jazzmen. One was **More Bloomin' Jazz** on Ameritone A-1364, and the other **Sing Your Favorite Hymns** on Ameritone A-1370. Details are:

Chet Jaeger; co; Al Jenkins, tb; Willie Martinez: cl: Morey Huff, p; Tommy Hearn, bj; George Olson, b; Tommy Raftican, d:

January, 1980

Titles: Copenhagen/Petite Fleur/My Honey's Lovin' Arms/Aunt Hagar's Blues/ That Da Da Strain/Fidgety Feet/Dippermouth Blues/The World Is Waiting For The Sunrise/Thou Swell/Willow Weep For Me/Sorry/Memphis Blues Ice Cream.

same.   c. March 1980

Titles: Over In Gloryland/Lily of the Valley/He Set Me Free/What A Friend In Jesus/Just A Little While To Stay Here/When The Saints Go Marching In/When The Roll Is Called/That Old Rugged Cross/I Shall Not Be Moved/How Great Thou Art/Down By The Riverside Just A Closer Walk With Thee.

On the hymns the band stays close to the melodies, but it has the opportunity to stretch out on the jazz standards, with the trombonist soloing on seven on them. My Honey's Lovin' Arms, Thou Swell, and Sorry have typical efforts.

With the Nightblooming Jazzmen Jenkins played the Pismo Beach festival in 1979 and the Sacramento Jubilee in 1980. As he says, "I did all this and still worked with Pete Daily and Johnny Lane - I was busy in those days."

Dan Barrett, the highly regarded trombonist of a later generation, admired the work of Al Jenkins in his apprentice days, as his appreciation elsewhere illustrates. He also plays what he calls "a little cornet" and occasionally he would play this instrument as a sub. In this capacity, he often found himself playing with Al Jenkins. The longest running of these dates was in the late 1970s, just short of a year of Sunday evenings, at Jack Murphy's, in the Johnny Lane band. Another Barrett/Jenkins engagement was at the Old Towne Mall in Torrance, where the band played in a gazebo in the fast food emporium.

Both Al Jenkins and Bob Higgins remember the Old Towne gig, a monthly date which lasted for about a year, between 1981 and 1982. Bassist Billy Hadnott was the leader, and one personnel included Bob Higgins, trumpet; Al Jenkins, trombone; and Gene Washington, drums.

Of life today, Al Jenkins says,

I am retired more or less... I work an occasional job with Johnny Lucas and a sub job with the Nightblooming Jazzmen.

And as Lucas comments,

He's playing as well or better than anybody around today. Some consider him one up on Teagarden in that he's a better ensemble man.

Lucas agrees that could be blasphemy to some, but it indicates the regard in which Jenkins is held. Collector Ron Clough, on hearing the Doc Evans recordings for the first time in many years, said he was quite surprised, "Everyone is much better than I remembered. Very Teagardenish trombone, I think, and very good, too."

Chicago trombonist Jim Beebe described Jenkins as "the perfect dixieland trombonist" and as "Teagarden with balls!"

Trumpeter Jimmy Ille said, without being prompted, "Doc Evans had one of the all-time great trombone players - Al Jenkins."

Al Jenkins' own favorites on trombone include no real surprises. He liked Lou McGarity, Cutty Cutshall, and Moe Schneider.

Warren Smith, Floyd O'Brien, and Georg Brunis were fine ensemble players. I have to marvel at Urbie Green's technique and range. Dan Barrett is playing great trombone these days. Bob Havens I like also. Trummy Young, Vic Dickenson, J.C.

Higginbotham, Tyree Glenn, played great. Jack Teagarden, of course. Still consider him one of the greatest jazz soloists.

And to that list of superior trombonists add another name, that of Al Jenkins.

Al Jenkins died on November 15, 1996 after being admitted to hospital suffering from pneumonia.

A tribute to Al Jenkins appeared in *The Mississippi Rag* for November 1994 entitled "The First Time I Heard Al Jenkins". This was written by Dan Barrett, hailed by critic Floyd Levin as "a leading trombonist of his generation". Barrett wrote of first hearing Jenkins:

> He literally had his own way of swinging ... He found just the right notes to insert the fullest harmony and delivered them with that utterly relaxed, irresistible swing. I felt I was in the presence of greatness.

In 1995 Arbors Jazz released "Dan Barrett Reunion With Al" on ARCD 19124. This CD contains 16 titles recorded at relaxed sessions in Newport Beach on March 5-6, 1993, with Barrett on cornet, Al on trombone and vocal, Rick Fay, reeds, Ray Sherman, piano, David Stone, bass, and Jeff Hamilton, drums. Jenkins was eighty years of age, so it would be unreasonable to expect him to sound the same as he did at 40, but the phrasing and the style are still present, on songs such as Oh, Baby, Darkness On The Delta, Bei Mir Bist Du Schoen, Girl of my Dreams and Rachel's Boogie. He has a vocal on I Can't Give You Anything But Love which is warm and friendly, indicative of the man himself.

Doc Cenardo: a great but unsung drummer

Towards the end of 1961, CBS television included *Chicago And All That Jazz* in its *Dupont Show of the Week* series. Near the end of the first half, on the screen came a few seconds of a silent movie with a bunch of young men running towards the camera. Twenty years later, Brigitte Berman's documentary *Bix* opened with the self-same scrap of film. The laughing young men were members of the Jean Goldkette orchestra and included was Bix Beiderbecke. These few brief moments contain the only known movie with the renowned cornetist.

Rumors of such a film had occasionally passed through the ranks of Beiderbecke buffs and collectors. Then, suddenly, there it was on television. But from where? "Where" was in the film collection of Enos Charles "Doc" Cenardo, a wonderful jazz drummer highly spoken of by contemporaries but almost unknown to most jazz followers.

He was born May 7, 1904, in Cuba to parents of Spanish extraction but, when he was still an infant, they moved to Ybor City, a suburb of Tampa, Florida, His father played the mandolin and his mother the guitar while tiny Enos tapped out rhythm on kitchen pans. He started piano lessons when he was seven but percussion remained the attraction, which his parents encouraged by buying him a drum kit for his tenth birthday.

Drummer Bill French recalls

> When he was around 8-10 years old, his parents packed him off to live with an uncle in Detroit. Putting him on the train in Tampa, they had packed a basket full of sandwiches, chicken, etc., and told the conductor to try to watch over him. He did because he got to Detroit safe and sound. He went to Eastern High School and I think he was in the band there, a marching band as well as a dance band.

Cenardo himself recalled the bands; other than that for parades, there was a concert orchestra and what he described as a jazz band. He joined the musicians' union in 1920 and the following

Doc Cenardo and Frank Gillis at a Dixie Five recording session, United Sound Systems, Detroit, Michigan, August 17-18, 1952

Left to right: Joe Marsala, Bill Bacin, Doc Cenardo, Lee Countryman, Los Angeles, April 18, 1968.

year he became a psychology student at the University of Illinois in Champaign-Urbana. He organized a jazz band and played nearby gigs and, says Bill French,

> ... played some football under Coach Zuppke who was one of the best in the USA then and for years afterward. All that in the early-mid '20s. Back in Detroit he even played some semi-professional football - he was sure big enough!

When weekends were free, Cenardo went into Chicago to listen to the great bands and was occasionally favored with invitations to sit in. One can imagine the effect of this on the youngster.

On his return to Detroit with his master's degree, he got a job in the Wayne County coroner's office where, for three years, his spare time was spent studying for a master's in criminal psychology. By now, the "Doc" nickname had been applied and continued for the rest of his life.

It was in this period that he joined the Goldkette organization, at first only in vacation time. Here is how Cenardo told the story:

> During the '20s and up to World War II. Jean Goldkette had a music-booking office in Detroit. He had many bands and I worked out of this office with these. His main band was known as the Victor band because it recorded for Victor. During the '20s there was an eight-piece called the Orange Blossoms and this played opposite the Victor band in the Graystone Ballroom. Tommy Gargano was the drummer and when he left to join the Wolverines, I joined the Orange Blossoms. I never did work with the Victor band but sat in with them several times. When that band went on the road, the Blossoms band was enlarged to 12 pieces and we stayed in the ballroom.

By 1929, the band was known as Henry Biagini's and was booked to play an engagement at the Casa Loma Club in Toronto.

> The Goldkette office split the band; half went to Canada and half stayed in Detroit where I remained with Biagini. Spike Knoblauch was the first sax man in the Biagini band so he became leader of the band that went to Canada. He changed his name to Glen Gray and the band became known as his Casa Loma Orchestra. The Biagini band made several recordings and I was on one of them but don't remember the label or the tunes.

It was during this time that Cenardo became a friend of bass man Steve Brown and, of course, Bix Beiderbecke. A little later, when the Blossoms band was playing at Island Lake, Bix spent an evening off sitting in.

From 1927 to 1930, Cenardo was with Dick Bowen's band at Detroit's Arcadia Ballroom along with Brown. The two then spent a while playing with various bands on the road, including that led by Henry Biagini. By 1934, the pair was with Sammy Dibert back in Detroit at the Arcadia and then with Morrey Brennan at the Graystone.

In 1937, Cenardo joined Glenn Miller's band. In the reference books he is named as Carney or Kearney.

> Carney was my stepfather's name and I used it for a long time in music circles. Kearney and Carney are pronounced the same in the eastern section of the USA so, when the Miller band played the East, the writers there spelled Carney as Kearney. George Simon and Glenn were real good friends and he played drums in the band until I could join.

Cenardo said, "I made at least twenty sides with Miller," but according to the discographies only six with him appeared. (Perhaps there were sessions for radio transcription discs?) The Brunswicks of November 29 and December 12, 1937, have been issued on compact disc: Sony-CBS 471656-2 in the U.S. and as 48831-2 in Europe.

Frank Gillis was playing piano in his own groups in the Detroit clubs during the 1930s. He said

> I'd heard of Doc Cenardo, the great jazz drummer. In the Fall of '39 he called me, 'I'd like to have you start working with me tomorrow night.' I said, 'Well, Doc, I can hardly do that. Being a union member, I have to give two weeks notice before I can leave the job.' He said, 'Don't mind that - I've already arranged for a substitute to take your place. You can start with us!'
> This says a lot for Doc. Very organized, very authoritative, not negative. People listened to him. We played the Ash-Trumbull Club, on the second story on the corner of Ash and Trumbull Streets in Detroit.

With Frank Gillis and Doc, tenor saxist Denny Doyle of Madison, Wisconsin, made up the Club's trio. Doyle was replaced around

June '40 by Bill Stegmeyer, then lately of the Bob Crosby band. About April of 1941, Bus Bassey, recently with Benny Goodman and then Artie Shaw, came in with his tenor, Gillis says that

> ... this was the finest jazz spot in Detroit from 1939 to around April '42. Local musicians plus such as Goodman, Shaw and Miller would sit in. Often as many as a dozen men would be on the bandstand. Hardly a night went by without at least one person sitting in.
> On one occasion, in July '40, Steg Meyer's clarinet was in company with Bartha's cornet, Fred Greenleaf, on violin rather than his trumpet, and Conrad Galvin on bass along with Cenardo and Gillis.

Bill French remembered that he

> ... didn't meet Doc until late '41 or '42 when he was at the old Ash-Trumbull along with Frank Gillis. There were always guys sitting in. One was trumpeter Andy Bartha who years later went with Pee Wee Hunt. Andy, a good friend of mine, later settled in Fort Lauderdale and had a fine group there for years. He died in the late '70s of cancer.

There was a big party and jam session at the Ash-Trumbull on the 27th of April, 1942, when Cenardo was drafted into the Army. Says Bill French,

> I think he went directly to Fort Leonard Wood, just south of St. Louis, and it was there that he met and married Tomi, his wife. Jack Teagarden was Doc's best man.

His qualifications became known and he was sent on courses in Army Intelligence, security and psychological warfare and was commissioned. At one time he was in charge of security at the San Francisco embarkation port and, in 1946 as Captain Cenardo, was in Germany with a unit on the war crimes trials. Discharged in April '48, he joined the reserves, remaining until '62 as full colonel.

Ruth and Bill Reinhardt had opened Chicago's Jazz, Ltd. nightspot in 1947 and, when they heard that Cenardo was back in Detroit, they sent for him to come as drummer in the house band.

Inevitably there were jam sessions promoted by such as John Schenck and at one such held at the Club Silhouette on May 16, 1949, Cenardo was one of the four drummers present.

For a while, Cenardo was in a band led by that other "Doc," Paul Wesley Evans, a fine cornet man from Minnesota. Two splendid sessions were made for the Art Floral label in Northfield on February 15 and October 30,1949, Russell Roth, writing in the 1953 *Record Changer* about the second of these, said,

> For once, he (Evans) had a proper personnel. Key men were A1 Jenkins, trombone; Johnny McDonald, clarinet; and Doc Cenardo, drums - journeymen musicians all.

The original issues were, of course, on 78s and now hard to find. However, in recent times George Buck has made them available on Jazzology LPs numbered J-85, J-86 and J- 87, including other Evans sessions with another drummer.

Cenardo's playing on these is a joy to hear and perhaps would repay study by some of today's drummers. Another plus on that second date, as well as on those without Cenardo that followed, is that trombone work of Al Jenkins, another neglected musician. Jenkins has been described as "Teagarden with balls," and he is quite astonishing on these mostly ensemble cuts.

In late May, 1950, Cenardo was with Muggsy Spanier's band along with Julian Laine, trombone; Darnell Howard, clarinet; Tut Soper, piano; and Truck Parham, bass, at the Silhouette. This appears to have been merely temporal as Sid Catlett was the regular man though perhaps sick at the time. Don Chester took over from Cenardo.

Back at Jazz, Ltd. for a spell, the band had Evans, Jenkins, Reinhardt (replaced for a holiday break by Charlie Spero), Mel Grant, piano, and Cenardo.

On August 17, 1950, in Detroit, Frank Gillis' Dixie Five cut eight sides for United Records. Four appeared on a couple of 78s but the whole session had to await 1988 and George Buck's Jazzology J-147 with Bartha on cornet; Clyde Smith, trombone; Eph Kelley, clarinet; Gillis, piano; Red McGarvey, guitar; and, together again, Steve Brown, bass; and Cenardo.

Cenardo worked evenings with the Dixie Five, says Frank Gillis, " ... each week in three locations in Detroit: The Wyoming Show Bar (Mondays); The Falcon Lounge (Tuesdays) and the Military Inn (Wednesdays)."

In 1951 the drummer was back at Jazz, Ltd. *Down Beat* that May noted Bill Tinkler, trumpet; Mole, trombone; Reinhardt, clarinet; Ralph Blank, piano; and of course, Cenardo, replacing Sid Catlett who had died that March. Around this time, with Doc Evans instead of Tinkler and Sy Nelson's bass added, the band cut four titles which formed part of the LP, Jazz, Ltd. Volume One. These appeared later on Atlantic 1261, then on CD, Delmark DE-226.

Cenardo remained in Chicago until 1957, working with Georg(e) Bruni(e)s and others at such places as the 11-11 Club. Just the same, the Reinhardts didn't entirely let him go as he did another recording session in '56 with Marty Marsala, trumpet; Harry Graves, trombone; Max Hook, piano; Kenny White, bass; and, of course, Reinhardt, clarinet. The five titles appeared on a 10" LP, Jazz, Ltd. JL-1003, and on Atlantic 12" 1338. Three titles (Savoy Blues, Bluein' The Blues, The Battle Hymn of the Republic) appeared on CD, Collectables COL-CD-6250.

Again in 1956, on the 14th of April at the Universal studios in Chicago, came a session for Buzz Seeburg, the juke box chief. This had a specially selected personnel under Muggsy Spanier's name: George Bruni(e)s, trombone; Peanuts Hucko, clarinet; Floyd Bean, piano; Remo 'Ray' Biondi, guitar; Sy Nelson, bass; and Cenardo. Ten titles were cut and pressed by RCA on 45 rpm discs for juke box use. Two attempts at the Star Spangled Banner apparently got no further! These were gathered together, along with a similar session without Cenardo, and issued on IAJRC 42. The liner notes tell the full story.

Trumpeter Jimmy Ille said,

Doc had an inheritance ... a lot of money, in '57. Doc and Tomi left town [Chicago] and went to the coast and bought a place out there in El Monte. There was a little cottage out the back and I rented that for two years. That was in the early '60s.

Bill French says

After the war, I only saw Doc a couple of times ...but when he came out here [the Los Angeles area] I began seeing an awful lot of him. I fondly recall some of the Sunday afternoons that I'd visit him at his Maxson Road home in El Monte. We'd sit around, tell lies and laugh, etc. Then he'd say, 'How'd you like a real chocolate malted milk?' It was delicious! Another favorite of his was chicken wings. He had a secret recipe for a delicious sauce and as far as I know no one ever knew the recipe. Doc could out-eat most people and when he was in Chicago, he and Nap Trottier would take care of prodigious amounts of spaghetti, or ribs or what-have-you at a sitting. He used to say to me (at the time I weighed in at a fast 130 pounds), 'Heck, I weighed that much when I was born!'

Cenardo worked in the L.A. area at such places as the Gas Light, the Millionaires and, with the Kid Ory band, at the Beverly Cavern. He said that the band - Andrew Blakeney, trumpet; Ory, trombone; Bob McCracken, clarinet; Bobby Van Eps, piano; Johnny St. Cyr, guitar; Bob Boyack, bass, and Cenardo - cut more than 20 tunes. For Verve on December 5, 1961, eight were made which appeared on an LP (VLP9015) which claimed "tunes made famous by Jelly Roll Morton" but, somehow, Do You Know What It Means To Miss New Orleans got in there." Jepsen's *Jazz Records* listed a dozen more (thus making up most of Cenardo's "more than twenty") made the previous day and not issued.

Al Jenkins recalled working with a band at The Roaring '20s, a Hollywood club often visited by Lucille Ball and party. The band was led by trumpeter Garner Clark with Bus Bassey, clarinet; Mel Bryden, piano; Woodie Bushell, bass; and Cenardo on drums. This would be around 1960.

Hal Smith recalls sessions with Cenardo present at The Pillars in Glendora and at the monthly Sunday afternoon meetings of the New Orleans Jazz Club of California. Another place was The Jolly Jug at 1612 North Tyler (later Santa Anita), South El Monte. This had featured jazz by trios plus sitters-in for several years. By 1967, the trio was established as Bill Wood, clarinet; Lee Countryman (another seriously neglected musician), piano; and Doc Cenardo, drums. The building was closed for renovations during the winter of 1968/69 but the trio was back until January the 20th, 1973, when new management changed to a Western music policy. Sitters-in that evening included singer Marge Murphy, Ralph Harden on trumpet, Marvin Ash, piano, Roger Stillman on bass and trombonist Al Jenkins.

Aside from music and soon after his arrival, Cenardo opened a TV repair shop (Bill French thinks it was on Melrose Avenue in west L.A.) but this venture soon failed. He then converted his garage into a repair shop for his "Tune In" service. He also worked days as a security officer for a large company in Commerce, a suburb not too far from El Monte.

Bill French said

On September 18, 1974, he reported for work around 9 a.m. and a few minutes later suffered a massive stroke. When he fell he sustained head and brain damage and was rushed to the hospital in Montebello. At 3:30 on the morning of September 19 he died. Tragically, Tomi was found dead at their home on Maxson Road on January 11, 1975.

During the October 1966 meeting of the NOJC of California, Doc Cenardo met Doctor Edmund Souchon who was on a visit to California from his home town, New Orleans. During conversation, Cenardo was told of the Jazz Museum in that city and, as a result, the tiny piece of film, with Beiderbecke and the Goldkette crew was presented by Cenardo the following year. (Presumably it had been made available to the CBS production unit for the 1961 Chicago show.) The film had been shot by Charlie Horvath, the band's manager, in June of 1927, and was given to Cenardo in 1950.
Bill French again:

After his death, Tomi had a big lawn sale in an effort to get rid of Doc's TV tools, equipment, et al. The day I visited her during the sale, she gave me anything I wanted of Doc's drum kit. All I took were his three best cymbals (Zildjians, of course!), one of which he used on the Glenn Miller records. Doc was never a show-off type drummer. That is, he rarely took a break nor did he want to. His mother told him not to concern himself with solos but to just keep time. And that he did, like a metronome.

Wayne Jones, talking of Cenardo heard at a session for the Purdue Jazz Society in West Lafayette, Indiana:

He was the first real drummer I ever heard. I was 16 and ready to hear that, though not fully accomplished mentally, and unready for the gloriousness and magnificence of it. I just knew it was great.

Hal Smith has the coda:

Doc Cenardo was a fine dixieland drummer. He had good time and played with imagination and interesting effects. At his best, his sound was reminiscent of Ben Pollack. Cenardo's use of heavy afterbeats on the snare and cymbals and cowbell, integrated into breaks and tags and kick beats with stick and pedal on the bass drum, are Pollack trademarks. Cenardo could drive a band with Wettling-like abandon, too - hear the Muggsy Seeburg sides. Admirably, he was able to fit in well with bands from Glenn Miller to Kid Ory.

Freddy Greenleaf: The little-known but talented

It is a continuing source of surprise that of the number of fine musicians playing traditional/mainstream jazz during the immediate post-war years, so many were present on just one or two recording sessions. Of course, a good performance on a single record may give an inaccurate impression of a musician's overall ability, so one must be cautious when making such assessments. With this in mind, let us consider the career of trumpeter Freddy Greenleaf, in the hope that readers may be encouraged to listen to his few recordings and, perhaps, to fill in the spaces in the following story.

He was born September 17, 1915, in the Michigan hamlet of Leonidas. Details of his siblings are unknown, except that he had a brother, Frank, of whom it was said, "played passable trumpet." At the age of 17, Freddy joined the Detroit-based band of Hank Biagini, worked with it at a New York ballroom, and then played one-nighters in Pennsylvania. His roommate and best friend in the band was Johnny Best. The late Joe Duren worked with Biagini and told John Miner of a tour "about 1932" of the New England states and the coal regions (presumably Pennsylvania and adjoining states). His best recollection of the personnel was: Hank Biagini, Johnny Best, Tweet Peterson, Freddy Greenleaf, trumpets; George Jean and one unknown, trombones; Joe Duren, alto, flute, etc.; Paul Wingate, Tony Zimmers, tenors; Bob Zurke, piano; Slim Fortier, guitar; John Fanscher, tuba, bass; Stan Fleck, drums.

Johnny Best told collector Larry Channave that Greenleaf was a fine player, and the Biagini band was good for its time. It worked around the Boston area, and Best recalled being paid $25 a week.

Freddy Greenleaf's activities are unknown for the rest of the 1930s. During his career he does seem to have switched from music to day jobs and back again. Kenny Davern has referred to Greenleaf working in a Detroit factory and playing on the weekends. In July 1940 he played violin on a session at the Ash-Trumbull Club in Detroit, alongside Andy Bartha, trumpet; Frank Gillis, piano; Conrad Galvin, bass, and Doc Cenardo, drums. He was in the

Jack Teagarden Sextet, 1954. Left to right: Fred Greenleaf, trumpet; Kasper Malone, bass; Ray Bauduc, drums; Kenny Davern, clarinet; Norma Teagarden, piano; Jack Teagarden, trombone.

Frank Gillis Band, Ash-Trunbell Club, Detroit, July 1940. Left to right: Conrad Galvin, bass; Bill Stegmeyer, clarinet; Doc Cenardo, drums; Andy Bartha, violin; Fred Greenleaf, trumpet. (Courtesy Frank Gillis)

service during World War II, as *Down Beat* reported that he had been studying clarinet in Detroit under the G.I. Bill. He was in Chicago at the end of 1948, playing in the Miff Mole band at the Bee Hive, alongside Darnell Howard, Art Gronwall or George Zack, and Baby Dodds.

A report by Jack Tracy in *Down Beat* for August 25, 1950, gives the band at Jazz, Ltd. as Greenleaf, trumpet; Miff Mole, trombone; Bill Reinhardt, clarinet; Mel Grant, piano; and Zutty Singleton, drums. Tracy writes,

> Searching around for a hornman to take Muggsy Spanier's place when he left the club to form his own group (this would have been about April, 1950), owners Bill and Ruth Reinhardt chanced upon Fred Greenleaf, who was out of music entirely and working a day job.
> He's a dandy. We're especially partial to the full, earnest tone he gets, plus the beauty of his ballad solos. On the latter he gets a sound not unlike Armstrong's. On up-tempo stuff, he fits in smoothly with the rest of the group, knows when to layout and let the other two horns fill the spaces.

By the end of 1950 Greenleaf was on the West Coast. When Jess Stacy opened for a four-week engagement at the Hangover in San Francisco on November 13, 1950, his band had Greenleaf, trumpet; Warren Smith, trombone; Albert Nicholas, clarinet; Paul Sarmento, bass; and Smokey Stover, drums.

Late 1951 Greenleaf was in Los Angeles, playing with the Ben Pollack band at the Beverly Cavern. Also in the band were Elmer "Moe" Schneider, trombone; Matty Matlock, clarinet; Ray Sherman, piano; Bernie Miller, bass; and Pollack, drums. Mary Greenleaf, Freddy's wife, told drummer Bill French that her husband had some of his greatest musical kicks while working in the Hollywood area alongside such notables as Eddie Miller, George Van Eps, Stan Wrightsman, and Nick Fatool.

He spent the last half of 1954 in the Jack Teagarden band, replacing Jackie Coon, at the Hangover in San Francisco. The personnel was Bob McCracken, clarinet; Norma Teagarden, piano; Kass Malone, bass; and Ray Bauduc, drums, plus Jack on trombone and vocal, of course. By August the band was on tour, including an appearance at the Three Dolls in Milwaukee. Shortly after this engagement McCracken was replaced by Kenny Davern. A photograph with Jimmy Dorsey was taken during a jam session on Jack Teagarden's birthday (August 20th), when the entire Tommy Dorsey orchestra, with Jimmy Dorsey, made a surprise appearance at the Bali Key (Kei?) Club in Brentwood, Pennsylvania. (However, *Tommy & Jimmy: The Dorsey Years* suggests this took place in Brentford close to Christmas 1954.)

This edition of the Teagarden sextet (Greenleaf, Teagarden, Davern, Norma Teagarden, Malone, Bauduc) recorded in New York for Period on November 12, 1954. Greenleaf solos on three of the four titles recorded, Riverboat Shuffle, King Porter Stomp, and Milenberg Joys. He is surefooted in the ensembles and contributes pleasant solos, with an occasional Bixian turn of phrase.

He recorded again on June 12, 1957, this time with Art Hodes, in a band which also included Dave Remington, trombone; Bill Reinhardt, clarinet; Truck Parham, bass; and Fred Moore, drums. Of the six titles recorded, three were issued on the Dotted Eighth label and have since appeared on Jazzology JCD-46. These confirm the comments made by Jack Tracy. Greenleaf takes a good solo on the fast tempo St. Louis Blues, a fair one on Livery Stable Blues, and displays his full tone and firm lead on Riverside Blues.

Dave Remington told Jim Beebe that he worked with Greenleaf at Jazz, Ltd. during 1956 and 1957. Greenleaf would come in from Detroit and play three or four weeks, and sometimes longer. He had an alcohol problem and this would get the better of him. Remington recalled Greenleaf as a tasty Bixian-Hackett cornetist-trumpeter, who was very intelligent, compatible and respected.

It seems likely that Fred Greenleaf remained in Detroit and abandoned music as a full-time occupation. He died there of lung cancer on January 1, 1979.

Jazz Ltd, 1950. Bill Reinhardt, clarinet; Fred Greenleaf, trumpet; Zutty Singleton, drums; Miff Mole, trombone; Mel Grant, piano.

Paul Jordan: Another Unsung Jazzman

Ups and downs! I've had 'em all! Never super-rich or super-poor, but I've tasted both ends, but mostly in the middle. My father was a prominent physician in Chicago, well-to-do, bright émigré from England. Worked his way through medical school as a chemist – and so on – loved music and bought me a piano at about age 4 and so on – well, I'm not going into all that – now! We had a car (among others) which was a JORDAN. I've got a terrific 45-year-old daughter named JORDAN JORDAN living in Chicago....

The above was included in a letter dated November 28/30, 1987, no address given, written by pianist and arranger Paul Jordan and addressed to "Dear Irmie". To place it in context, the lady in question forwarded the letter to bassist Harlow Atwood and in October 1995 he wrote to me:

... passing on to you a letter written by the late Paul Jordan, the man who wrote much of Artie Shaw's wartime book with the full string section and a superb jazz pianist. Paul's Indian princess (genuine) wife had died the year before this 1987 letter and concerned over his depressed state of mind, I induced a rather naughty lady I know in Las Vegas, whom I'd nicknamed Irmie-Squirmie, to initiate a correspondence with Paul ... After long consideration, I decided to send you the letter, since it is a surviving document of a shamefully neglected jazz man of the mid-century.

Jordan's letter includes a great deal of domestic detail, talk of his cat and of meals and cars, but in addition to the above there is a mention of his first wife, June, Jordan's mother, and of his recently deceased wife, who was called Betty, as well as "my fantastic medical bills and loss of financial assets [which] wiped us out". He refers to a possible visit to suburban Littleton, which would seem to confirm the report that he spent his last years in Denver.

In the letter he also speaks of being jilted at the age of eighteen and burying himself in music. From this he developed his approach to emotional difficulties – "This will not do. What I have to do is HAUL OFF – and do something I LIKE TO DO."

Although Atwood exaggerates when saying that Jordan "wrote much of Artie Shaw's wartime book..." the pianist did receive a certain status because of his few yet individual arrangements and compositions for Shaw. Despite this, little biographical information has been published about him. Gunther Schuller has given his birth date as 1916[1], which fits the above details, and we know he died between 1988 and 1995. Fortunately his introduction to the piano at the age of four clearly qualified him to become part of the Chicago jazz scene for thirty years or so.

The first reference to Jordan is in connection with Floyd Town and his Men About Town, who opened an engagement at the Triangle Café on July 1, 1933. Altoist Bill Dohler recalled Paul Jordan, almost certainly, on piano. If Jordan was present, he would have been about 16 or 17 years of age.[2] The others were Johnny Mendell, trumpet, Dohler, Johnny Lane, altos, Town, tenor, Pat Pattison, bass, Don Carter, drums. It is unclear if Jordan was with Town during 1934. He was not in 1935, when the pianists were Art Hodes and then Tut Soper. Therefore it might be that he began working for Floyd Town when the band played at the Via Lago Café on 837 Wilson Avenue, either from March to July 1936 or, if one believes publicity material, from January until August 1st, 1936. The probable personnel for this period was Dick Donahue, trumpet, Bill Dohler, alto, Johnny Lane, clarinet, Floyd Town, tenor, Paul Jordan, piano, Norman Van Hook, bass, Don Carter, drums. Anita O'Day was persuaded to sing at this venue, probably after her regular gig. In her autobiography she wrote, "I remember Paul Jordan was on piano, Bill Dohler on alto sax." She refers to "some other sharp cats in the band. But the one who caught my eye was a tall drummer...." (namely, Don Carter).[3]

O'Day also suggests that Maurie Stein took over the Via Lago crew for an engagement at the Chez Paree.

(Harlow Atwood said that when Anita O'Day left Gene Krupa in 1946 to work as a single "the book she carried was written by Paul Jordan").

A West Coast tour was planned for the latter part of 1936, and in 1937 the Men About Town opened at The Midway Café, across the street from the Midway Gardens, followed by several months at the Storke Club on the north side of Chicago. They opened for an "indefinite stay" at the Hotel LaFontaine in Huntingdon on

December 31, 1937. In September 1938 they had another long booking at the Pla-Mor Café. An unidentified newspaper cutting dated January 5, 1938 gives the same personnel as above, except that Al Gold was the clarinettist.

The Town band had folded by the end of 1938 and the period 1939 to late 1941 is one of the many gaps in the Jordan chronology. When Jordan does reappear it is in connection with one the biggest names in the big band field.

Ray Conniff told Michael Zirpolo that while the Artie Shaw band was playing in Chicago at the Chicago Theatre in October 1941, Jordan visited him backstage and "showed him some of his composition/arrangements, with the hope that Conniff would then show them to Shaw. (He did.)"[4] Shaw was impressed and Jordan began scoring for the band almost immediately. His arrangement of Carnival is dated as early as November 17, 1941, while Suite #8 was included in a Spotlight Bands broadcast of December 8, 1941. On December 23, 1941, January 20 and 21, 1942, Shaw recorded nine of Jordan's arrangements, four of them original compositions.

Commenting on the December titles in the *IAJRC Journal* for June 2011, Zirpolo notes: "The two Jordan originals were the ethereal Evensong (Dusk), one of the most evocative of all Shaw recordings, which is pure concert music, and Suite No. 8 which is half atmospheric concert music and half romping jazz." (Zirpolo feels that the version of *Evensong*, recorded by the Smithsonian Masterworks Orchestra, is superb, better than the Shaw original.[7])

In his article, "Artie Shaw and his Symphonic Jazz" (part two) in the Summer 1998 issue of the *IAJRC Journal*, Zirpolo writes that "Paul Jordan's debut on record could not have been more auspicious" and cautions, "To say that the American pop music audience was not ready for Jordan's extraordinary talent would be an understatement." From the January 21 date he selects *Carnival* as representing "as perfect an example as is extant of the brilliance of Paul Jordan." He has pointed out that Jordan was of a generation that included Gil Evans (b. 1912), Eddie Sauter (b. 1914), Billy Strayhorn (b. 1915) and Bill Finegan (b. 1917).[5] These were young men who were changing the ways of writing for the big swing bands.

Shaw, commenting sixty years later in 2001, upon the demands of his audiences, wrote: "However, within these limitations I managed to make a number of records I felt were musically interesting, stuff like Paul Jordan's Suite #8, Two In One Blues, Evensong and so on."[6]

Arrangements from the Artie Shaw library are housed at the University of Arizona and Michael Zirpolo has traced the following Paul Jordan items from the University's index.[7] Some have previously been credited to Lennie Hayton.

Evensong (Jordan)	Victor 28-045	(12-inch)
Suite #8 (Andante) (Jordan)	Victor 28-045	(12-inch)
Two In One Blues (Jordan)	Victor	20-1526
Carnival (Jordan)	Victor	27860
I Don't Want To Walk Without You	Victor 27746	(vocal arr.)
Somebody Nobody Loves	Victor 27798	(vocal arr.)
Hindustan	Victor	277980
Not Mine	Victor 27779	(vocal arr.)
Absent Minded Moon	Victor 27779	(vocal arr.)
Old Rip		unrecorded
I Said No!		unrecorded
Suite #4 (Lento & Allegro)		unrecorded
Someday Sweetheart		unrecorded
Ev'rything I Love		unrecorded

Pearl Harbor ensured that Jordan's association with Artie Shaw was brief, the leader disbanding after the Victor recording session of January 21, 1942.

A *Down Beat* feature referred to Bud Freeman having the house band at the Sherman Hotel in Chicago "around 1942" with Bill Dohler, alto, and Paul Jordan[8]. One could guess that Jordan left Freeman to play piano and arrange for the Bob Chester orchestra, possibly from May 1942 to mid-1943, or perhaps into 1944. He is listed for Chester Bluebird recordings on May 27 and June 30, 1942. A review of the band in *Billboard* (October 10, 1942) lists the rhythm section at that time as Paul Jordan, piano, Bobby Gibbons, guitar, Hank Wayland, bass, and Tony Romersa, drums. Three World Transcription titles on Golden Era LP-15003 are alleged to be from 1940 but credit Jordan on piano. One could easily accept that the few bars of interesting piano on Strictly Instrumental are by Mr. Jordan.

It is possible that Jordan stayed with Chester into 1944. Billboard, in a January 8, 1944 review of the orchestra, referred to an original by pianist Paul Jordan, Rollo Get With It.

He may have been working with Bud Freeman again in 1946. He recorded two titles with Freeman for John Steiner's Paramount label, Bop Boose and Blue Lou. Probably from the same session, with Bud Freeman, are two titles on Gold Seal 402 under Jordan's name, Goin' Far Away and Blues For Peanuts. The piano solos on these four titles, on which he responds well to Freeman, are all modern in approach, well-crafted and worth hearing. One can speculate that these two Gold Seal originals, which are not credited, are Jordan compositions.

Listed as September 1946 recordings are two titles (The Footwarmer/Lament For A Water Buffalo) by Paul Jordan's Octet on Gold Seal 403. The personnel is Bob Durfee, clarinet, Bill Dohler, alto, Boyd Rolando, tenor, Jordan, piano, George Barnes, George Allen, guitars, Mike Rubin, bass, Frank Rullo, drums. Two unissued titles from this period (Rumpus, The Sissy Policeman) could perhaps be from this session and all four might even be Jordan originals.

1947 is blank, but *Down Beat* for July 14, 1948 reported: "Paul Jordan, fine young pianist and ex-Artie Shaw arranger, is playing in a strip joint, the Silver Palm, with three pieces." He was still there at the end of 1948, with *Down Beat* (January 14, 1949) stating: "One time Shaw arranger (Evensong, Two-In-One Blues) Jordan is currently playing at the Silver Palm, a strip house on Wilson and Broadway. His cohorts are drummer Ross Morrison and tenorist Charlie Clark."

We come to 1950, when *Down Beat*'s Chicago office advised: "Paul Jordan band backing Anita O'Day at the Hi-Note: Boyd Rolando, tenor, Verne Rammer, bass, Elmo Luperini, drums" (May 19, 1950 issue) and "Paul Jordan combo back at Hi-Note: Denny Roche, trumpet, Buddy Nichols, bass, Guy Viverous, drums" (June 16, 1950 issue). O'Day also recorded four titles for London on January 5, 1950 with Paul Jordan's Sextet, though only two, Blues For Bojangles/Your Eyes Are Bigger You're Your Heart, were issued. The sextet includes Boyd Rolando, as well as John Carroll, trumpet, George Barnes, guitar, Mel Schmidt, bass, and Frank Rullo, drums.

It has also been reported that Jordan led a band in the 1950s, at the Panther Room of the Sherman Hotel, which included

Coleman Hawkins, tenor, and Max Miller, presumably on vibes.[9] Bud Freeman, in his autobiography, said that about 1950 he took a sextet into an East St. Louis club for three weeks. The group included Ruby Braff [spelt Brath] and Paul Jordan.[10]

Down Beat's Chicago office (January 25, 1952) reported: "George Barnes is leaving ABC staff to go out on his own with a trio in New York City. Present plans call for a trio to include Paul Jordan on piano and Irv Kluger on drums." There was no confirmation that these plans were fulfilled.

Another large gap, then in 1956 he is in the recording studios in Chicago again. There was a session for Argo, with Cy Touff as leader, and one for Dot with Russell Procope. With Procope on alto were Earl Backus and Remo 'Ray' Biondi on guitars, with Jordan, Schmidt and Rullo as the rhythm section.

The Cy Touff band consisted of Muggsy Dawson, cornet, Touff, bass-trumpet, Mike Simpson, clarinet, Paul Jordan, piano, Mel Schmidt, bass, Frank Rullo, drums. Six titles were recorded and released on Argo LP606, **Doorway To Dixie**, together with four titles by Miff Mole and his band from 1950, Don Ewell on piano, originally on Premium. The titles by Touff were all dixieland standards (At The Jazz Band Ball, Basin Street Blues, Struttin' With Some Barbecue, Royal Garden Blues, South Rampart Street Parade and Muskrat Ramble), but played with a mainstream feel. Cy Touff had a foot in both jazz camps of the day and Jordan, who solos on all titles but the last, again has a modern approach without disturbing the equilibrium of the group.

Jack Tracy's sleeve note to Argo LP606 says, "Three more studio musicians make up the rhythm section". This comment could explain why little is known about Jordan's activities during the 1950s and into the 1960s, though studio musicians often return to jazz in their free time.

At some point in the 1960s Jordan is reported to have moved to Denver and his comment about Littleton would seem to confirm this. As one report said, after the Artie Shaw period he lived and worked in obscurity.

Despite the limited amount of evidence available - the arrangements for Artie Shaw and the few recorded titles heard – there would seem to be justification for Harlow Atwood's claim that Jordan was "shamefully neglected".

Undoubtedly there is more information about Paul Jordan somewhere. Perhaps someone did interview him in Chicago or even in Denver and these stories are waiting to be found or published. Was there an obituary in a Denver newspaper? As an inexperienced internet surfer my searches have been almost fruitless, but one lives in hope. In addition to his contribution to the Artie Shaw orchestra, Paul Jordan merits his place in Chicago jazz history.

Comments on the titles by Anita O'Day on London, the Russell Procope on Dot and the Paul Jordan on Gold Seal 403 would be very welcome.

Of course, I now regret not pursuing Harlow Atwood for more of his recollections of the life and music of Paul Jordan.

A more detailed listing of Argo LP-606 appeared in Discographical Forum on page 55 of the *IAJRC Journal*, December 2015, issue.

Additions received from Chris Kaufmann and Robert L. Campbell

From Chris Kaufmann's Internet searches:

Paul Jordan was born August 25, 1916 and died July 23, 1989, in Denver, Colorado. Last known address: 80212 Denver, Denver, CO. [U.S. Social Security Death Index 1935-2014]

No details are given, but according to John Steiner he attended Roosevelt Military Academy in Aledo, IL. [Steiner Collection, University of Chicago]

An article in *Down Beat* by Ted Toll was headed "Fine Men Scramble To Play With Band That Never Works". [*Down Beat*, March 15, 1941]

"Music and Rhythm" for May, 1941 had a feature article by Paul Eduard Miller entitled: PAUL JORDAN STARTS WHERE ELLINGTON STOPS. This referred to a concert held March 31, 1941, featuring the Paul Jordan Orchestra and the Max Miller Trio. The orchestra personnel was: Nicky Craig, Carl Knauer, Mickey Traisel, trumpets; Lloyd Wilson, Bob McReynolds, Ernie Kolstad, trombones; Bill Dohler, Charlie Spero, altos; Verne Anderson, Johnny Bothwell, tenors; Jordan, piano; unidentified bass and drums, presumably. "When the band opened a series of Monday-nighters at Chicago's Panther Room late in April, Warren Smith had replaced Kolstad, Pat Trapani, Wilson; and Jimmy Zito, Knauer."

Then followed some biographical details, touching upon the influence of Duke Ellington and the amount of hard work and study Jordan had undertaken. [ibid]

Jordan took piano lessons from the age of 8 to fourteen. "He had aspirations to follow in his father's footsteps and become a doctor. But his father's sudden death when Paul was 13, forced him to change his plans." [ibid]

"At 18 he joined the musician's union and for the next five years gigged around the local Chicago bands, particularly those of Floyd Towne and Carl Schreiber." "Jordan began writing and arranging professionally in 1936. He composed some music on the serious side, as for example a *Suite For Strings* and two *Tone Poems*." [ibid]

A "Partial List of Jordan's Compositions" was: *The Private Dining Room Suite* (3 parts); *Ballad*; *Suite No. 8* (2 parts); *The Jewel Suite* (5 parts); *Sleeper Jump*; *Carnival*; *Lament For A Water Buffalo*; *The Baccilus Suite* (3 parts); *Etude For Alto*; *Old Rip*; *On The Fire*; *Sleeveless Errand*; *The Chant*; *Two and One Blues*; *Night Out*. [ibid]

Under the headline PAUL JORDAN JOINS SHAW AS ARRANGER *Down Beat* for December 1, 1941, announced:

> Paul Jordan, whose "band that never works" has been a sensation with Chicago musicians and critics for the last year or so, has joined Artie Shaw as an arranger. Jordan signed with Shaw on November 13 and joined the band in New York a day later. The first number Jordan will write especially for Shaw's instrumentation is *Dance of the Drunken Spirochete*.
>
> Jordan is a young musician who has been gigging around town on piano for several years. He's never attracted any attention to himself as a performer having preferred to devote most of his time to writing. [condensed from *Down Beat*, December 1, 1941]

Artie Shaw, with his 32-piece orchestra, scheduled to play a charity event at the Aragon Ballroom on December 29. "Shaw will play a number of [Paul] Jordan's unique songs." (*Chicago Tribune*, December 21, 1941)

A Paul Eduard Miller production, "Operations Jazz," was scheduled for the Opera House in Chicago on October 13, 1946. Featured were groups led by Sidney Bechet, Dizzy Gillespie, Gene Sedric, Bud Freeman, Max Miller, George Barnes, Jimmy

McPartland and Paul Jordan with his Octet. The Octet personnel was similar to that for the Gold Seal recordings, but it was really a ten-piece, with Jack Cavan, trumpet, Charlie Spero, clarinet, Bill Dohler, alto, Boyd Rolando, tenor, Jordan, piano, George Barnes, George Allen, guitars, Mike Rubin, Abe Luboff, basses, and Frank Rullo, drums. [*Chicago Tribune*, September 29, 1946, and Robert L. Campbell website]

> Paul Jordan, a jazz genius born under the wrong star, is finally playing his own kind of music again behind the warbling of Anita O'Day at the Hi-Note. Among his noncompos compositions are Lament For A Water Buffalo and Maid With The Flaccid Hair. Dig the guy, he may be uncovered. [*Chicago Tribune* April 21, 1950]

A review for the following record appeared in Billboard for August 11, 1956:

Paul Jordan's Orchestra
(appears to be piano and drums)

Miami Beach Rhumba	Deed 1021
Crazy Carousel	Deed 1021

The following additions are from Robert L. Campbell, The Red Saunders Research Foundation

They add unissued titles to the Paul Jordan Octet session and add a previously unlisted Max Miller session. A newspaper clipping provides news of work with other performers and of appearances in Denver and Colorado Springs in 1964.

BOB CHESTER and his ORCHESTRA
Joyce LP4005, Spotlight on Bob Chester and Teddy Powell, includes six tracks by Chester from May and August 1943 broadcasts. The four tracks from 4 August have Chester announcing The Footwarmer and Jordan's presence.

PAUL JORDAN OCTET
(Bob Durfee, cl, as; Bill Dohler, as; Boyd Rolando, ts; Paul Jordan, p; George Barnes, George Allen, e-g; Mike Rubin, b; Frank Rullo, d).
United Broadcasting Studio, Chicago – September 1946

UB-2477	Lament For A Water Buffalo	Gold Seal 403

UB-2478	The Footwarmer	Gold Seal 403
	Down A Flight	unissued
	New Blue	unissued
	Mirage	unissued
	Evensong	unissued
	Rumpus and the Sissy Policeman	unissued
	Suite No. 8	unissued
	Major Triad Was Loaded	unissued

These titles were scheduled for issue on the still-born Green label.

Note that Durfee plays both clarinet and alto, and that Rumpus and the Sissy Policeman is one title, not two as suggested in Lord.

PAUL JORDAN QUARTET

(Bud Freeman, ts; Paul Jordan, p; Mike Rubin, b; Frank Rullo, d).

United Broadcasting Studio, Chicago – September 1946

UB-2479	Goin' Far Away	Gold Seal GS402
UB-2480	Blues For Peanuts	Gold Seal GS402
	Ragamuffin'	unissued
	B Flat	unissued

These titles were scheduled for issue on the still-born Green label.

MAX MILLER and Life Records All Stars

(Miller, vb; Paul Jordan, p; Parke Hill, e-g; Ernest Shepherd, b; Terry Nolan, d; Wellington Blakey, vo).

Chicago – early 1952

| KB1698 | Only For You (Roth) | Life B-1011, B-5001 |
| | Cross Me Off Your List (Roth) | Life B-5002 |

Backings to these discs are by Max Miller Trio, without Jordan.

Sources:

"The Swing Era", by Gunther Schuller
"Floyd Town: His Story", by Iris Town & Derek Coller, *The Mississippi Rag*, February 1990
"High Times, Hard Times" by Anita O'Day
Michael Zirpolo, e-mail, July 15, 2015
Michael Zirpolo, e-mail, July 15, 2015
Artie Shaw, "Self Portrait", Bluebird CD set
Michael Zirpolo, e-mail, July 20, 2015
Down Beat, January 14, 1949
redsaunders.com
"Crazeology" by Bud Freeman, with Robert Wolf

Muggsy Spanier: the Horn of Truth

Francis Joseph Spanier, known to all as Muggsy, was born to immigrant parents in Chicago in 1901. His mother was an FBI (Muggsy's jocular expression for Foreign Born Irish) who moved to Chicago via Boston; his father came from France. Young Muggsy grew up close to the teeming north side of the young, virile city where the vast cultural mix offered many beneficial European influences, not least in popular music.

The situation was not limited to Chicago. It was happening elsewhere and especially in the southern city of New Orleans where the music soon to be known as Jazz was taking shape. The search for work elsewhere caused many of that city's musicians to try their luck in Chicago which gained considerably by the arrival of the Original Dixieland Jazz Band, the New Orleans Rhythm Kings and King Oliver's Creole Jazz Band, soon to reveal its full glory with the subsequent addition of a young Louis Armstrong.

Spanier and many others of his generation heard the music of these bands, were excited by it and wanted to take part. Instruments were bought, often from pawn shops, and the youngsters worked hard at mastering them, eventually achieving sufficient competence to try for work. Spanier started on drums, becoming good enough to play in his school band, but it was the cornet of King Oliver that appealed to him and he switched instruments, making the band on cornet by the time he was in his early teens.

He joined the Musicians' Union in 1919 and by the following year he was playing professionally in various Chicago clubs and dance halls. Violinist Sig Meyer led one of the bands from which Muggsy and others travelled to Richmond, Indiana, in February 1924 to record seven tunes under the name of The Bucktown Five.

Our first CD opens with two of these recordings. Really A Pain, on which Spanier shares composer credit, is a bright number, typical of the era, and is entirely ensemble with solo breaks. It is well-rehearsed but is certainly jazz. Even more so is Steady Roll Blues which is not of the traditional 12-bar construction but has ensemble verse and chorus which gives way to Volly De Faut's clarinet and

Muggsy Spanier at the Blue Note, Chicago, 1951.
(Courtesy John Miner)

then Muggsy, making his first recorded solo. He makes no secret of his admiration for Oliver and his breaks are wonderfully confident.

Spanier had yet to achieve the sound which made his playing so instantly recognisable but at least one aspect of it is apparent on the next date - Muggsy's power and strength in leading an ensemble through two medium-paced popular songs. It was April 1928 and a scratch band of young enthusiasts were recording as the Chicago Rhythm Kings. There is no doubting the boss horn and the only pity is that the solo space assigned to Mezz Mezzrow's tenor on I've Found A New Baby did not go to the cornetist. But Muggsy held no grudge and when he was in Paris with the Ted Lewis band a couple of years later, he came across a review of the French release and wrote across the top of the page: "Show This to Mezzrow."

Spanier was one of Ted Lewis's featured 'hot' soloists and is heard in this capacity from a January 1930 date. Lewis was a vaudeville entertainer who played gruesome clarinet - and knew it! He also 'sang' in a semi-spoken manner, but he loved his band. The Lonesome Road, from the stage production Show Boat, has a male vocal quartet with Lewis preaching and Muggsy blowing with his inimitable display of emotion as he drives the congregation in a searing close. Muggsy's special ability to play blues and ballads from the heart is heard often in this compilation.

Dip Your Brush In The Sunshine, a cheer-up song from the Depression years, offers a fine clarinet solo by Benny Goodman which is then eclipsed completely by Spanier's intense muted chorus, encouraged by Lewis to "Paint it red, Muggsy!" Two months later on a Red McKenzie record, Muggsy followed a Coleman Hawkins solo and once again 'cut' his illustrious colleague. Hot jazz, indeed!

In December 1936, the cornetist switched to Ben Pollack's Orchestra, taking over from Harry James as the Jazz soloist. The band travelled extensively and early in 1938 was working in New Orleans when Muggsy complained of stomach pains and collapsed with a perforated ulcer. At the point of death, he was saved by Dr Alton Oschner who, taking a chance, drained the fluid and eased Muggsy's weakened breathing. The recovery, even after discharge from the Touro Infirmary, took many months, but the indomitable Spanier practiced hard to keep his *embouchure* in shape.

He recorded privately in New Orleans (the records have yet to surface) before returning to Chicago. By April 1939 Muggsy

Spanier's Ragtime Band was in full cry at the Sherman House Hotel and in July recorded four titles for RCA Victor's Bluebird subsidiary. A further 12 tracks were cut over three sessions in New York and the whole collection was later released as a 12-inch LP under the universally-adopted title **The Great Sixteen**. Two of those July numbers are here. The Big Butter And Egg Man, recorded by Louis Armstrong in 1926, is brimful of joyousness, with Spanier (a middle-register man) reaching for the heights encouraged by the cries of trombonist George Brunies. Someday, Sweeetheart, on the other hand, is a yearning love song with the cornet expressing all its sadness. Like some other jazz musicians, Spanier was certain that knowing the lyrics of a song enabled him to better interpret the number.

At the Jazz Band Ball dates from 1917 when it was composed and recorded by the Original Dixieland Jazz Band. It steps out with an effervescence rarely - if ever - matched, despite the subsequent countless interpretations it inspired. Then comes the Spanier theme, dedicated to the hospital in which he had his brush with death - Relaxin' At The Touro. This gently-swinging performance demonstrates, perhaps more than any other, Muggsy's way with a mute and his ability to express his emotions, in this case just what that life-saving visit meant to him. It is a classic performance, and, by way of a bonus, this and the other three Ragtime Band tracks are from takes different to those usually chosen for issue.

Changing fads in popular music led to the disbanding of the Ragtimers and mid-1940 saw our hero sat in the brass section of Bob Crosby's Orchestra. Much of the band's output was very commercial and when the opportunity came to record a couple of tracks with songstress Lee Wiley and pianist Jess Stacy, Muggsy grabbed it. Down To Steamboat Tennessee is a blues which Wiley invests with a fervour that would have done credit to Bessie Smith, while Sugar is transformed from a popular song into something quite special, aided by a lovely muted chorus on the cornet.

In 1941 Spanier left Crosby and formed his own orchestra. It was a very good swing band with an excellent personnel which, after some out-of-town gigs, played for dancing at the Arcadia in New York. With the wonderful New Orleans clarinetist Irving Fazola in its ranks, the band recorded our next four. With one exception, they are first-class big band performances quite typical of the era, as are the following four recorded with a somewhat different line-up and including the obligatory girl singer on More Than You Know. The solitary exception is Hesitating Blues which is by an octet from the band and played in the manner of the Ragtimers of fond memory.

Although the big band continued to work regularly, Spanier started to feel the effects of the draft as his musicians were called into the armed forces for service in World War II. By mid-1943, Muggsy took ill with the problems he faced, and the orchestra folded. After a period of recuperation, he found himself freelancing in New York.

Milt Gabler was not only a record producer but also a good friend to musicians and he assembled the next band for his Commodore label. The jazz is not quite 'Ragtime Band' but is certainly in the tradition of the swinging, extemporised music to be heard in such New York establishments as Nick's in Greenwich Village. Oh, Lady Be Good! has that cornet, as ever, driving the ensemble, with the baritone saxophone of Ernie Caceres replacing the usual trombone. Spanier played September In The Rain as a feature when he was with Pollack and here he takes a full chorus before giving over to the piano of Dick Cary, whose talents are so often taken for granted.

In the summer of 1944. Muggsy spent a few weeks with his old boss, Ted Lewis, but was soon back in New York where he recorded again for Gabler. With Miff Mole adding his trombone skills to the ensemble, we hear what has become known as 'Nicksieland' jazz - a free-flowing, sophisticated way of interpreting the music of earlier times. Riverside Blues, a 1923 King Oliver speciality, is given powerful but respectful treatment in a gesture towards Muggsy's mentor of two decades ago. Clarinetist Pee Wee Russell offers typical examples of his unique, love-it or hate-it style, as he does on the next date which has Lou McGarity in the trombone chair, his performance reflecting his experience in the big bands. Bassist Bob Haggart's whistling on the blues is unusual but it works well enough although soon eclipsed by the excellent instrumental choruses that follow.

The second disc opens with September In The Rain, taken from the same session as Oh, Lady Be Good! and then parades the complete set of 12 titles from two 1946 sessions. Original issues from the first date named all the musicians except Muggsy who was billed as 'Surprise star cornetist.' Cliff Jackson, who was often used as intermission pianist at Nick's, being considered more 'Harlem' than 'Chicago', plays with the band here and fits in well, also contributing a pleasant vocal on Rosie. Russell's singing on Take Me To The Land Of Jazz comes out just as he might have interpreted it on his horn, but he then confounds the listener by soloing quite differently. He makes a tender contribution to the love song I'd Climb The Highest Mountain which closes with typical Spanier lead.

Muggsy and Pee Wee engage in some hokum on Pee Wee Squawks with Russell singing a couple of blues stanzas, while he obviously enjoys his lead role on the opening of Sentimental Journey, playing different variations on the alternative take.

Spanier formed a band of his own again in the Fifties and went on the road. While the personnel inevitably changed, the repertoire stayed within the boundaries of jazz standards and good popular songs. The group which made our final session had been together for some time and was well-settled, with British trombonist Ralph Hutchinson and the Mexican, Phil Gomez, completing the front line on clarinet. The rhythm section consisted of Harlem swing pianist Red Richards, Chicago-based Truck Parham on bass and Kansas-born George Wettling on drums.

In 1954 the band made two sessions for Decca on September 2nd and 3rd, and was due to open in Toronto on the 6th, but the opportunity came to cut an LP for the Weathers label on the 4th and it was a band of tired musicians who struggled into the studio to record what is now a collectors' item. The nine tracks they cut are all presented here. The performances show the band in its usual exuberant form with not even a hint of strain.

At the beginning of 1957, Spanier and his wife moved to Sausalito, just across the Golden Gate bridge from San Francisco. Muggsy's health was not good and he gave up touring almost entirely, taking the opportunity to settle down with steady work in the locally-based Earl Hines band. He and Ruth were happy in their pleasant home where Muggsy pottered in the garden and walked his dogs, always taking time to keep his *embouchure* in trim by daily practice. He died on Sunday, February 12th, 1967.

Through most of his career, Muggsy lied about his age. Maybe vanity caused him to claim he was born in 1906, but his real birthdate was November 9th, 1901. One thing for sure - he always told the truth through his cornet. Muggsy was special, indeed!.

Muggsy Spanier: Richmond and Chicago Days

The basic facts of Muggsy Spanier's life and career, from his birth in Chicago on the 9th of November, 1906, to his death in Sausalito on the 12th of February, 1967, have so often appeared in print (and are admirably summed-up in John Chilton's *Who's Who In Jazz*) that there seems to be little point in repeating them here.

Let's look, then, at the man behind the cornet from which for over forty years came the punchy, driving lead which swung ensembles so uncompromisingly. With Muggsy in there blowing it just had to be jazz and it had to swing, the feeling very intense, the tone very hot and it mattered not whether the tune was a Dixieland warhorse, played for the umpteenth time, or a nice old pop tune.

Although Muggsy fronted a big band for a couple of years in the early 'forties and, by all accounts, enjoyed it, there is no doubt that he was happiest with a smaller outfit. "I have always preferred small group work and this is not because I don't like large bands," he told David Sessions, "but there is something less contrived in a small group—a chance to stretch your imagination, as it were, and, by and large, you must have better musicians. I love the free-wheeling privileges which are a constant challenge both as to execution and improvisation."

He didn't like the banjo-tuba rhythm of the "revivalist" era. Not for him the slavish copying, clinkers and all, of the old records.

I like four beats and, even on the Ted Lewis records, that's what I played. I'm probably dead wrong but, if so, so is Louis because in his band you don't hear the heavy kerboomchunk sound. For me, I think you should feel rhythm as you listen rather than hear it. That's why I like a bass fiddle and a guitar. These give you a wonderful rhythm section, along with piano and drums, of course, and they swing a band.

So it was always clean-cut swinging music for Muggsy. Good men alongside him and good tunes to play. No need for fancy arrangements and screeching high notes. His admiration for Armstrong is well known and obvious in his playing. But his tastes were by no means limited, because he enjoyed the playing of men of schools well away from his own kind of jazz — Ben Webster, Dizzy Gillespie, Benny Carter, Coleman Hawkins and so on ... the good men, the swingers, the non-phoneys.

Despite the tough appearance, the tough nickname, the as-you-would-expect tough Chicago voice — to hear him pronounce 'hundred' as 'hunnert' told all — and the tough, fightin' cornet playing, despite all this, Muggsy was a kind and gentle man. Through the years of scuffling and touring and the tiredness, he maintained standards set in his early days of fair dealing with his fellow musicians. A man with the ability and interest — the stamina, too — could be assured of having a job with Muggsy for as long as he wanted it and for as long as the work came in. Mind you, he would have to be on the stand on time and in good shape, for Muggsy was a stickler for presentation — if you looked good, you played good. Always impeccably turned out himself (for years he went to a Canadian tailor whose cutting suited him; the hang of the jacket, when the arms were up holding the cornet, was important), he expected similar standards from his sidemen.

Muggsy had his moments, of course, and we all know the story of a jazz critic who felt the sharpness of his tongue. The story is true but, as always, the years softened the edges so that a couple of decades or so later when the critic lunched with Muggsy and Mrs. Spanier everything went well and, as might be expected, the incident was not mentioned!

In common with many musicians, Muggsy didn't really enjoy making records. His was that sort of temperament which, in the studio, got him up-tight. The results rarely satisfied him and the restrictions imposed by the session director were annoying. "I think if he could have been leader, director and engineer," Mrs. Spanier once told me, "he would have felt differently — given, too, no time limits (and there always are)." There were the occasional exceptions: Muggsy enjoyed hugely his first session for Mercury where director George Tasker was entirely sympathetic and the only restriction would have been the necessary one of the time limit imposed by the 78 r.p.m. record.

"Some men don't mind," continued Mrs. Spanier, "and others do and Muggsy happened to be one of those who felt restricted in a studio. He enjoyed jam sessions and, if all the men were sober and on their toes, he didn't care whether it was recorded or not.

He would have loved the V.J.M. records for they are 'live' and 'free-wheeling', as he used to say, and the men were not bound in any way by a director."

One might well wonder, then, how it was that Muggsy managed to turn out so many fine records both as leader and sideman. The answer has to be that he was a damned fine jazzman and a pro and so, come what may, a good performance had to result. The nub of the matter is that Muggsy was a dedicated and determined musician and this came through in his playing. And he communicated with the listener so that somehow you felt you knew him. (When you think about it, there aren't too many musicians of which the same can be said.) This was why Muggsy Spanier was a successful jazzman. In financial terms, maybe not always, maybe even not too often, certainly not often enough, did he make it. But in what he said to us through his cornet there were few to match and even fewer to surpass him.

The Bucktown Five

Just who organised this session and who was the leader remains unknown. Muggsy Spanier was a natural leader and, of course, his instrument is that which leads the good jazz ensemble. This is a basic fact in the music and, in these performances, he leaves us in no doubt that he knew the role he must play. Not to be the star performer with the others tagging along but to be a part of the whole, showing the way with both strength and sympathy.

Even so, there can be no doubt that the outstanding men on these seven titles are Spanier and Volly De Faut. As a band, though, the quintet hangs together beautifully. The three horns balance each other admirably in ensembles whether improvised or lightly arranged. Arranged, I like to think, not in the usual sense of being committed to paper but organised and practiced at rehearsals.

Guy Carey's trombone is righteously New Orleans tailgate and pushes the ensembles along well. In solo he is — let's be kind — too straight. Even so, this was not entirely unusual at this time: compare Jesse Barnes on the Midway Garden Columbias (their Buddy's Habits should be noted alongside the version presented here) and even the superb George Brunies, surely the finest of the white New Orleans trombonists, was rarely a great soloist. Carey was no Eddie Edwards or Santo Pecora but he knew what he had to do and he did it well.

The two-man rhythm team is more than adequate. Mel Stitzel's piano is light but rhythmic. I have him down as an admirer of the playing of 'Miss Lil' in the Oliver band. Marvin Saxbe's banjo is dextrous enough and, as I say, these two men together are fine backing the few solos and they are first-class in the ensembles. Here was a quintet of the same instrumentation as Armstrong's Hot Five but nearly two years earlier and producing fine jazz.

De Faut, who recently died, was another of the many fine clarinetists who never got sufficient recognition. His recorded output is meagre and, in fact, a high percentage of the really worthwhile part of it is included here on one side of this record. His playing obviously fits into the school headed by Leon Rappolo: clear, pleasant tone and flowing phrases dancing nimbly in ensemble and calm and swinging in solo. Here he complements Muggsy's cornet very happily and he takes his breaks quite beautifully. Really A Pain is all ensemble with breaks and De Faut's playing here is excellent. Move on to Chicago Blues and the clarinet is often quite superb.

On every track, Muggsy demonstrates how well he had soaked up the jazz he had enjoyed in Chicago and consider, too, that not too long before this session he had reached the ripe old age of eighteen! What he plays here would not have shamed a man ten years older and much more experienced. As it is, the results are astonishing. King Oliver was his man and it shows so often in what he plays. Yes, here and there comes a phrase which makes you say 'Louis!' (and this becomes more apparent in the later tracks on this record) but Oliver has to be the major influence and it still came through in performances of many years later.

This session was Muggsy's first-ever in a recording studio and was a remarkable debut. Curiously, perhaps, only two titles include solos by the cornetist. However, when you take stock of the overall content, no one musician is favoured. But we are conscious of our man almost all the way through and we mustn't regret for a moment the decision that was taken not to give more space to individual efforts. The sides are not without their flaws but these may easily be forgiven for there is much to enjoy. In Someday Sweetheart Stitzel plays the verse very pleasantly and at the same time gives Saxbe ample time to switch from banjo to guitar for his duet with De Faut (and surely there was something original about a clarinet-guitar duet!). Saxbe's little stumble is maybe briefly annoying but can be immediately forgiven and forgotten because the thing is so well presented.

The Stomp Six

Although the front line here is identical to that of the Bucktown group, the results are somewhat different. There is the obvious replacement of banjo by the good brass bass of the obscure Joe Gish and the addition of the lively drumming of Ben Pollack. So the sound is much fuller. The crude electric recording quality doesn't help and I believe these would have sounded better coming from Gennett's acoustic studio. Even so, what strikes home right away is the greatly increased heat and fervour in Muggsy's cornet playing which, after brief introductions, commences both titles.

Why Cant It Be Poor Little Me is a nice little tune and everyone does well. De Faut's clarinet, with the bass prominent, is a delight, as is Muggsy's break in the ensemble, while Pollack demonstrates his prowess with cymbals. Everybody Loves My Baby has Muggsy revealing more of Armstrong as an influence and Carey's solo is a great improvement on what he does on the Bucktown sides. De Faut again shines in a controlled, hot solo. The Charleston beats in the ensemble raise a smile every time.

Charles Pierce and His Orchestra

The first of the Pierce Paramounts was the subject of the very first reissue specifically aimed at the jazz collector. It now seems astonishing that the time between the original issue and the reissue was less than eight years. The labels of the latter record (UHCA 1/2) have the legend, "Dubbed and re-pressed ... November 1935 and issued for UHCA members."

Whether or not there was ever such an organisation as The United Hot Clubs of America, the "members" had to wait until early 1941 for the next Pierce reissue which was on 71/72. For some strange reason, Milt Gabler numbered each side of his records and so this was the thirty-sixth in the series. If anyone had wondered why this should be, its importance (or lack of it) would have been lost in the problem: does the personnel include Muggsy Spanier and Frank Teschemacher?

Maurie Bercov was consulted and he insisted that he, not Tesch, was the clarinetist and he thought Muggsy was on cornet. On the other hand, Dan Lipscomb and Ralph Rudder were equally sure that the cornet had been played by Charlie Altiere. Spanier himself said he was certain he had made the sides and one would think he would know. The critics and collectors wrangled for years and it wasn't until fairly recently that the matter was resolved. What had become quite apparent, by careful listening, was that Muggsy was not on Jazz Me Blues and Sister Kate as they appeared on the UHCA record. After much longer drawn out dissent, Bercov was settled on for the clarinet work and this was how the personnel appeared in the discographies.

Then, just a few years ago, a collector turned up a copy of the Paramount which contained quite different versions of the two tunes —and the cornet just had to be by Spanier while the clarinet was certainly by Teschemacher. This "new" record bore the take numbers shown in the accompanying discographical data and these indicated re-makes. Aural comparison demonstrated that these had been done, at the same session as the hitherto solitary Nobody's Sweetheart and thus the whole thing fell neatly into place some four decades after the sessions took place. All these recordings are included in this LP.

In stylistic terms, these are much more in the muscular 'Chicago' manner than the white "New Orleans" Dixieland of the Bucktown Five. The music is perhaps tinged with tension as though the men were determinedly setting out to play jazz while the others somehow just 'up and did it'. Coming through this feeling, though, is the Muggsy cornet which, in Bull Frog Blues, has something of the majestic manner of Louis and sounds extremely relaxed against the nervous rhythm. On China Boy he is much more typical of the Spanier we all got to know some years later. Note, too, the good sound of the two cornets and the clarinet with the saxes in the closing ensemble.

As already observed, the earlier versions of Jazz Me Blues and Sister Kate quite obviously (now) have cornet by someone other than Spanier. That heard lacks the easy flow contained in the later ones. One can but wonder at the taste of the fellow who chose the non-Muggsy takes for the bulk of the pressings of the original Paramount record! Spanier plays extremely well on Jazz Me Blues, including a fine break, and leads a closing ensemble which has more of the Dixieland about it than do most of the period's Chicago style records. Sister Kate is taken at a much livelier tempo than the earlier version, with Spanier again in good form both solo and lead. The banjo coda is a giggle!

Nobody's Sweetheart is very much Chicago in style with Tesch and the drummer working well and some good Muggsy. This session was unusual in that a trombone was used and Jack Reid plays suitably and satisfactorily, throughout.

The Jungle Kings

Although probably far less well known than the Brunswick coupling by the same personnel but as the Chicago Rhythm Kings, these sides have everything which makes 'Chicago Style', The first (December, 1927) in the school are often cited as the epitome and they do have the advantages of OKeh's vastly superior recording quality and of Bud Freeman's tenor sax instead of that of Mezz Mezzrow. The dreadful tone and poor phrasing of the latter and the somewhat unclear Paramount recording are, by my reckoning, more than compensated for by the inclusion of Muggsy rather than Jimmy McPartland.

Add to this the wonderful knocked-out sound which the band achieves — and Red McKenzie's gruff singing rates the same adjectival praise—and the pulsing shuffle rhythm of Jim Lannigan's brass bass and Eddie Condon's banjo. These sides have a wonderful atmosphere which conjures' up Prohibition and gangsters and speakeasies and the rest of the legend. The 1927 sides sound too clean, if you see what I mean.

Friars Point Shuffle has Muggsy playing what we have come to expect from him: strong firm lead in ensembles. The same again, of course, in Darktown Strutters Ball, but on this he also solos on the verse and does a beautiful job with fine tone and phrasing and laying back here and there on the rhythm.

Muggsy Spanier made hundreds of records in the forty years that elapsed after the first on this collection. Most had the benefits of improved techniques in both playing ability and recording quality and many by the use of more capable and compatible fellow musicians. Those presented here, however, have a freshness and unsophisticated eagerness which is a delight. They also illustrate the early development of a first-class jazz man who gave enormous pleasure to untold numbers of devotees many of whom, let us not forget, came to the music because of his playing.

Muggsy Spanier In New Orleans 1938 -1955

Any writer/researcher will tell you the same: go to publication and the next thing you know more information starts to roll in. Either you just philosophically ignore it or, never despairing, put it all together and eventually find an outlet to which, hopefully, your book's readers will have access.

Muggsy Spanier: The Lonesome Road was published towards the end of 1995 by Jazzology Press and this put the writer in the privileged position where his readers can be reached with that additional information. The Winter/Spring 1998 issue of *Jazzbeat* had two pages covering the later contributions to our knowledge of the life, times and work of Francis Joseph Spanier.

Thereafter, things had been pretty quiet. Inevitably, there have been some compact disc compilations but these have all been of previously issued recordings. Until now, that is, and here it's confession time because there should have been a note somewhere of the rumors which circulated long ago: Spanier had recorded in New Orleans before returning to his home town, Chicago, in 1938 following his discharge from the Touro Hospital.

Sixty years on, early in 1999, came a cassette from New Orleans-based trumpeter Plato Smith. This is what his accompanying letter said:

> When Joe Mares (brother of Paul and owner of Southland Records and a great friend of many musicians) died, he left me all his musical memorabilia. Among it were a number of 16" transcriptions (and) one of them should be of interest.
> The transcription label was written in pencil and said in large letters: 'Muggsy 1938'. Listed below was the personnel: Muggsy, Bujie Centobie (cl), Julian Laine (trb), Armand Hug (p), Chink Martin (b), and Monk Hazel (d).
> There is no announcer and, judging by the length of the numbers, it's very doubtful that this was from a radio show. Joe had friends at several local radio stations and I would guess that he had this made in one of the studios.

Muggsy Spanier at Grandview Inn, Columbus, Ohio, March, 1956.
(Courtesy Ed Lawless)

Plato went on to say that this (and other Mares acetates) had been passed to George Buck so a fast letter to Hal Smith, then working in New Orleans, got the search ball rolling. George had completely forgotten about it but Hal and Barry Martyn found the acetate and this compact disc was on its way.

Spanier's playing was always full of his enthusiasm for the music but here that seems even more apparent. This was a man who very nearly died earlier that year and had been told that his chances of playing his cornet ever again were remote. That old Irish spirit of showing what you're made of — "Come on, we'll show 'em" — just never failed him. His exuberance and vitality are astounding.

Bear in mind too that, prior to the 1938 trauma, the last six-piece band he'd recorded with was the rather under-wraps New Orleans Rhythm Kings early in 1935. Years of well-paid work with Ted Lewis hardly provided opportunity for the real thing — yes, plenty of solos but that's not 'our' Spanier — and not much more when he switched to Ben Pollack at the end of 1936.

Put all that together and here's a man so elated that, when given the opportunity by Joe Mares, he plays so ecstatically. We must allow that he will surely have played in clubs, sitting in with local musicians, getting his lip back into shape, picking up from where he left off long ago. And so, when it came to the recording session, the others — Laine, Centobie, Hug, Martin and Hazel — seasoned veterans all — are infected with that elation and turn in a first class job. Inevitably, there are moments which tell us that these are not well- rehearsed and polished performances which we expect from a regularly performing bunch of musicians but we all enjoy the casual air of 'let's get together and play' affairs.

With these four tracks we are listening to Spanier's inspiration for the time-honored Ragtime band he put together the following year back home. All these years on we can only wonder at Joe Mares apparent reluctance to make his session available to Spanier admirers.

Turn to the top of page 91 in the *Lonesome Road* book and remark the hiatus for the second half of 1955 until that October. Some of the reason lies in our next batch: Spanier spent some time in New Orleans and it is likely that this was for another of his meetings with Dr. Alton Ochsner. He would do this when he felt that his health was worrisome and, of course, not exactly helped by the rigors of touring which, he found, could be alleviated by alcohol.

Again, we can be sure that the cornet traveled with him and that he would sit in with the bands in the joints in the Quarter. What is certain is that Doctor Edmond Souchon recorded this informal session. There's much fun here including Doc's two vocal choruses on "C" Blues with Muggsy commenting through his plunger the while. Souchon switches from guitar to banjo for Darktown Strutters Ball and works his way to the vocal refrain with chanting by the others including, we like to think, Spanier.

The 1952 session was played by Spanier's regular band. Ralph Hutchinson, a Britisher and a Bill Harris admirer, had no difficulty in providing the right tailgate trombone for ensembles and blew virile solos. We don't know how and where Spanier heard him but presumably he was not playing in the then modernist way. He was asked to replace his old instrument and he joined the band, taking over from Harry Graves, in April, 1951.

Darnell Howard had been with Muggsy since the Spring of 1950 when he put together the band which, with the inevitable changes, he toured through much of the decade. Howard, of course, was a vastly experienced musician having worked in bands since the teens of the century. If he'd needed any 'traditional' clarinet experience it would have come in the 1940s with Kid Ory. He knew all the right songs.

As did pianist Floyd Bean and bassist Truck Parham and they, with drummer Barrett Deems, provided the rock solid rhythm was well as having the stamina to keep up the very fast tempos called for. A *Down Beat* writer called it a 'portable heating system'. Bean remarked that this was a 'show band' in the sense of putting on a show for the clients in the clubs where it played. Apart from including features for individuals, such as Floyd's Mr. Piano Man, there were those fast tempos as demonstrated here in the hectic At the Jazz Band Ball.

Spanier always denied that he played 'Dixieland' — he played jazz and it swung and it didn't need labels — so it was perhaps curious that he used the word several times in his spoken passages during this transcription session. However, it's fairly obvious that he's reading from a script and we like to think that he may have protested.

This collection serves to add much to our knowledge of Muggsy Spanier's working life. More importantly, we have that much more of his music and collectors will be grateful to all those who, one way or another, did so much to preserve it.

The reason Muggsy Spanier appears on American Music is simple. For the first eight songs on this CD, all of the accompanying musicians are from New Orleans. What a discovery these first songs are!!! Recorded two years before the Kid Rena Delta Session officially launched the revival in the Crescent City, these titles, along with the rare 1955 session fill an important gap in the history of New Orleans music.

The "Here's To Vets" segment (tracks 9 through 13) was added to fillout the CD & came from station acetates, giving first class reproduction.

MUGGSY SPANIER IN NEW ORLEANS - American Music AMCD109

Muggsy Spanier, cornet; Julian Laine, trombone; Bujie Centobie, clarinet; Armand Hug, piano; Chink Martin, string bass; Monk Hazel, drums, mellophone-1.

New Orleans – 1958

Dippermouth Blues
Tin Roof Blues
Sweet Lorraine
Blues   -1

The opening cornet solo on Sweet Lorraine is perhaps by Johnny Wiggs, rather than Spanier.

Muggsy Spanier, cornet; Red Mackie, piano; Edmond Souchon, guitar, banjo-2, vocal; Sherwood Mangiapanne, string bass; unknown female singer*.

New Orleans – August 14, 1955

The One I Love Belongs To Somebody Else	
"C" Blues	vES
Darktown Strutters Ball #1 -2	vES*
Darktown Strutters Ball #2 -2	vES*

Muggsy Spanier, cornet; Ralph Hutchinson, trombone; Darnell Howard, clarinet; Floyd Bean, piano; Truck Parham, string bass; Barrett Deems, drums.

New Orleans – April 15, 1953

Relaxing At The Touro
At The Jazz Band Ball
Tin Roof Blues
Dippermouth Blues
Relaxing At The Touro

Notes on Other Chicago Jazzmen

All the major names associated with Chicago jazz, stars such as Bud Freeman, Art Hodes, Eddie Condon, Pee Wee Russell, Wild Bill Davison and Max Kaminsky, have entries in *The New Grove Dictionary of Jazz* or in John Chilton's *Who's Who of Jazz*. Very many of them have had autobiographies or biographies published, some of which are listed in *Recommended Reading*. Other many fine musicians - Bud Jacobson, Boyce Brown, Joe Marsala, Frank Melrose, Johnny Mendell, Pete Daily and others - can also be found in Grove or Chilton, but many are not. Here are a few, just the tip of the iceberg, of those who are not.

ARON, Sammy (bass)

Born Chicago, 1917. Played with wide variety of bands. 1942, The Townsmen, instrumental/vocal group in Chicago clubs. 1943 at Blinkin' Pup with Larry Grady, vibes; 1943-44 with Lawrence Welk; 1945-50 with Chet Roble Trio (Boyce Brown on alto); 1951-88 with the Don White Trio, apart from 1961 with German band. Retired in 1988.

BEEBE, Jim (trombone)

Born in Omaha, May 24, 1931. As a schoolboy was taken to Jazz, Ltd. (Miff Mole) and Rupneck's (Floyd O'Brien) – decided to become a jazz trombonist. After service in Marine bands, played with Bob Scobey (late 1950s), Clancy Hayes, Jazz, Ltd., Dukes of Dixieland and many others. Then became a well-established Chicago band leader. Recorded, among others, with Scobey, Wild Bill Davison, Little Brother Montgomery and his own bands. Died LaCrosse, Wisconsin, August 29, 2004.

BILLINGS, Frank "Josh" (drums/suitcase)

Born c. 1903. In Chicago 1925 to 1940 as "career jazzfan". Worked and recorded with revived Mound City Blue Blowers (Red McKenzie) (1929-31). His Baggage Busters, with Tut Soper, piano; and Jack Goss, guitar, played some 1945 Chicago concerts. Moved to New York for non-playing role with Eddie Condon's entourage. *Down Beat* reported: "In recent years he was a successful lithographer". Died New York City, April 1957.

BLANK, Ralph (piano)
Played with Louis Panico at the Canton Tea Gardens in 1935, was with Sophie Tucker in 1936. Worked for Ted Weems for a time, starting in 1940. "Worked for years in Europe," then taught piano "to Chicago's 400." With Freddy Wacker and the Windy City Seven in the mid-1950s. Also played at Jazz, Ltd. Recorded with Jazz, Ltd. and Wacker (1957).

BURKIS, Dash (drums)
In 1928 worked with Bunny Berigan and Bill Dohler in dance hall band in Champaign, IL. All except Berigan were from Chicago's Lake View High School. 1929 worked with Wingy Manone at My Cellar. Dash was a great time drummer, said Tut Soper. Became manager of the North Star Inn. Recorded with Wingy Manone (1930).

COUSINS, Bob (drums)
Born c. 1930. Records include the Salt City Six, Dave Remington, Jan Scobey and a concert with Soprano Summit (1976).

CUNNINGHAM, Jimmy (trumpet)
Born c. 1934. Died July 12, 1956 in a car accident. Car went off the expressway going home from the Red Arrow, where he had played with Sid Dawson band since 1953. Also played in Johnny Lane's band. Influenced by Wild Bill Davison. Recorded 1955 with Dave Remington's Dixie 6.

DAWSON, Byrne (Muggsy) (trumpet)
In the U.S. Army during the Korean War. Played regularly with Art Hodes Band and recorded with him in 1954 and 1956. Moved to New York about 1959, where he was working as a freelance artist, when he died October 23, 1962 at the age of 32.

DAWSON, Sid (trombone)
Born c. 1929. Worked in sales for some years. Recordings include Dave Remington, Smokey Stover and own band.

DOHLER, Bill (alto/clarinet)
Born February 6, 1907 as William Hildebrand, but took his step-father's surname. In Wild Bill Davison's Beau Brummels strolling quartet at the 1933 World's Fair, then at Sherman Hotel. Played with Floyd Town and most everyone in Chicago. In the army WW2 (in Florida). In later years taught saxophone. Recorded with Paul

Jordan, Bud Freeman; one title under own name. Died February 24,1993. Bud Freeman called him: "a very fine, elegant alto player".

ESTERDAHL, Lennie (guitar/banjo) Worked and recorded with Pete Daily in L.A. at least 1947 to 1954. Recorded with Johnny Lucas (1954) and unissued titles in 1925 with Wingy Manone for OKeh. Died February 25, 1968.

FIEGE, Dick (cornet)
Recorded with Charlie Pierce orchestra for Paramount. In 1941 was in the Lutheran Sanatorium, Wheatridge, Colorado, suffering from tuberculosis.

GORMLEY, Hap (drums)
Recorded with Art Hodes (1954/1956), Dave Remington (c. 1959-1961), Wild Bill Davison (1964), Washington Square Stompers (1966), Gary Lawrence (1976/1980).

GRANT, Mel (piano)
Worked with Bud Jacobson mid-1940s, and with Freddy Martin orchestra about 1944. Recorded with Joe Venuti (1929), Doc Evans (1947/50/58), Muggsy Spanier (1953), Dave Remington (1960). Solo titles for Joco.

HENKE, Mel (piano)
Played in various club around Chicago during the 1930s. Later with Horace Heidt's orchestra. Worked in radio studios. Moved to Los Angeles about 1947. Recorded for Victor, Contemporary, etc.

HIGGINS, Eddie (piano)
Born February 21, 1932. Moved to Chicago from Cambridge, Massachusetts, to study at NW University School of Music. Did army service in the mid-1950s. Played with dixieland groups, toured with Jack Teagarden for six months, appeared at various Chicago clubs, including Jazz, Ltd. House pianist at the Chicago House jazz club early 1960s to 1969, working with major jazz players and in a variety of jazz styles. Recorded with Eddie South, Lee Morgan, Wayne Shorter, including numerous solo and trio albums, many for the Japanese Venus label. Closer to dixieland are titles with Jack Teagarden, Bobby Gordon, Jan Scobey and Tommy Saunders. Moved to Fort Lauderdale, Florida, in 1970, where he died August 31, 2009.

HUNTER, Bud (tenor/clarinet)
In Gene Kerwin band at Canton Tea Gardens in 1929. Helped to found the Chicago School of Music in late 1940s. Recorded with Bud Jacobson 1941.

JAMES, Jimmy (trombone)
Played with the Tiny Hill orchestra for many years, but settled in Chicago about 1948, playing with dixieland groups such as Danny Alvin's and Johnny Lane's. Recorded two rare 78s with Jimmy Ille and George Zack in Chicago, 1950. Died December 10, 1954 of a heart attack, aged 33.

JONES, Wayne (drums/writer)
Born Lafayette, Indiana, May 21, 1933. After military service, lived in Chicago, working with a variety of jazz groups, including the Chicago Stompers, Ted Butterman, Gold Coast Jazz Band, Terry Waldo and The Sons of Bix, but with the Salty Dogs forty years. Many recordings, including with the groups mentioned. Prolific writer of sleeve notes and record reviews. Died Chicago, May 30, 2013.

KUHN, John (tuba)
A native Indian, he left the Fort Shaw Indian School in Montana to join a wagon show. Played with Pat Conway's band and seven years with Sousa, and in orchestras conducted by Saint-Saens and Toscanini. Also with Isham Jones. On NBC "Farm and Home Hour" broadcasts at least from 1930 to 1937. His jazz claim was his presence on Elmer Schoebel's 1929 Brunswick recording. In *Leader of the Band* by Gene Lees: "It is said that he was the finest tuba player in jazz or dance music at that time".

LINCOLN, Del (trumpet)
Played with Danny Alvin, George Brunis, etc. Died in Chicago in early 1959, at the age of 55.

MASEK, Joe (tenor)
Played with Ted Lewis and Henry Busse. Worked in Chicago radio studios in the 1930s and 1940s. Recorded with Charlie LaVere (1935).

McPARTLAND, Dick (guitar/banjo)
Born 1905. Brother of Jimmy McPartland and worked frequently with him. Became a booker, but continued to play into the 1940s on

records and at jazz sessions, including Squirrel Ashcraft's Monday night gigs. Recorded with Original Wolverines (11927/28), Jack Teagarden (1933) and his brother 1936 and 1939. Ceased playing about 1948 due to the heart problems. Became a cab driver. Died December 1, 1957.

NORTH, Dave (piano)

Became associated with the Austin High Gang about 1922. Recorded with Bud Freeman (1928). Retired from full-time music in 1930; became an electrician and then owned a print shop.

PODALSKY, Murph (piano)

Originally dance band musician, but affected by jazz bug in 1921. Played with everyone in Chicago until he left full-time music in 1943. Became wealthy as a land developer. Buddy of Eddie Condon.

REMINGTON, Dave (piano/trombone)

Born October 10, 1926. Worked and recorded with Salt City Five, Dukes of Dixieland and at Jazz, Ltd. Head of Rockford College music department 1970-1974. To New York as pit musician. 1996-2006 at Interlochen Arts Academy, Beulah, MI, teaching piano and jazz improvisation. Recorded several LPs with own band; also with Art Hodes (1955), Dukes of Dixieland (1965), and Dick Ruedebusch (1967). Died June 8, 2007.

SCHENCK, John (promoter)

For a time was very active in Chicago. Died in Los Angeles, May 28, 1955 aged 30.

SMITH, Leroy (clarinet)

Worked with Pete Daily in Chicago. Entered military service about 1943, leading own unit.

Died March 5, 1948 of uremic poisoning.

JOHN STEINER

Born July 21, 1908; died June 3, 2004. The doyen of Chicago jazz historians. In partnership with Hugh Davis was responsible for numerous releases on the Steiner-Davis label. He became the owner of the Paramount record label, with many reissues resulting.

TINKLER, Bill (trumpet)

Born 1916 in Murphysboro. Became professional in 1933. Worked with the bands of Benny Strong (1 year), Eddie Howard (3 years) and Lawrence Welk (two years), then to Chicago. Played at Jazz, Ltd and with Johnny Lane and George Brunis. Recorded with Miff Mole for Premium and on Argo LP. Moved to Arizona about 1980, playing mainly dance music but organised jazz sessions.

TROTTIER, William "Nappy" (trumpet)

Born October 3, 1925, he worked with Frank Gillis and briefly with Jack Teagarden's big band. Moved to Chicago in early 1950s and worked with George Brunis; at Jazz, Ltd; and led own band (through 1962) at the Velvet Swing. Recordings with Al Capone Memorial Jazz Band, and with Art Hodes, including appearances by Albert Nicholas, Barney Bigard and Volly De Faut. There was also "an under-appreciated gem of a session with Don Ewell, Marty Grosz and Earl Murphy" for Audiophile. Retired due to ill-health in mid-1970s. Confined to wheel-chair. Died in Appleton, WI, September 21, 1997.

VIERA, Norman W. "Pete" (piano)

Born 1908 Jacksonville, Illinois. Worked with Louis Panico and Mezz Mezzrow. With Bob Crosby orchestra the summer of 1939. Recorded with Louis Panico, Wingy Manone and Bob Crosby. Died c. May, 1960.

WACKER, Freddie (drums/leader)

Served in the U.S. Navy. Raced cars in Europe after the war. President of company he founded, 1948-1986. Recorded at a Squirrel Ashcraft Monday night session in 1953. Organised his own band, the Windy City Seven, in 1955 and it recorded in 1957 and 1965. Died June 16, 1998, aged 79.

WILEY, Earl (drums)

Born Kewanee, IL, September 15, 1900. Worked with Tony Catalano on Streckfus steamboats. Moved to Chicago around 1920; played for Mike Fritzel, Gene Green, Eddie Tancil and, in 1933, Johnny Lane. Led own Dixieland group. Recorded with Bud Jacobson's Jungle Kings. Moved to New York in 1944.

And to conclude, space should be found to document a few more writers who researched jazz in Chicago. In addition to the doyen of them all, John Steiner, mentioned in the Recommended Reading list, they should include Jim Gordon, drummer Wayne Jones, and Tom Gilmore, together with George Hoefer and Pat Harris, the *Down Beat* representatives in Chicago.

Selected reading

George Avakian: sleeve notes to *Chicago Jazz*, Columbia CLP632

Derek Coller: *Jess Stacy: The Quiet Man Of Jazz* (Jazzology Press, 1997)

Eddie Condon, with Thomas Sugrue: *We Called It Music* (Corgi Books, 1962)

Pete Daily: article, Pete Daily Writes On Frank Melrose (Piano Jazz, No. 1, 1945)

Sandor Demlinger and John Steiner: *Destination Chicago Jazz* (Arcadia Publishing Inc., 2003)

Jean Porter Dmytryk: *Chicago Jazz And Then Some, as told by one of the original Chicagoans, Jess Stacy* (BearManor Media, 2010)

Bud Freeman, as told to Robert Wolf: *Crazeology* (Bayou Press, 1989)

Richard Hadlock: *Jazz Masters of the Twenties* (Collier Books, 1974)

Nat Hentoff & Albert J. McCarthy (editors): *Jazz* (Cassell & Co. Ltd, 1959) (chapter, *Chicago*, by John Steiner)

Robert Hilbert: *Pee Wee Russell, The Life of a Jazzman* (Oxford University Press, 1993)

Art Hodes and Chadwick Hansen: *Hot Man, The Life of Art Hodes* (Bayou Press, 1992)

Thomas Jackrell: article, *The Last Chicagoans* (Joslin's *Jazz Journal*, August 1991)

Max Kaminsky with V.E. Hughes: *My Life In Jazz* (Andre Deutsch Limited, 1964)

Keith Keller: *Oh, Jess! A Jazz Life* (Jess Stacy) (The Mayan Music Corporation, 1989)

William Howland Kenney: *Chicago Jazz* (Oxford University Press, 1993)

Wingy Manone and Paul Vandervoort: Trumpet On The Wing (1948)

Mezz Mezzrow and Bernard Wolfe: *Really The Blues* (1946)

Paul Eduard Miller (editor): *Esquire's 1946 Jazz Book* (A.S.

Barnes & Company, 1946). (chapters, *Thirty Years of Chicago Jazz*, by Paul Eduard Miller, and *Chicago Jazz History* by Paul Eduard Miller and George Hoefer)

Frank Powers: article, What Is Chicago Style – A Comprehensive Look (San Diego Dixieland Festival programme, November 28-December 1, 1996)

Frederic Ramsey and Charles Edward Smith (editors), *Jazzmen* (Harcourt, Brace & Company Inc., 1939) (chapter, *The Austin High School Gang*, by Charles Edward Smith)

Charles A. Sengstock, Jr.: *That Toddlin' Town: Chicago's White Dance Bands and Orchestras 1900-1950* (University of Illinois Press, 2004)

Richard M. Sudhalter: *Lost Chords: White Musicians and Their Contribution to Jazz 1915-1945* (Oxford University Press, 1999)

Bert Whyatt: *Muggsy Spanier: The Lonesome Road* (Jazzology Press, 1995)

Hal Willard: *The Wildest One, The Life of Wild Bill Davison* (Avondale Press, 1996)

Laurie Wright (editor): *Storyville* 2000-1 (*Storyville*, 2001) (chapter, *The New Orleans Rhythm Kings*, by Tom Buhmann)

Original Publications

George Brunies: The Tailgate Supremo
Jazz Journal, May 2002   Bert Whyatt

Jack Pettis: More On....
The Mississippi Rag, April 1993   Derek Coller

Frank Snyder: (Rhythm King Drummer)
The Mississippi Rag, April 1983   Derek Coller

Elmer Schoebel: Pianist, Composer, Pioneer Arranger
IAJRC Journal, June 2010   Derek Coller

Rod Cless: The Forgotten Ones
Jazz Journal, May 1999   Bert Whyatt

George Snurpus: Elusive Jazzman
Storyville 160, December 1994   Derek Coller

Maurie Bercov: Following Tesch
IAJRC Journal August 2007   Whyatt/Coller

Floyd O'Brien: He Played Jazz Chicago Style
IAJRC Journal, Spring 2002   Derek Coller

Oro 'Tut' Soper: Chicago Pianist
The Mississippi Rag, March 1992 Bert Whyatt

Tut Soper's Memories of Chicago
IAJRC Journal, December 2010   Bert Whyatt

Floyd Town: His Story
The Mississippi Rag. February 1990 Derek Coller

Johnny Lane: "Played With Gusto"
Storyville 1996-7   Derek Coller

George Zack: The Unforgettable
The Mississippi Rag, January 1998 Bert Whyatt

Jack Gardner: "A Truly Lusty Pianist"
IAJRC Journal, September 2010 Derek Coller

Chet Roble: A Chicago Pianist
Storyville 164, March 1992   Derek Coller

Floyd Bean: The Forgotten Ones
Jazz Journal, May 1999   Bert Whyatt

Bill Reinhardt: Jazz, Ltd. – And More
Storyville 154, June 1993   Coller/Whyatt

Bill Reinhardt: Jazz, Ltd. – And A Little More
Storyville 1996-7   Coller/Whyatt

Dan Lipscomb: Talk About Two-Handed Piano

                unpublished   Derek Coller

Frank Chace: Chicago Clarinet

        Jazz Journal, December 2008   Coller/Whyatt

Jimmy Ille: Cornet Player From Biwabik

        IAJRC Journal, Summer 1994   Derek Coller

Al Jenkins: Knocking Down Walls

        The Mississippi Rag, November 1994 Derek Coller

Doc Cenardo: A Great But Unsung Drummer

        The Mississippi Rag, December 1993 Bert Whyatt

Freddy Greenleaf; The Little-known But Talented

        The Mississippi Rag, October 2003 Derek Coller

Paul Jordan: Another Unsung Jazzman

        IAJRC Journal, December 2015   Derek Coller

Paul Jordan [additions]

        IAJRC Journal, Fall 2016

Muggsy Spanier, 1924-1928

        Retrieval FJ-108   Bert Whyatt

Muggsy Spanier In New Orleans 1938-1955

        American Music AMCD-109   Bert Whyatt

Muggsy Spanier, 1924-1954

        Avid AMSC 695   Bert Whyatt

Also by Derek Coller and Bert Whyatt

by Derek Coller

Jess Stacy: The Quiet Man of Jazz, Jazzology Press, 1997
Clarinet Marmalade: The Life and Music of Tony Parenti,
    Jazzology Press, 2003
Strictly A Musician – Dick Cary, Dick Cary Music Company,
    2012
*Superstride: A Biography and Discography of Johnny
    Guarnieri,* dist. Jazzology Press, 2018

by Bert Whyatt

*Muggsy Spanier: The Lonesome Road. A Biography and
    Discography,* Jazzology Press, 1995
(with Sonny McGown) *The Jump Records story: A discography,*
    IAJRC, 2006
(with George Hulme) *Bobby Hackett: His Life in Music,*
    Hardinge Simpole, 2015

Sig Meyer and his Druids
Left to right: Arnold Loyacano, George Petrone, Marvin Saxbe, Horace Williamson, Sig Meyer, Volly De Faut, Bob Pacelli, Floyd Town, Muggsy Spanier. Chicago - c. 1924.
Some of the inter-connections: Spanier, De Faut and Saxbe were in The Bucktown Five; De Faut and Loyacano were in the New Orleans Rhythm Kings; Spanier played with Floyd Town.

Index

The term "writer" covers a host of activities, including those of poet, critic, reviewer, columnist, researcher, author of books and/or articles, musicologist and historian.

D

Dailey, Dan (actor) 203

Daily, Pete (co) 109, 157, 158, 247, 248, 293, 295, 297, 299

Dameron, Tad (p) 227

D'Amico, Hank (cl, as) 59, 69

Daniel, Ray (cl) 77, 237

Dapogny, Jim (p) xiv, 36

Darensbourg, Joe (cl) 141, 142, 231

Darrington, Frankie (vo) 72

Daugherty, Doc (club owner) 98

Davern, Kenny (cl) xiv, 34, 261, 262, 263, 264

Davis, Hugh (record producer) 95, 297

Davis, Jack (tp) 124

Davis, Johnny (tp, leader) 67

Davis, Maxwell (leader) 56

Davis, Spanky (tb) 67, 192

Davies, John R.T. (collector) 223

Davison, Wild Bill (co) vi, 7, 8, 45, 92, 104, 142, 147, 157, 159, 220, 246, 293-295, 300

Dawson, Muggsy (co) 75, 76, 87, 141, 245, 270, 294

Dawson, Sid (tb) 135, 146, 221, 294

Dayton Hotel 165

Dean, Sammy (d) 198

Deems, Barrett (d) 197, 199, 225, 291, 292

De Faut, Volly (cl) viii, 12, 88, 95, 113, 114, 118, 134, 275, 283, 284, 285, 298, 304

DeHaven, Doc (reeds) 66, 93

Delaunay, Charles (discographer) xviii

Delbridge, Del (leader) 118

Del Monico's 67

de Lys, Bobby (d) 28

Delta, The 173, 177

DeMichael, Don (d, vb, writer) 100, 103, 104, 115

DeMille, Cecil B. (film director) 233

Demlinger, Sandor (writer) 299

De Muth, Gerry (writer) xvi, 143

de Naut, Jud (b) 247

Dengler, John (tp, reeds) xv, xviii, 75, 219, 224, 225

De Paris, Sidney (tp) 200

De Paris, Wilbur (tb, leader) 32, 45

De Salvo, Emil (p/acc) 52

Desert Inn Hotel 247

Dever, John (collector) xvii

Devoe 11 (see De Fau)

Devore, Dave (b) 199

Dexter, Fred (leader, vl) 181, 188, 189

Diamond, 'Legs' (see Maritote)

Diamond, Lou (d) 130, 237, 247

Dibert, Sammy (leader) 254

Dickenson, Vic (tb) 162, 249

Dietrick, ---- (club owner) 126

Dixieland All Stars 74

Dixon, ---- (leader) 12

Dixon, Ray (p) 74, 145, 198

Dmytryk, Jean Porter (writer) 299

Dodds, Baby (d) 1, 12, 76, 87, 95, 96, 113, 128, 156, 166, 263

Dodds, Johnny (cl) 1, 39, 41, 54, 186, 221

Dohler, Bill (as) 26, 73, 96, 102, 107, 114, 122, 124, 125, 127, 134, 136, 166, 266, 268, 269, 271, 273, 294

Dominque, Natty (tp) 76, 87, 221

Donahue, Dick (tp) 107,122, 125, 127, 136, 266

Dooley, Phil (tp, leader) 63

Dorseys 14, 90

Dorsey, Jimmy (reeds, leader) 168, 190, 201, 243, 264

Dorsey, Thomas A. (p, composer) 37

266

Kuhn, John (tu) 123, 296
Kuriss, Theo (g) 201
Kweskin, Jim (vo) 225, 230

L
La Casita 45
Lacey, Steve (ss) 33
Laine, George 'Papa Jack' (d, leader) 5
Laine, Julian (tb) 97, 256, 288, 290, 292
Laine, Alfred 'Pantsy' (co, d) 5
Lake, Sol (p) 237
Lamare, Hilton 'Nappy' (g, bj, vo) 70, 71, 137, 142, 147, 157, 218, 234, 246, 247
Lambert, Lloyd (b) 238
Lamm, Bob (tp) 240
Lancaster, Burt (actor) 237
Landis, Chubby (reeds) 201
Landrey-Dorley orchestra 49
LaFontaine Hotel 127
Lane, Johnny (Italiane) (cl, leader) vi, xvi, 52, 61, 63, 64, 74-76, 96, 97, 107, 122, 124, 125, 132, 133, 134-147, 167, 174, 235, 246-249, 266, 294, 296, 298, 301
Lane, Larry (vo) 143
Lane, Leona (Johnny's wife) (vo) 143
Lane, Lucille (vo) 247
Lang, Eddie (g) 14
Lanigan, Jim (b) 1, 62, 76, 79, 80, 88, 95, 96, 114, 128, 182
Lanigan, Jr., Jim(cl) 128
Lanin, Sam (leader) 39
Lark, The 142
Larkin, Philip (writer) 229
Larsen, Paul (writer) 72
LaVere, Charlie (p) 71, 72, 84, 86, 105, 108, 296
Lawless, Ed (photographer) 289

Lawrence, Gary (leader) 295
Lawson, Yank (tp) 45, 226
Laylan, Rollo (d) 66, 93, 110, 199
Lee, Carroll (p) 197, 244
Lee Guber's Swing Rendezvous 32
Lees, Gene (writer) 296
Leins, George (p, leader) (also known as Lyons) 179
Leland Hotel 64, 134
Leonard, Will (writer) xvii
Lerner, Al (p) 164
Les Rois du Fox-Trot 40
Levant, Phil (leader) 94
Levee Loungers, The x, 242, 243
Levin, Floyd (writer) xvi, 250
Levinson, Peter (writer) 164
Lewine, Harris (writer) 26
LeWinter, Dave (p) 52, 64
Lewis, Bobby (tp) 199, 204
Lewis, Ted (cl, vo, leader) 5, 7, 8, 41, 60, 65, 132,134, 144, 277, 279, 281, 290, 296
Lent, Freddie (p) 147
Liberty Club 108
Liberty Inn 94, 96, 107, 108, 136, 170
Lido, The 177
Liefert, John (collector) 16
Lightfoot, Eddie (d) 97
Lincoln, Abe (tb) 137
Lincoln, Del (tp) 76, 146, 296
Lincoln Gardens 1, 60
Linwood Inn 179
Lipscomb, Dan (p) xvii, 208, 210, 211, 212, 213, 214, 215, 286, 302
Lipscomb family, 211, 212, 213
Lishon, Henri (leader) 65
Little, Danny (tp) 145
Livingston, Fud (cl, ts) 62
Lodice, Charley (d) 246, 247
Logan, Bob (tb) 70
Lollobrigida, Gina (actor) 237
Lombardo, Guy (leader) 39, 67

Long, Slats (cl) 188
Lord, Tom (discographer) xviii,
    113, 274
Lovett, Bill (cl) 40
Loyacano, Arnold (b) viii, 12, 19,
    23, 118
Loycano, Arnold (see Loyacano)
    11
Luboff, Abe (b) 273
Luby, Ray (d) 235
Lucas, John (Jax) (writer) xvii, 96,
    158, 162, 165, 243
Lucas, Johnny (tp) 143, 246, 247,
    249, 295
Lugg, George (tb) 22, 26, 93, 98
Luke, Charlie (composer) 37
Lund, Jack (hall owner) 22
Luperini, Elmo (d) 269
Lyman, Abe (leader) 162
Lyman, Bernie (leader) 39
Lyman, Tommy (vo) 34
Lynch, Catherine Ann (vo) 16
Lyons, Art (cl) 198, 200, 244
Lytell, Jimmy (cl) 151

McBee, 'Mac' (cl) 76
McCann, Lloyd (p) 146
McCarthy, Albert (writer) xiii,
    xvii, 170, 299
McCloud, ---- (b) 64
McCoy, Clyde (leader) 105, 108
McCracken, Bob (cl) 98, 108, 156,
    178, 246, 258, 263
McDonald, John (cl) 244, 256
McDonald, Joyce Lacy (p) 197
McGarity, Lou (tb) 225, 249, 279
McGarvey, 'Red' (g) 256
McGhee, Brownie (g, vo) vi
McGuire, Frank (club owner) 134
McHargue, Rosy (cl) 64, 70, 120,
    163, 166, 203
McKay, Jay (Pettis family
    member) 16

McKendrick, Mike (g, bj) 196, 199
McKenzie. Red (vo) 1, 3, 41, 54,
    162, 170, 182, 189, 277, 287, 293
McKenzie, Tom (p) 147
McKinstry, Ray (ts) 44, 152
McLean, Scott (cl) 236
McMickle, Dale 'Mick' (tp) 188
McPartland, 'Dick' Richard (g, bj)
    1, 60, 62, 66, 76, 95, 113, 124,
    127, 131, 163, 182, 296
McPartland, Hayden (g) 128
McPartland, Jimmy (co) xvi, 1, 3,
    43, 54, 60, 62, 63, 68, 76, 80,
    127, 128, 131, 163, 174, 179, 181,
    182, 185, 221, 273, 287, 296
McPartland, Marian (p) 76, 80, 128
McReynolds, Bob (tb) 271

M
Mackey, Chuck (tp) 73, 86
Mackie, Red (p) 292
Madhouse, The 237
Madison, Rich (helicon) 99, 185
Magnusson, Tor (discographer)
    xvii, 167
Maher, James T. (writer) xiv, 35
Mahlberg, Cy (leader) 181
Mahony, Dan (discographer) 158
Malone, Kasper (b) 262, 263, 264
Mangiapanne, Sherwood (b) 292
Mann, Jerry (mimic) 92
Mann, Marion (vo) 182
Man(n)one, 'Wingy' Joseph (tp,
    vo) 7, 37, 47, 49, 52, 62, 67, 71,
    85, 86, 90, 98, 108, 136, 138,
    144, 162, 163, 182, 190, 194, 219,
    231, 244, 247, 294, 295, 298,
    299
Marable, Fate (p, leader) 58, 116
Mares, Joe (record producer) 288-
    290
Mares, Paul (tp) viii, 1, 5, 11, 17,
    19, 23, 38, 43, 125, 136, 288,

Mezzrow, Mezz (real name, Mesirow, Milton) (cl) xvi, 2, 12, 45, 60, 62, 64, 66, 67, 68, 81, 85, 227, 277, 287, 298, 299
Michaels, 'Hots' (p) 176
Mickey's 178
Midnight Ramblers 93
Midnight Serenaders 110
Midway Cafe 126, 266
Midway Dance Orchestra 21, 28, 283
Midway Garden Dance Orchestra 25, 34, 36, 39, 119, 129
Midway Garden(s) 21, 27, 34, 36, 54, 118, 126, 208, 215, 266
Military Inn 256
Miller, Bernie (b) 263
Miller, Eddie (ts, cl) 7, 59, 65, 69, 70, 85, 182, 218, 226, 263
Miller, Glenn (tb, leader) 84, 160, 188, 254, 255, 259, 260
Miller, Max (p, vb) 167, 270-274
Miller, Paul Eduard (writer) 271, 272, 299, 300
Miller, Punch (tp) 231
Miller, Ray (leader) 39, 105
Miller, Tommy (tb) 92
Miller, William H. (writer) xvi, 71, 73, 82
Milligan's (restaurant) 206
Millionaires, The (club) 258
Mills, Irving (producer) 15, 16, 21
Miner, John (photographer, researcher) xvii, xviii, 130, 135, 136, 145, 187, 190, 197, 236, 244, 261, 276
Mintz, Herb (leader) 118
Minuet, The 96
Miranda, Carmen (vo) 206
Mississippi Six, The 179
Mitchell, Tony (cl) 238
Moeller, Harold (tp) 92
Mole, 'Miff' Irving (tb) vi, 8, 43, 45, 74, 136, 156, 183, 189, 195, 198, 218, 230, 234, 236, 256, 263, 264, 270, 279, 293, 297
Moncrief, Burt (tp) 70
Montgomery, 'Little Brother' (p, vo) 74, 79, 293
Mooney, Joe (p) 190
Mooney's 235
Moore, 'Big Chief' Russell (tb) 198
Moore, Bill (b) 235, 236
Moore, Billy (d) 75
Moore, Freddie (d) 32, 74, 196, 198, 205, 264
Morgan, Cody (collector) 13
Morgan, Lee (tp) 295
Morgenstern, Dan (writer) xiv, 35, 45
Morley, Sheridan (writer) 206
Morrell, Charlie (cl) 74
Morris, Dolph (b) xv, 54, 247
Morris, Earl (writer) 125
Morris, Ralph (vo) 123
Morrison, Ross (d) 269
Morrison Hotel, Chicago 27
Morrow, Buddy (tb) 85, 86
Morton, Ferdinand 'Jelly Roll' (p, composer, leader) 13, 35, 36, 37, 39, 40, 224, 258
Mossier, Arnold 'Arnie' (co) 34, 40
Moulin Rouge, The 146
Mound City Blue Blowers 293
Mountjoie Knights Templar Order of Masons 58
Muelbach Hotel 151
Mueller, John (b) 214
Muggsy Remembered 84
Murphy, Earl (d, b) 44, 75, 76, 97, 204, 298
Murphy, Marge (vo) 258
Murphy, Norman (tp) 76, 104, 192, 195, 198, 199, 203-205, 225
Murphy, Turk (tb, leader) 34, 221

Milton Keynes UK
Ingram Content Group UK Ltd.
UKHW022008090823
426617UK00005B/77